W9-BBE-899

# Betty Grable
## The Reluctant Movie Queen

DOUG WARREN

ST. MARTIN'S PRESS
NEW YORK

B
Grable

Betty Grable
Words & Music by: Neil Sedaka and Howard Greenfield

For information, write: St. Martin's Press,
175 Fifth Avenue, New York, N.Y. 10010
Manufactured in the United States of America

Warren, Doug.
Betty Grable, the reluctant movie queen.

1. Grable, Betty, 1916-1973. 2. Actors–
United States–Biography. I. Title.
PN2287.G66W3 791.43'028'0924 [B] 81-5749
ISBN 0-312-07732-7 AACR2

Design by Manuela Paul

10 9 8 7 6 5 4 3 2

## ACKNOWLEDGMENTS

*This list identifies many who provided information integral to this biography. Without their generous contribution of time and effort, it would have been impossible to write the book. The order in which the names are listed says nothing of the importance of their contribution, but only of the chronology of the interviews. Many thanks to each of you.*

Jeff Parker, Bob Remick, Steve Preston, Vivian Blaine, Kevin Pines, Marjorie Arnold, Michael Levitt, Leonard Scumacci, Marie Brasselle, Sonia Wolfson, Jet Fore, Lucille Ball, Tony Charmoli, Paula Sloan, Art Kassul, Pan Berman, Jessica Yahner, Max Showalter, Victor Mature, Richard Lamparski, Anthony Coogan, Ron Alexander, Jane Ardmore, Lee Doyle, Duchess Tomasello, George Raft (via Linda Rafful), Betty Baez, Sugar Geise, Charles Le Maire, Bill Smith, Muzzy Marcelino, Charlie Price, Anthony Slide, Morey Amsterdam, Gene Lester, Jimmy Cross, Ham Waddell, Frank Powolney, Vernon Scott.

## SPECIAL ACKNOWLEDGMENT

*In Chicago there is a collection of Betty Grable memorabilia that is second to none. It belongs to Leonard Scumacci, who must qualify as one of the world's foremost authorities on Betty Grable. Without the generous sharing of his photo collection, too many of these pages would remain blank. I give my heartfelt thanks.*

# Part One

# Chapter 1

It is early February of 1973. The setting is the Alhambra Dinner Theatre in Jacksonville, Florida. On stage, the famous gin rummy scene of *Born Yesterday* is in progress. The scripted impudence of Billie Dawn is gauged to mangle the nerves of her opponent, Harry Brock. Her chatter is continuous. Periodically she says the word "Gin" and proceeds to win the hands with annoying regularity. But in this performance there is an added bit of action. At varying intervals, Billie flicks her fingertip against the charms of her gold bracelet.

The audience chuckles in its appreciation of the stage business, without knowing that this is an improvisation for the personal benefit of Art Kassul, the actor playing Brock. Betty Grable, as Billie, is using the device to acknowledge the gift Kassul has given her, the bracelet with gold charms that depict scenes from the show. It is her way of saying thanks without being gooey about it.

It was never easy for Betty Grable to accept gifts, no easier than it was for her to field compliments regarding her persona or her work. She seemed to have a built-in personality device that prohibited effusive displays of sentimentality, a curious inner compulsion that would cause her to slip away quietly, for example, to avoid a meaningful goodbye. It was just one of the quirks that made Betty Grable what she turned out to be.

On this occasion—there were other behavioral peculiarities recognized by the cast. Something had changed since the troupe had toured together three years earlier, there was a new preoccupation on the part of the star.

Betty had always enjoyed sightseeing excursions in the past, but she passed them up this time around, and there was none of the former pub-crawling after the show. It was apparent she was more pensive as she stood in the wings awaiting her cues, and it was obvious she was physically drained after the final curtain. She seemed physically heavier, a bit plump actually, and some of the cast members noticed that she never allowed herself to be seen without a wig or a fall.

When Betty was asked about this by one of the female members of the cast, she tossed it aside by saying her hair had thinned as a result of wearing wigs when she'd played *Hello Dolly* seven nights a week for eight months in Las Vegas.

Art Kassul also noticed the difference in the relationship between Betty and Bob Remick. When he had been with Betty in 1968, it seemed Remick was in command. It seemed to be the case of an older woman inexorably smitten with a younger man, while the younger man maintained full chauvinistic control. Now, the roles were reversed, and it was now Bob who seemed to be dancing to Betty's tune. "Remembering their previous relationship," said Kassul, "I was surprised to see they were still together. But I was happy about that . . . to see Bob had real feeling for her."

Kassul also noticed that Betty's stage wardrobe had become much more seductive. "Initially," he explained, "she was subdued in her dress, as though attempting to tone down her sex image. In fact, she wore only one dress that revealed her legs. On tour, she was wearing pajamas when she came downstairs to play gin, but at Jacksonville she wore a sexy black nightie. It was as though she were saying, 'It's still there, kids . . . look it over.' "

Word circulated soon enough that Betty was under treatment for lung cancer. She had been hospitalized for four months in California in the spring of 1972 and had received cobalt treatment. After recuperating at home in Las Vegas for the better part of a year, she had felt strong and thoroughly bored, and so, when the offer came to revive *Born Yesterday* at the Alhambra Dinner Theatre in Jacksonville, Betty accepted readily. She was able to bring together most of the cast members from an earlier road company of the show and returned once more to the boards.

Betty was initially under the impression the engagement was for only two weeks, but it turned out to be for a month. She agreed. At the end of the four-week engagement, the management asked for an extension. Betty could have left then, since the contract was fulfilled, but, as was so often the case in the past, her thoughts turned to "the kids"—the members of the cast who needed the money. She extended another four weeks, and, when the theater was still selling out each night, a further extension was requested. This time she was forced to refuse.

It was no longer a matter of simple exhaustion; the pains in her lower abdomen were beginning to rule her. Betty had to give up. She was all right once she was on-stage, but the moment she exited, deep nausea would take charge. The bathroom had to be kept clear to enable her to rush there to vomit the moment she was off. The engagement closed after eight weeks, and it was the first time in the theater's six-year history that an attraction ran that long to sell-out houses.

Ham Waddell, who has designed the sets for the theater since it opened in 1967, said there had never been a show that commanded such local appeal. "My worst enemies were asking my influence to get them tickets at any price," he said. "The people adored Betty. She was bigger than life."

Betty believed she might have taken on too much too soon after her hospitalization. She was confident that after a few week's relaxation she would again be strong enough to work, to honor her commitment to do *No, No Nanette* in Australia. It was something she wanted to do very much.

In 1969 Betty had traveled abroad for the first time in her

life, when she went to London to play the title role in *Belle Starr.* The musical was a dismal failure, but the trip was glorious. She had inhabited the planet for fifty-five years and had seen only two countries, and she hoped to correct the travel deficit in the years to come.

While in Jacksonville, social activity was minimal, but it didn't halt altogether. The cast members had a standing invitation to come to Betty's apartment on their night off to play poker. This time around, Betty didn't hang-in around the clock as she would have before, but she did play for an hour or two, and seemed to enjoy it thoroughly.

Duchess Tomasello, a cast member, recalls, "Betty was so cute. She had these pet phrases of hers. Like, if she would make a blunder at the card table, she would say: 'Oh, shit, she cooed!' "

Another actor, Lee Doyle, remembers one of the few nights Betty joined them in a restaurant for dinner. They had eaten and were in front of the restaurant waiting for Bob Remick to bring the car around. "Betty went over to the gutter and picked up one of those floppy plastic six-pack holders," he said. "She put her finger through one of the holes, and flaunted this thing in front of us. She said 'George Raft gave me this. Do you think it's too flashy?' "

Art Kassul said he had never worked with anyone who was as much fun as Betty. "And she was a fine actress . . . much better than she thought she was, and she was always coming up with bright little ideas to add sparkle to her performance. I could tell by the glint in her eye when something was coming. But I would get impatient with her, because she was so self-effacing. When I'd tell her she was good, she would insist she wasn't. It seemed to embarrass her to receive a compliment."

Kassul described a performance when Betty inadvertently allowed a cigarette to fall from an ashtray onto the seat of the couch where they were sitting. Kassul saw it smoldering away on one of the cushions. "I was holding a drink," he said, "and it occurred to me that in gesturing I might be able to spill some of the drink on the cigarette. I did it, and the water hit the cigarette perfectly, a thousand-to-one shot. Betty saw what happened and broke up. If it hadn't been for that, the audience would never have been the wiser, but she couldn't help herself. Her sense of humor simply couldn't be reined."

The aftermath of the scorched couch was recalled by Lee Doyle. The couch was returned to the dealer who had loaned it, and it was set aside for repair. A customer noticed the couch and was told what happened to it. "You mean Betty Grable sat on this couch," the woman exclaimed. "I'll take it, burn and all."

When this was recounted to Betty, she howled with laughter and proceeded to improvise a routine about the "burnt holes" she had known in Hollywood. She capped it off by saying it was a pity she had been cured of her bladder problem—"I could have peed on every piece of furniture, and made the furniture guy a fortune." She recalled then that Louella Parsons had been notorious for having had chronic problems with her bladder. "But, somehow," said Betty, "that never increased the value of anything."

Betty usually reserved her energy during the day so she could reach a peak by showtime, but on one occasion she was up and out by mid-afternoon. Her destination was the Thunderbird Hotel, where whe had been invited to attend rehearsals for a show that was doing a one-nighter there. It was an appearance of the Harry James Orchestra.

As she sat and listened to that sweet trumpet sound, the years must have fallen away to a time when her dreams were all ahead, when she was young and romantic and hopeful. How many hours had she sat like this, listening to its heady call—at the Hollywood Palladium, the Astor Roof, some dive in Chicago? Times had changed; people had changed; but this was the way things were. She visited with Harry for several hours and promised to return for the late show after her final curtain.

She felt good. She even invited Art Kassul to get a date and join Bob and her at Harry's performance. Art got the date and was pleased to see Betty so vibrant and alive. But Betty's happy intentions were overruled by reality. The play's performance sapped every bit of energy she could muster. She had no choice but to hurry home afterward. She apologized to Kassul and insisted he go on without her. He did and was surprised to discover that Betty had called to make sure that his dinner check was charged to her.

Later Betty confided to Kassul that she still loved Harry James and probably always would. This February afternoon in Florida spent in the company of the man she would always love would have to last Betty an eternity. It was the last time she ever saw him.

One of the weekly card games at Betty's will never be forgotten by Art Kassul. He had given a cast party a few nights earlier, and Bob Remick told him how proud Betty had been of the way Kassul had handled the event. Art assumed Betty had enlisted Bob to pass along the praise because such remarks weren't easy for her. Kassul accepted the compliment graciously and felt good about it. That was early in the evening.

Later, when the other guests were gone and Betty had been asleep for hours, Remick and Kassul were having nightcaps together in the kitchen. Betty had seemed in particularly high spirits that night, and Kassul mentioned it. He said he was happy to see she was feeling better. Remick absorbed the remark, then, with tears in his eyes, he slowly lowered his head to his arms on the kitchen table. A few moments later, he pulled himself together enough to tell Kassul what no one else knew. It was only a matter of time. Betty didn't know it, but her cancer was terminal.

The pain in Betty's stomach wasn't imaginary, nor was her waning energy. She returned to St. John's Hospital in Santa Monica not long after the closing of *Born Yesterday* in Jacksonville, and a tumor was removed. The cancer in her lungs had been arrested, but the disease had spread throughout her body.

There would be no trip to Australia, nor would Betty play Billie Dawn again. The standing ovations in Jacksonville were Betty Grable's last hurrah.

# Chapter 2

The illustrious career that came to an end with the final curtain of *Born Yesterday* at the Alhambra Dinner Theatre in Jacksonville had begun somewhere in St. Louis approximately fifty years earlier. The scene may have been at a neighborhood school auditorium or at a local amateur show. Or her child's voice may have been heard straining to the popular tunes of the day over one of the city's radio stations.

Betty Grable was pressed into a variety of performing arts lessons and classes before she turned four. Within a couple of years she was a capable tap-dancer and a not-too-bad alto saxophonist. She could strum madly on a ukelele, was learning trap drums, and managed, at the very least, to sing on key.

It may appear that a child prodigy was on the loose, a moppet genius whose first words out of the cradle were, "Let me entertain you." But this was not the case. It was more a matter of a malleable child being programmed into a specific mode of life. The maestro—or Svengali, depending on viewpoint—was, in this instance, Betty's mother.

For Lillian Grable, it seems to have been a matter of dire necessity to bestow a performer upon the world. It isn't clear if it was a need to bask in reflected glory or to participate vicariously in another's adventures, but the compulsion, whatever its origins, was clear and unrelenting. She tried first with her older daughter, Marjorie, but failed. Then Betty, more amenable, and fortunately more talented, came along and filled the bill.

The impetus behind Lillian's ambition perhaps had something to do with her infirmity, a stiff hip that rendered her an ambulatory cripple; daughter Marjorie recalled that her mother had a very lovely singing voice, but she didn't remember any confessions of show business aspirations. It is also possible that Lillian's father, Charles Hofman, influenced her, since he was known to have been an accomplished cellist. Marjorie was unable to attest to his talents, however, because her only memories of Grandfather Hofman were of a pensioned old man with only one hand. The other had been lost many years earlier when he was short-fused by a Fourth of July cannon cracker, which cut short any musical ambitions he may have had.

Very little family history was passed along to the Grable offspring. Lillian was never a family person, and, while her husband, Conn Grable, was much more gregarious, his socializing never included relatives. The Grables were, for the most part, an isolated family unit—self-contained, loners.

Lillian, who had an older brother and two sisters, was born May 29, 1890 to Charles and Elizabeth Hofman. Charles was of German ancestry, and his wife, the former Elizabeth Goodenough, was of English stock.

Lillian may have recounted childhood recollections to her daughters over the years, but among the few remembered by Marjorie was Lillian's account of her visit to the magnificent St. Louis World's Fair of 1904. The fair, officially designated the Louisiana Purchase Exposition, provided the background for the 1944 Judy Garland musical *Meet Me In St. Louis,* but Lillian Hofman made an important meeting at the real fair. It was there she met Conn Grable, and they would marry three years later.

"I don't know if they were introduced, or if they picked each other up," said Marjorie, "but mother was young, because she hadn't turned eighteen when they were married."

Conn, born to John and Lavinia Grable in 1885, was christened John Conn Grable, but his first name was never used. His father was of Dutch heritage, and his mother, Lavinia Conn, was Irish. Conn had four sisters.

John Grable died when Conn was very young, which made it necessary for him to go to work when he finished grammar school. He became a board boy for the St. Louis Stock Exchange, one of the lads who entered the stock quotations on the blackboard after they came over the ticker tape from New York. "He eventually became a stockbroker," said Marjorie. "He had an office in downtown St. Louis with a man named Orthwein and was enormously successful before the crash."

Marjorie was born to Conn and Lillian April 17, 1909, and a brother, John Karl, came along five years later. But he was doomed to an early demise. At twenty-two months he contracted whooping cough and pneumonia. Deep snow made it impossible for little John Karl to get help, but the doctor sent word by telephone to put the child in a tub of hot water. Conn was further instructed to attempt drawing the phlegm from his throat with his fingers. "Daddy tried to do it," Marjorie said, "but the baby bit daddy's forefinger clear through to the bone. He carried the scar all through life. John died in early 1916, when mother was beginning her pregnancy with Betty."

The birth of John Karl complicated Lillian's hip condition, and she was warned not to bear any more children. The warning came too late, however, because Lillian was already pregnant with Betty. On December 18, 1916, the birth occurred without complication, and Ruth Elizabeth Grable first saw light of day. Throughout her life Betty was reminded of what Lillian went through to bring her into the world. When Betty demonstrated recalcitrance in her early training regimen, Lillian did not hesitate to use this device to bring her into line.

Lillian's difficulty with her hip had been prevalent since she was quite young, but she never explained what caused it. Marjorie often wondered if her mother was stricken with polio. Her hip had become enlarged, frequently causing Lillian to lose her balance and fall. Each fall would complicate the condition by loosening the socket. She refused to discuss the matter. She was often taken to a doctor by a friend, but would announce only that she would be away for the afternoon. Surgeons eventually fused the hip in its socket, and for many years Lillian was confined to a wheelchair. Lillian despised her invalidism. Later, only a cane was needed as an aid to her mobility, but she resented even this. Often, much to Betty's dismay, Lillian would abandon the cane just when she would need it most, when she was a bit on the tipsy side.

The Grables had a comfortable home in the German section of South St. Louis, but, because of Lillian's ambulatory difficulty, they decided to move to an apartment hotel. They chose the Forest Park Hotel on Lindle Avenue, in what was then the west end of town. It was only a block from a delightful park and close to one of the better metropolitan zoos. The apartment was spacious, but had only one bedroom. Still there was room for everyone to do what they had to do—there was certainly room for the wood platform Conn had built to accommodate Betty's tap-dancing practice, and there was a piano. All meals were eaten downstairs in the hotel dining room.

Throughout Betty's life her friends were aware of her strange proclivity for wetting her pants. It seemed impossible for her to give full vent to laughter and control her bladder at the same time. And if there was one thing Betty had to do, it was laugh, consequences be damned. One of the earliest accidents recalled by Betty occurred when she was a very small child in St. Louis.

Lillian Grable, ever inventive, covered Betty's tiny body with a concoction of lavender makeup to make her appear stark white under glaring stage lights. Betty got a glance at herself in the dressing room mirror and started to giggle. The more Lillian chastised her, the worse the giggles became, until the inevitable happened. Betty wet herself, ruining the costume and turning her painted body into a smeared disaster area. Lillian failed to appreciate the humor of the situation and gave Betty a smart crack across the cheek.

Lillian was obsessed with bringing Betty before the public eye. If there were no amateur shows or auditions available, she would arrange impromptu gatherings to put Betty on display. Even on vacation Lillian would organize entertainment in resort hotel lobbies to show off the family star. Betty would tap dance, blow her sax, and sing to Lillian's delight. There is no record of the audience reaction to such command performances, but it didn't really matter—not to Lillian. She had no doubts regarding her daughter's talents, and no power on earth could convince her otherwise.

"Mother was lucky," Marjorie said, "because I sure flunked everything. My piano, singing, and dancing lessons cost daddy a fortune. I couldn't carry a tune and didn't know one foot from the other. Then mother started me on violin lessons, which was the final straw. Daddy came home one night and said, 'One of us goes, the violin or me.' I said, 'Daddy, don't push your luck.' But he won out. They finally gave up on me altogether. Then Betty came along, and it started all over again. But with Betty, at least they had some talent to work with."

After moving to Forest Park, Lillian enrolled Betty in the rather exclusive Mary Institute. Before Betty had her pencils organized in her new desk, Lillian was at work campaigning for special treatment for her gifted daughter. The pleas were apparently ignored, because Betty was not chosen to be one of the predebs in the school's fortnightly ball. The affront was more than Lillian could bear. Betty was pulled out of the school with a yank that could have caused whiplash.

As a child, Betty made many vaudeville appearances and was on the same bill with stars such as Jack Haley and Bert Wheeler. On one occasion she was included in a bill with Jane Froman, who was a favorite star of Marjorie's. Otherwise oblivious to Betty's show business forays, Marjorie took notice this time and happily used her connection with Betty to get backstage for a Jane Froman autograph. Marjorie, eight years older than Betty, was at an age when girls were easily star struck, and this was a highlight of her life.

Several years later, when Marjorie was enrolled at the University of Missouri at Columbia, Betty paid a visit to the campus (with her mother and father). "Betty and I went horseback riding," Marjorie recalled, "and that day I was thrown. We came back to the Kappa house for Sunday dinner, and I realized something was wrong. I called my beau, and he took me to the hospital where it was discovered I had broken my pelvis. I was put in the hospital, and the family stayed on to be near me. A few days later momma was looking through the local newspaper and saw that a Hollywood talent scout was in town. Bingo—she was down there! He told her to bring Betty to Hollywood. I have no idea who it was. He may have been from RKO. But that was when momma made up her mind to leave St. Louis."

There was a delay, while Marjorie recuperated from her accident, and she missed a year at college. Conn bought a seven-passenger, custom-built Lincoln for the journey and did all the planning for the trip, but it was never his intention to remain in Los Angeles with the family. He would stay long enough to establish Lillian and Betty in an apartment and then return home. This was fine with Lillian, because Conn had pledged to finance the movieland adventure and, despite the impending stock market crash, would continue to do so.

"Mother had mapped out her life," said Marjorie, "and daddy and I didn't fit into the picture at all. Mother charted her road and got there. She was a very strong-willed woman."

With one spouse as fiercely driven as Lillian, one might expect the other spouse to be passive. Marjorie insisted this wasn't the case. She said her father was very strong and assertive and was very strict in issuing discipline; he was, however, warm and jovial as well and possessed an unflagging sense of humor, which was obviously inherited by Betty. Conn was known as "Bud" by his cronies, and he spent a good number of hours with them in nearby clubs. Lillian never joined in.

Conn was also generous. The Christmas before the departure to Hollywood, he presented Lillian with an expensive diamond bracelet, and for the trip he bought a fur blanket in which Lillian could ride in the Pullman-sized backseat like a queen.

This was not the first family trip to the West Coast. They had been there on two previous occasions, but not with an eye toward remaining. This trip was the important one, and Marjorie and Betty often reminisced over it in later years.

It was one of those seemingly interminable odysseys that was recalled more as fiction than fact. There was the imperious Lillian perched in the middle of the broad backseat, with her fur blanket drawn over her lap, like Queen Victoria. There was the harassed Conn Grable some five feet in front of her, guiding the huge auto over the primitive highways. There were the orders from the queen, the myriad stops, and the unending complaints regarding the shabby hotels in the jerkwater towns along the way. Then, finally, there were the Rocky Mountains.

Lillian was horrified at the residue of previous landslides along the narrow mountain highways and was stricken with terror by the ragged edges of some spans of road where actual highway had chipped off and plummeted over seemingly bottomless cliffs. At each hairpin turn the children were enlisted to take turns in running ahead to peer around the other side. When the way was clear, the girls would wave the car forward and stand by until it had safely negotiated the turn.

To Betty and Marjorie the trip was a truly unique experience, and they considered themselves special in their right to declare that they had crossed the Rocky Mountains on foot. They each swore that this was not much of an exaggeration.

After a long, hot trip over the Mojave Desert, the mammoth sedan climbed the final mountain range, and descended into an irrigated wonderland. For miles in every direction there were seemingly endless groves of bountifully-laden orange trees. A sign near a roadside stand said: "All the orange juice you can drink for 5¢." It must have read as a symbol to Lillian that the land of plenty was clearly at hand.

The first West Coast dwelling for Lillian and Betty was close to the Ambassador Hotel on Wilshire Boulevard. It was closer to downtown Los Angeles than to Hollywood, but the nearby restaurant shaped like a brown derby hat was a ready reminder that Hollywood was not far away.

It was now the summer of 1929, and, as Conn and Marjorie went sightseeing, Lillian was already laying the cornerstones for the Betty Grable career. Betty was enrolled at the Hollywood Professional School, whose students were movie brats, some with contracts, others with hope. She was set for dancing lessons at the Ernest Belcher Academy and would be coached in acting at the Albertina Rosch School. This would not be a summer of languishing on the beach for Betty; she had come to California to work.

At the end of his vacation, Conn said farewell to his family, including Marjorie, who remained with her mother until time for fall enrollment at college. Back in St. Louis, Conn found himself thrust into long hours of work to make up for the backlog that had accumulated during his absence. Then, when the way was finally open for new business advances, the bottom dropped out of everything. On October 29, Black Thursday, the stock market crashed.

It was back to square one for Conn; all his reserves were soon dissipated, and stockbroking was probably the worst profession in the country. Conn never again knew affluence, but his mathematical acumen kept him working for others. He was able to eke out enough income to keep Marjorie in college and continue the weekly stipends to Lillian and Betty.

As far as Lillian was concerned, the Depression simply meant that she and Betty would have to accelerate their efforts. She kept knocking on doors, parading Betty before casting directors, and taking her around to auditions. She managed to buy a relic of a roadster devoid of a top, in which Betty was transported to beauty contests, little theater gigs, and casting calls. When the rains came with winter, nothing was curtailed. The only difference was that Betty would be there on time—but wet.

A friend of Betty's came to Hollywood from St. Louis at the same time she did, and they planned to work up an act together. The girl friend, Emelyn Pique, danced while Betty blew on her sax. They had the routine honed and polished and ready to go, but before their debut Emelyn backed down. The perky youngster was offered a job in New York as a single and jumped at the chance. Betty was left holding the sax. Her friend remained in New York throughout most of her career and became quite well known under the name Mitzie Mayfair.

A few weeks after being abandoned by Emelyn, Betty answered a chorus call at Fox Studios for a film called *Let's Go Places.* Because of her pretty young face, her precociously abundant figure, and her facile foot work, Betty was signed. Although Betty was only thirteen at the time, Lillian had hustled false identification that proved she was fifteen, the minimum age for chorus work at the time.

Betty ran home to tell Lillian the good news, but her mother failed to respond with excitement. Lillian had known it was only a matter of time. She had spent ten long years preparing her daughter for this break in show business, and at last Betty's foot was in the door. Betty had been only an aspirant yesterday, but today? Today she was in the movies.

# Chapter 3

Betty may have blended into the scenery in *Let's Go Places,* but not as far as Lillian was concerned. Only a few days later, Lillian was cracking her cane against the Fox casting office door, with her daughter, the film actress, in tow. She was there to point out that her daughter was no common hoofer. She could also sing, play the sax and drums, roller skate, ice skate, do acrobatics—in fact, practically anything an imaginative director could dream of in a musical.

It isn't known if the casting director was beaten down by Lillian's supersalesmanship, or if he could see Betty's potential. Whatever his reasoning, Betty came away with a studio chorus contract with an assured sixty dollars a week for a year. At age thirteen, a whole year seemed to be a great deal of security indeed.

Since Fox was investing in their young chorine, they lost no time in coming up with her second assignment. She was outfitted for the chorus line in the El Brendel starrer, *New Movietone Follies.* In this picture she was almost as obscure as in *Let's Go Places,* but in the first film she had been hidden by blackface makeup. In this one she was recognizable, which spelled her doom at Fox. With recognition came knowledge of Betty's tender years. Her security went up in a puff of smoke; she was fired.

Betty, childlike and easily defeated, came home to her mother with an attitude of having tried but lost. She had had her fling in movies and supposed that now it was time to try something else. Such an attitude was totally alien to Lillian's nature, and Betty wasn't permitted even five minutes of self-pity. The trusty roadster was cranked up, and mother and daughter drove to the casting offices of Goldwyn-United Artists.

Lillian was uncanny in such matters, as if she were equipped with a special radar system that sensed difficulty and divined solution. She had learned that the people at Goldwyn were considering the organization of a stock chorus line to serve as repertory hoofers in the studio's musicals. At this time casting was underway for the movie adaptation of the Broadway hit, *Whoopee,* starring Eddie Cantor.

Times were tough, and everybody knew it. For this casting call 1,500 girls turned out, each hopeful for a miraculous break in the movies or, at the least, a few weeks salary to put food on the table. Betty went through her smiling paces and was one of the lucky girls hired for the pony line. This assignment closed Betty's first year in the movies, and she hadn't done badly at all—for a tot who had just turned fourteen.

Betty's vitality and healthy good looks, coupled with her work in *Whoopee,* earned her a Goldwyn contract, and once again she was puppy-dog happy. The studio loaned her out soon afterward for a United Artists remake of *Kiki,* starring the immortal Mary Pickford. When her bit part was finished, she was once more a Goldwyn Girl in the Eddie Cantor film *Palmy Days.*

Betty was a taunting and untouchable adolescent when she wore the Goldwyn Girl banner in *Palmy Days,* and her fully budded charms did not escape the notice of one of the fellow cast members, who was at least twenty years her senior. The actor, playing the role of Joe-the-Frog, was George Raft. Betty was, of course, far too young for the Latin-type lover, but it didn't really matter. There was no way on earth this ingenue could be placed in compromising circumstances. Betty was watched like a stack of gold bullion at Fort Knox, which was not far from the value her mother attached to her blossoming offspring.

There were a few dates, however, and Raft was a model of decorum. If Lillian were unavailable as chaperone, it was Betty's older sister Marjorie who would take responsibility. There was always someone of authority very close at hand. They went to a fight or two, watched a few ball games, and were seen regularly at the Six-Day Bicycle Races, but then, as Raft put it himself, he "tossed her back into the pond." What he did, actually, was place Betty on hold, where she would remain, as far as he was concerned, for the better part of a decade.

A look at her published credits suggests that Betty worked around the clock in 1932, but most of her film assignments required little of her time. In *The Greeks Had a Word For Them,* Betty did nothing more than model a Chanel gown; in *The Kid From Spain,* she donned the Goldwyn Girl scanties for a single production number; and in Columbia's *Child of Manhattan,* she played a bit part for which she received seventh billing. But this loan-out to Columbia marked the end of her Goldwyn-United Artists contract. She was confident when option time rolled around, but was once more met with rejection. Her option was dropped without ceremony.

There were two other films logged for Betty in 1932, but they came late in the year. She was also inviegled into a spot in the Frank Fay–Barbara Stanwyck road show, *Tattle Tales,* but because of Fay's inability to remain sober, the show closed early.

The full impact of the Depression was making the entertainment industry reel at this time, and to be out of work was tantamount to queuing up in the bread line. But the Grable luck—whether it was Lillian's or Betty's—held true. Just as Betty and her mother were packing up to leave San Francisco, Lillian had a flash of pure inspiration.

The major cause for Frank Fay's booze-out during *Tattle Tales* was his reunion with longtime imbibing buddy, Ted Fio Rito. Fay had been maintaining reasonable success at sobriety until the two cronies got together to hang one on. Fio Rito loved to drink, but he could function under the influence. Not Fay, he would get so drunk he couldn't stand on the stage, let alone remember lines and speak them coherently. The show had to shut down. Since it was Fio Rito's influence that caused Betty's sudden case of unemployment, it should be Fio Rito who came to her rescue.

With this conviction firmly in mind, Lillian limped across the street to the St. Francis Hotel and cornered the millionaire bandleader. He had attended the show's rehearsals; he had seen Betty's perky rendition of "I'll Take an Option On You;" he could see how adorable she was. Didn't he think she would be an asset to any show? Before Lillian left the hotel suite, she had him convinced that Betty should join his band as a vocalist. The salary would be seventy-five dollars a week, and there would be free room and board at the hotel. Everything had already been packed, so all Lillian and Betty had to do was carry their bags across the street and move in. The next evening Betty was beaming her personality at the Junior League customers in the Mural Room of the St. Francis. The high-society clientele were entranced by the youthful energy Betty added to the rather sedate ensemble.

Muzzy Marcelino, Fio Rito's guitarist and one of the vocalists, said Betty was cute and energetic and made a nice appearance before the band, but her voice wasn't good enough to make recordings with the orchestra. There were two sessions a month and regular network radio broadcasts, but Betty was excused from those dates. The lead male vocalist was always included, however, with his rich baritone talents. This was young Leif Erickson, who would become a successful movie actor a few years hence.

It was autumn when Betty joined the band, and she remained with them until the following summer, and the months were not exactly uneventful. Betty was in her sixteenth year by this time, and there were certain physical awakenings to deal with. The twinges had been recognized before, surely, but had been willfully restrained. On this occasion, however, Betty's libido burst into full blossom. She found herself deeply enamored of the handsome young drummer with the band, Charlie Price.

Charlie was only nineteen, but he was earning more than a hundred a week and tooled around San Francisco in a gleaming 1932 Oldsmobile cabroilet, with leather seats under the canvas top and a rumble seat behind. It was there that Lillian sat when she accompanied them on their dates. Muzzy and his girl friend often double-dated with them.

"We would all be bundled up in the front of the car," says Marcelino, "and would deposit her mother in the back. We would ply her with wine, so by the time we reached the beach, our rendezvous point, she would be passed out in the rumble seat. It was the only way we would get any freedom from her. Betty's mother was always there."

Charlie Price said that Monday was the band's day off, and he and Betty often used it to go dancing or to the movies, and they frequently attended the Fox Theater, where a 110-piece symphony orchestra was in the pit. "Mrs. Grable was always with us," he said. "She didn't like the idea of Betty getting serious about anyone, and I never had any hard feelings about it. I could see her side of it."

When the contract came to an end at the St. Francis, Betty toured much of the country with the band in a custom-made, double-deck Greyhound bus. The tour eventually ended up with an extended date at the Ambassador Hotel in Los Angeles.

Muzzy Marcelino recalled an incident aboard the bus that illustrates Betty's capacity as a "spoiled brat." Betty got into a quarrel with viola player Norm Bobnik. "All of us wore striped trousers with morning coats, complete with spats," said Marcelino. "At the height of the fight, Betty grabbed Norm's striped pants and stuffed them into the john, which, of course, stopped up the plumbing. Then she got his viola and tried to push it out of the window of the moving bus. It was worth at least a couple thousand. Someone grabbed her just in time. Fio Rito wasn't a task master, but he laid it on Betty that time. She almost got fired."

Betty liked the adventure of road touring, but, with her mother omnipresent, it amounted to long hours, hard work, and a scarcity of personal pleasure. Not that her life in Los Angeles had been a never-ending gambol, but there, at least, she had had considerably more freedom. To Betty, "liberty" was nothing more than the name of a five-cent magazine.

If, on the other hand, Lillian felt the inclination to party, she did not hesitate to lock Betty up in the hotel room while she went out. This restraining measure had not been used for a while, but it had been employed often enough in the past for Betty to fear its revival.

Betty was generally obedient to her mother's commands, but, even when she was young, there were moments of rebellion. Lillian usually countered these outbursts with the tried and tested application of guilt. "If I had taken the doctor's advice, you wouldn't be alive today." Or, "If it weren't for you, I wouldn't be walking with a limp." The device was usually, but not always, effective.

It wasn't that Betty stood toe-to-toe with her mother and slugged it out. She tried to avoid such drastic confrontations, because she knew Lillian would never give in. Instead, Betty listened passively to the chastisement and then proceeded with whatever she had to do. It would start all over again at their next encounter, but, if that was the price for a moment of freedom, Betty paid it.

Now, with Betty so demonstrably smitten with the drummer, Lillian was bewildered. She had the feeling she was losing control. In frustration, she called her husband, Conn, displaced now for more than three years. She said Betty was not responding to discipline, and the time had come for him to come West. Since the SOS involved his loving daughter, Conn lost little time in responding to the plea. By the time he finally cleaned up his affairs in St. Louis, the band had returned to Los Angeles for its date at the Ambassador.

During the early Thirties, Betty and her mother lived in the Canterbury Apartments on the southeast corner of Yucca and

Cherokee in the heart of Hollywood. One of Betty's few girl friends at the time, Sugar Geise, lived only a block away at the La Leyenda. They became friends as they made actor's rounds together, and for several weeks both were chorus girls in an Olson and Johnson review. That was in 1930, and their friendship lasted several years, until their careers finally separated them. Sugar became a star dancer at the Florentine Gardens in Hollywood and remained there for many years.

"Betty and her mother had the apartment on the second floor of the Canterbury," she said, "just above the lobby. The rooms were on the south side of the building facing Hollywood Boulevard. My most vivid recollection is of her mother standing for hours in the kitchen ironing those organdy dresses for Betty to wear when she was singing with bands. I never saw her mother mistreat her in any way, and they were always together. Betty didn't have many friends."

Their first meeting was in 1930, when they were on a chorus interview. Betty was wearing a lavender and cream-colored swim suit with a lavender beret. Sugar remembered her as being very striking to the eye, but somewhat lacking in disposition. "Later we were such good friends that I never really noticed," she said. "But so often others would mention how quarrelsome and complaining she always was. She wasn't the least bit conceited, though, and didn't act superior in any way, but she was rather crabby, I guess. I think she got her disposition from her father. He could be plain nasty. Later on both our families lived at the Knickerbocker, and I remember her father would get mad at the Filipino bell boys, and would call them 'Pineapples'—to their faces. Lillian actually had the nicest disposition of the three."

Sugar says the catalyst that compelled Lillian to call Conn out from St. Louis was a letter Betty had written to Charlie Price. She gave it to Lillian for mailing, but, before doing so, Lillian opened it up and read it. Betty's serious intent was expressed in the letter, and Lillian was nonplussed. Betty was furious that her mother read her private correspondence, but that changed nothing. Lillian began to crack down and sent for Conn to help.

Conn cornered Betty soon after joining them in Hollywood and proceeded to lay down the law. He forbade her to see any more of her adored musician and, furthermore, declared that she would be returning to school. Lillian may have panicked a little at this ad lib, but Betty handled the matter with aplomb. "I'm not going to be a scientist or a banker," she argued, sensibly. "I'm not going to become a bookworm either."

The quarrel probably expanded from there, but Betty struck truth in her opening statement. She asserted she would never become a scientist or a banker, which was true, but, although she couldn't have been aware of it then, she was destined to become one of the country's better-known students. Not in real life, of course, but on the screen. Betty, in the prime of youth and nubile cuteness, would soon become the almost perennial movie-world coed. Meanwhile, as for the love affair, it would cool slowly but surely. The Fio Rito band went on the road again, and Betty remained in Hollywood. Absence, in this case, did not make her heart grow fonder.

When Betty was only eight, she won a Charleston contest in St. Louis on a vaudeville bill headlined by comic Bert Wheeler. At the time he said, "Sometime you'll be in Hollywood. Look me up, and I'll do everything I can to help you."

It would be unthinkable that Lillian would have passed up an invitation this clearly stated. The odds are that she was rapping on Wheeler's door before she and Betty had fully unpacked. But three years had passed since the Grables hit the West Coast, before Wheeler's help found her a job. Betty landed the role of a prison warden's daughter in the Wheeler and Woolsey movie, *Hold 'Em Jail.*

Next, Betty free-lanced in the independent production of *Probation,* in which she was given ninth billing. She went on to make a series of two-reel shorts for other independent producers. Three of them were directed by Fatty Arbuckle, who was working under the name, William Goodrich. He had been blackballed out of the business as a result of the notorious sex scandal that had taken place a decade earlier. He was never convicted of a crime in connection with it, but his career was through. He could only work under assumed names, which made sense, but, strangely, Betty also used a fictitious name, Frances Dean, in these films.

Betty was cast in the 1933 Fox film *Cavalcade* as "Girl on Couch." The movie would win the Academy Award for that year, but Betty would share little of its glory. She teamed up again with Ted Fio Rito, but only to work in the film, *Sweetheart of Sigma Chi* at Monogram. She then landed a stewardess role in the RKO production, *Melody Cruise,* and received fourth billing at Columbia in *What Price Innocence.* In this she played the girl friend of Jean Parker, the female lead. This was her meatiest role of all, but the melodrama was a critical embarrassment in its attempt to decry the dangers implicit in sexual innocence. It was an anachronistic commercial for birth control, essentially, but the message came in strident tones at a time when even whispers on such a subject were taboo. *The New York Times* review stated: "The film has none of the subtlety, indirection or dramatic power needed to make the theme palatable for the public screens."

Betty was on an extended roll, but it finally came to an end. When no further film work was forthcoming, she was pleased to accept another band gig. This time she would join the Ted Whidden orchestra at the San Francisco Mark Hopkins Hotel. Several weeks later the band moved down to the Miramar Hotel in nearby Santa Monica. It was here she was noticed by certain powers at MGM, who signed her for the role of Cayenne in the comedy, *Student Tour,* starring Jimmy Durante. This marked the beginning of Betty's own student tour. She played her first coed role. Another of the students in the film was newcomer Nelson Eddy, whose stardom would be earned later on. This wasn't the vehicle to advance anyone. *The New York Times* said: "The script possesses the sparkle and the wit of a performing elephant, and the headlong speed of a Step 'n' Fetchit."

Before *Student Tour* could be held against her, Betty struck pay dirt. Her new agent, Vic Orsatti, landed her a featured role in the forthcoming RKO film, *Gay Divorcee.* The part wasn't a big one, but was unique in that Betty was to do an important dance number in which neither of the stars would be involved. The stars in this case were Fred Astaire and Ginger Rogers; Betty performed the "Let's K-nock K-nees" number with comedian Edward Everett Horton.

On the strength of her appearance in *Gay Divorcee,* Betty was once more signed to a contract. RKO dyed her hair platinum, Harlowed her brows, and gave her the ingenue lead in *The Nitwits,* another Wheeler and Woolsey starrer.

Betty's next assignment was *Old Man Rhythm,* in which she played a rosy-cheeked coed. Joining her with beany and saddle shoes was another fresh-faced contractee, Lucille Ball. Before her mood changed, Betty, the up-and-coming college-kid was farmed out to Paramount to give school cheers in *Collegiate.* The star of *Old Man Rhythm* was Buddy Rogers. In *Collegiate,* Joe Penner was featured as the inheritor of a girls' school, which he converts into an academy for chorines. Betty got lost in the crowd.

Betty returned to RKO for another Astaire–Rogers musical, *Follow the Fleet,* but there was no specialty number for her in this one. She played one of a trio of showgirls, in a cast that included Lucille Ball and Harriet Hilliard.

Pandro S. Berman produced *Gay Divorcee, By Your Leave,* and *Follow the Fleet,* all of which included Betty in the cast, but Berman had no knowledge of her existence until years later. "She was such a child then," he explains. "I never really got to meet her. I would know her socially years later, but during the early years I only recall a nice little school girl who came along about the same time as Ann Miller."

While these are the recollections of the man who produced three of her early movies, it was probably the consensus of reviewers and moviegoers alike. If an analysis were made of the Betty Grable rise to stardom, it would seem a miracle that she was ever signed by a studio. It seemed inevitable that once Betty was under contract, all initial enthusiasm began to fade. She bobbed around from one campus fling to another, ending up unnoticed by all but her most stalwart fans. Her roles in most of the college capers weren't noteworthy enough to elicit even minimal mention in the reviews. It was apparent that just being there wasn't enough. There seemed to be a missing ingredient that neither Lillian nor Betty were able to see.

From the time Betty was little more than a tot, she had presented the surface appearance of womanhood. Her straight, exercised legs were nicely developed; her breasts were full and provocative; her face, while scrubbed and youthful, suggested adulthood; but, actually, Betty was a toy woman. She had not yet turned into an adult.

Her sexuality seems to have awakened on schedule, but she failed to exude the look of it. She didn't possess that vital look, that essence of completeness. But then an incident arose that changed Betty measurably. She met someone who brought her alive.

It took place on a typically sunny day in late summer, 1935. Betty was aboard the S.S. *Catalina* for a day's outing to the island. Mamma was along, of course, and also on board was a young male film personality, one the entire world would recognize. Betty had crossed paths with him once or twice before, but nothing had come of it. This time, however, the chemistry seemed to blend. He greeted Betty amiably and introduced himself to Lillian. "Hello, Mrs. Grable," he said. "I'm Jackie Coogan."

Lillian's expression brightened. Yes, of course, she had been reading about young Mister Coogan. What a shame his father was killed in that horrible accident the previous spring. But what else was it she had been reading? Wasn't there some talk about an imminent inheritance? As she recalled, Jackie Coogan was destined to come into something like four million dollars on his twenty-first birthday.

Lillian commented on how grown up he had become and offered all the requisite platitudes regarding memories of his childhood acting accomplishments, and then she asked the question: "Just how old are you now, Jackie?"

"I'm twenty," he told her. "I'll be twenty-one in October."

"Sit down, Jackie. Please, sit down."

That was approximately how the relationship began between Betty and the world's first child superstar. It was the first time in Betty's nineteen and a half years that she had met an attractive young man of whom her mother seemed to approve. Jackie was a singularly charming person, but how could he be otherwise after mingling with presidents and royalty? He was fairly tall, slim, and broad-shouldered. The more Betty looked him over, the better she liked what she saw.

Betty's missing ingredient soon became manifest. She began to glow with the expression of womanly love, and, due to Jackie's fame, her glow was seen by millions.

# Chapter 4

Betty was never bold among strangers, and even after achieving stardom she was seemingly stunned that anyone could want her autograph. She kept a low profile, but, when bolstered by the company of the right pal, she could be irrepressible. She was always more motivated by a good time than by any ambition for career success.

Paula Stone, whose later marriage to Mike Sloan kept her name sounding pretty much the same, was a buddy of Betty's from the days when both of them were under contract to RKO. She holds vivid memories of the high jinks that surrounded Betty all the way back to the Thirties and the good times they always had together.

"I remember Lela Rogers [Ginger's mother] used to give acting lessons on one of the RKO sound stages," said Paula, "and Betty and I went a few times. It was always Betty's idea to get into these self-improvement programs. She was always studying, working, trying to improve herself. Another time she kept after me to take tap-dancing lessons with her. She was always very persuasive, and hated to do anything by herself. So I took tap with her, despite the fact that I had been taught by Bill Robinson, one of the best teachers in the world."

Paula, who years later became a Broadway producer, came from a theatrical family. Her father was the famous vaudevillian and actor Fred Stone. Her cousin was Milburn, who played Doc for so many years in "Gunsmoke." She was happy to reminisce over the carefree outings she and Betty had, like the time they all went to the amusement pier in Santa Monica. "Betty was so beautiful in white slacks," she said. "She was eating corn-on-the-cob, and was singing "Chloe" between bites. It was always something like that."

Everyone who knew Betty agreed that she was extremely funny, but examples of her humor are difficult to come by. She wasn't a storyteller and didn't tell jokes. She possessed an indefinable irreverence manifested in asides, wisecracks, plays on words, and ribaldry that was ever present. All her life Betty seemed more like the bad boy in class, rather than the sweet-faced angel of her appearance. She was highly skilled when it came to simulated burping, for instance, and would gladly demonstrate her ability to anyone present, no matter where she might happen to be. One of her favorite vehicles for demonstration was the song "Take Me Out To the Ball Game," but she would sing it: *"Burrrrp* me out to the ball game, *burrrrp* me out with the crowd. . . . " And the burps that replaced the words of the song were grand and resonant, loud and clear.

Unlike many others who were always on, Betty was as good an audience as she was a performer. She would fall apart with laughter at the slightest provocation. Betty had the rare ability to find humor in almost anything. Paula gives an example.

"I was taking singing lessons from Mrs. Gumm, Judy Garland's mother," Paula said. "She became impatient with me during one of the lessons and called Judy inside to help me. Judy had been skating outside with Jackie Cooper, and they both skated inside when Mrs. Gumm called. Judy stood beside the piano and sang the passage divinely. Her mother said that this was how she wanted me to do it. I was almost in tears. I said 'I can't sing like that.' "

Betty listened in amusement and asked Paula what the passage was that had given her so much trouble. "Betty was driving at the time," said Paula, "and when I repeated the phrase she fell over the steering wheel in hysterics. It was 'Jebeetah jebahta joobee doodee wah,' and Betty thought that was the funniest thing in the world. We harmonized all the way home to jebeetah jebahta joobee doodee wah."

When Betty started earning money during the mid-1930s, she redecorated her bedroom and hurried Paula over to see it. "She bought a canopied bed," said Paula, "and the whole room was done in white with lots of red bows everywhere. The room was like a candy box. She insisted I stay over so I could sleep in the canopied bed. I'm sure that today even Betty would realize there was something in the decoration she had dreamed of as a little girl."

The little girl in Betty emerged regularly throughout her life. It was almost as if she were constantly seeking the childhood that had eluded her.

Another friend who dates back to the RKO days is Lucille Ball. She recalls the great times they had together at parties. "I was always sure I'd have a good time if Betty was there," she said. "She was the funniest person I ever knew, and everyone loved her. She had what I call a kind of kinky, curly, wonderful way of looking at things."

Lucille also was one of the first of her friends to learn of a Grable peculiarity: her penchant for sleepwalking. "We were on tour for some reason," said Lucy, "and were booked into this hotel. Betty's mother asked for the ground floor, but there was nothing available on any of the lower floors, so I was asked to sleep in the room next to Betty's, and her mother would sleep on the other side. The reason, I was told, was that Betty walked in her sleep, and we had to be careful. That was all I needed, right? I didn't sleep a wink. I spent the whole night looking in on Betty. And sure enough she did get up and start walking, and headed right for the window. Thank God, I was there. Her mother told me to just quietly turn Betty around and lead her back to bed, which I did. I would have bet that Betty was playing a joke on me, but, knowing her, she would have had to break up somewhere along the line. She got back into bed and didn't recall any of it the next morning."

It would be interesting to hear the psychological explanation for Betty's somnambulism. Was she subconsciously trying to escape the restrictions imposed by her mother? Whatever its causal factors, the anomaly was one Betty would always live with and was the cause for her avoiding the higher floors of hotels during her travels.

Many years later, Betty was again faced with a hotel that had no room on the lower floors. This time it was at New York's Waldorf Astoria. She had the bellman stack furniture against the balcony door. "You don't have to worry, Miss Grable," said the bellman. "We're on the thirtieth floor. . . . No one could possibly get in from the balcony."

"I know," she told the puzzled young man, "but I can get out."

Lucille Ball was close to Betty during several of her single years, and was very much on hand during Betty's courtship days with Jackie Coogan. She recalls the party atmosphere created by Betty and Jackie, and how well suited they seemed for each other at the time. But, they were, of course, very young, and weren't prepared for the conflict that life can provide.

Lillian was ambivalent regarding the engagement. She and Conn didn't forbid it, however, because neither expected a marriage to follow. They elected to allow nature to take its course.

What no one had counted on was the other Lillian in the picture. If Lillian Grable was strong and manipulative, Lillian Coogan, Jackie's mother, was shrewd and cold as marble. There was no way on earth she would condone the alliance, and when Jackie revealed the engagement she employed every means short of physical force to break it up. She knew Betty's RKO contract wouldn't permit her marriage until her twenty-first birthday, which gave her more than a year to place obstacles in the way.

When the publicity broke on the Coogan/Grable engagement, Betty's name became an almost overnight household word. Her obscurity was behind her, and no matter what else came about, she would begin to ascend the long ladder to success. Betty had that glow about her now, and, thanks to the publicity, the movie fans in Cleveland and Keokuk could see it.

Franchon and Marco, the vaudeville packagers, knew a good thing when they saw it. They offered the young lovers a tour across the country that was difficult to turn down. They were seeking the proper personalities to MC a show called *Hollywood Secrets,* and this was where the search ended. The show was first-class and well produced, and RKO approved Betty's acceptance of the offer. It was launched December 11, 1935.

The show received excellent reviews at each stop along the way. In Boston, a reviewer said, "Jackie is as good a performer as in his baby days, and Betty Grable is even prettier in person than on the screen."

"There's an interesting sketch in which Miss Grable and Coogan appear as movie stars. It actually shows how pictures are made with an authentic set, director, mike, and other necessary details. Besides serving as an education, this little playlet is highly amusing and well acted."

One of the highlights of the trip for Betty was her appearance in hometown St. Louis—the return of the conquering heroine. She was accompanied as always by Lillian, and Conn traipsed along for good measure. In a news conference, the discomfiture of her parents was apparent to newspersons when the discussion involved Betty and Jackie's forthcoming marriage.

"Not for a long time," replied Betty, when asked when the wedding would take place. "My contract has something in it that says I mustn't marry until I am twenty-one. That will be a year from next December. There'll be plenty of time to prepare for the wedding I want to have. And to get a house. I want a dear little, white colonial house with early American furniture. We want to live in the little college town of Westwood."

Betty's canopied bed and red bows idealism was prevalent now that she was projected into marriage, and she and Jackie had no qualms when the press pried into the matter of what difficulties were encountered in putting off their wedding. It was clear to one and all that the big question was when the lovers would go to bed together, but, in keeping with the times, the inquiry was couched in euphemism. It was Conn who laid the question to rest.

One of the newspapers quoted Conn's reply:

> "I hope it will be years yet," growled Conn Grable, local bond salesman, who, while business isn't so good, has been traveling with his wife and daughter. "Betty could break her contract, of course, but that isn't so good for a girl in the picture business. I'd like to see her in a starring role with a good dancing partner before she quits. Why, she hasn't even been to New York yet. She's billed there on this tour at the Roxy."
>
> Lillian contributed. "We think they'll both be better satisfied to settle down to a married life when they've had a chance to establish themselves professionally," she said. "It isn't that Jackie isn't ready and able to support a wife. It was love at first sight with him. They met on a weekend trip to Catalina. He wanted to carry her right off on a honeymoon around the world. For a week he argued with me. But I was determined it should not be one of these Hollywood fly-by-night affairs. And Mrs. Coogan, too. She doesn't want Jack to be a loafer. After Jack has established himself, and after Betty has had her chance, then there will be plenty of time to settle down. Then there won't be so much chance for recriminations about what they might have accomplished if they had not married so young."

Betty was asked to what she attributed her success, and the reply was the one she had made so many times before, and would make so many more times in the future. It was almost as if she had been prerecorded. "My mother," she said at once. "My mother made me what I am. I would never have done all the drilling, studying, practicing, if my mother hadn't been right in back of me, pushing, urging me on. While I was still at the Mary Institute here in St. Louis, my mother kept me taking dancing lessons, music, singing, modeling for photographs and style shows, getting me auditions and engagements; then when I was thirteen she took me to Hollywood and has stayed with me constantly, coaching me and encouraging me every step of the way. I had no ambition of my own."

An interviewer said this about Jackie: "He is a clean-cut, broad-shouldered, athletic looking youth, five feet eight inches tall. His hair is slicked back, and even now growing thin at the temples. His smile is reminiscent in its wistfulness. As he bade farewell to his guests, he said rather wearily, 'Next time you see us I hope we will be just Mr. and Mrs. Coogan.' "

Betty did become Mrs. Coogan, and she held off to within a month of her birthday, even though the RKO contract clause was no longer a problem. RKO had dropped their long-budding starlet in early spring 1937. Paramount had been standing by and signed her almost immediately, which might not have been the case had it not been for all the publicity she received as Coogan's fiancee. She signed with Paramount May 19, 1937, and became Jackie Coogan's bride the following November 20.

While the Coogan relationship had been still in the going-steady stage, Betty pounded out several other RKO assignments. She was given fifth lead in a melodramatic exposé of the prison parole system called *Don't Turn 'Em Loose,* starring Bruce Cabot. She then regained access to the Fox lot (by then Twentieth Century-Fox) on a loan-out for *Pigskin Parade.* Betty provided little more than set decoration for this light entertainment, which became notable only as an introductory vehicle for Judy Garland and Tony Martin.

Paramount welcomed Betty to the lot by giving her the female lead opposite Buddy Rogers in *This Way Please.* The movie made no lasting impression in the annals of motion picture history, but it did serve to introduce Jim and Marian Jordan to the screen as Fibber McGee and Molly. It was also a comeback attempt for the fading Buddy Rogers—which failed. *The New York Times* liked Fibber McGee and Molly, but wasn't moved by the comedic attempts made by Rufe Davis in the same film. The review referred to Betty only once: "Buddy Rogers is romantically reinforced by the beautiful Betty Grable." Mary Livingstone was also in the film, minus Jack Benny, and became good friends with Betty as a result of this first meeting.

Betty was next assigned to the Judy Canova comedy, *Thrill of a Lifetime,* in which she played the love interest opposite Leif Erickson. Once more, if nothing else, Betty came away with a lasting pal. This time it was Dorothy Lamour.

In her book, *My Side of the Road,* Lamour commented, "I was rushed into *Thrill of a Lifetime* starring Judy Canova. . . . I played myself in a cameo spot and sang only the title song. But working on this film I began a lifelong friendship with one of the sweetest women in the world. Betty Grable had played a couple of featured roles and still hadn't reached her peak. But I knew that with the proper exploitation by a big studio she could become a top star."

As for Betty's dramatic accomplishment in the film, the *New York Herald* had this to say: "Miss Grable could stand a lot of dramatic coaching." By the time the film was being released, Betty was beginning to grow accustomed to the sound of "Mrs. Jackie Coogan."

Following the November wedding, Betty felt reborn as a legal lover and housewife and wore her freedom as a badge. They laughed together, played and partied as though life was a three-act comedy.

Lucille Ball recalls the fun and frivolity that surrounded Betty and Jackie, and pinpoints one elaborate costume party Betty gave for Jackie in the lobby of the Knickerbocker Hotel. "We all dressed up as babies," she said. "Tony Martin was there, Cesar Romero. I can just see Cesar whirling Betty around the floor, and believe me, the floor would clear. There were diapers, bonnets, baby carriages, and nursing bottles. It was great fun."

What Lucille Ball was recalling was a party that took place long before the Grable-Coogan marriage. It was in October of 1935 in honor of Jackie's big twenty-first birthday. That was when his inheritance was supposed to come through, and it was an event to commemorate. Betty thought it auspicious enough to finance the entire celebration.

Sugar Geise recalls it well, because she and Betty were close pals at the time, and both lived in the hotel with their families. "Lucille Ball came as one of the Dionne quintuplets," says

Sugar. "Everyone was in costume except Betty, who came in an exquisite gold-lamé gown. I think Betty may have been between studios at the time, but she paid for everything. Everyone was there, including Betty's bulldog, Bing."

Jackie might have become alarmed when his twenty-first birthday came and went without reward, but not seriously. He had been able to draw enough periodic monies to maintain his life-style and was confident the big money was on its way. He also believed that all he needed to collect his inheritance was to ask for it—which, for a while, he failed to do.

It was, after all, common knowledge that Jackie's father had salted away millions during the productive run of Jackie's career, and that half the fortune would go to the boy. It was published information.

What Jackie hadn't taken into account was the importance of the marriage of his mother to Arthur Bernstein, the accountant for the Jackie Coogan Corporation. Jackie despised him, and Bernstein made clear his own contempt for Jackie. He went so far as to throw Jackie out of the corporate offices when his engagement to Betty became known. Lillian Bernstein made a call to Lillian Grable at that time, which could have cued Jackie in on what was to follow. Jackie's mother told Lillian: "If Betty thinks she's marrying a rich boy, she's mistaken. Jackie is a pauper."

The significance of the call was minimized at the time, because it was recognized as a last-ditch effort of a possessive mother to protect her son from the clutches of someone she considered a designing woman. But when Jackie got around to making his demands, he learned the extent of his mother's ruthlessness. He also learned for the first time what it was like to be penniless. Between his mother's calculated scheming and his stepfather's ability to handle the machinations, Jackie was rendered almost helpless. It became clear at once that the only road to justice would be by way of litigation, and the litigious road would be long and tortuous.

# Chapter 5

According to Anthony Coogan, Jackie's son by his second wife, Flower Perry, it is questionable that Jackie would have sued the estate for what was rightfully his. Jackie, like Betty, was vital enough when it came to beach parties, dances, and other forms of fun and games, but when it came to business acumen, he was sorely lacking. It was true also that he was not a fighter—not unless he was shamed or goaded into it. He would more likely have drifted along accepting whatever crumbs his fiercely domineering mother might have tossed his way.

Anthony believes it was Lillian Grable who coerced Jackie into the complicated litigation that eventually resulted in the heralded Coogan Law, which today guarantees child performers a fair share of their accrued show business profits.

The scenario Anthony sees is one of Lillian Grable dogging Jackie with references to the old wreck of a car he was driving, when the Coogan garages had held Rolls Royces in those earlier years, and asking how he expected his lovely wife to live in comparative squalor, when all that money was there waiting to be claimed. She probably also suggested that Bernstein was running a couple of businesses out of the Coogan office and charging all the expenses back to the company. And what about Jackie's personal humiliations at the hands of Bernstein when he was bodily ejected from the office?

Betty wasn't in line for much personal gain, because, for the protection of both youngsters, attorneys had been hired to design an iron-clad prenuptial agreement that assured there would be no free ride for either of them. Betty was, however, entitled to some sort of financial contribution from her husband, no matter how idyllic the marriage was in its early stages. To this point, it was Betty who was footing most of the bills.

As the legal battle ensued, Paramount was taking keen interest in their rosy-cheeked contractee. Betty's stock was appreciating by leaps and bounds, because, whether rich man or pauper, Jackie Coogan was big news, and, as his bride, Betty was sharing the publicity. To cash in further on the marriage, Paramount offered Jackie acting parts in a pair of Betty's films. The roles weren't important, but his name would surely draw additional box office revenues. Jackie, penniless, signed the contract with gusto.

*College Swing* was the first Grable–Coogan vehicle, but they weren't exactly alone in the production. Joining them in the film directed by Raoul Walsh were George Burns and Gracie Allen, Martha Raye and Bob Hope, Edward Everett Horton, John Payne, and a newcomer named Jerry Colonna. Acting as the radio announcer was a young actor named Robert Cummings.

The *Hollywood Reporter* loved the epic campus romp, but *The New York Times* was somewhat less enthusiastic: "*College Swing* like all other 'big' pictures, is bound to have something in it to displease all tastes," said the Bosley Crowther review. "To give you a general idea of its proportions: It has Jackie Coogan, of the front pages, and Betty Grable, who shag through the entire action, though it apparently covers several days."

Concurrently to Betty's and Jackie's shagging in *College*

*Swing,* the newspapers were publishing daily accounts of Jackie's lawsuit against his mother and the Coogan corporation.

Jackie had orchestrated his case very secretly, with a battery of lawyers working for him on a contingency basis. He was certain he would win, and the press was almost unanimously on his side. He played to them, by seeing that the subpoenas would be served to his mother and Bernstein on a Friday afternoon. This gave him the opportunity to plead his case before the public before the Bernsteins had time to collect their thoughts. The following Monday morning Bernstein's entrance into City Hall was covered by newspapers and newsreel cameras that captured his cockiness in every detail. He strutted before them, reeking of sarcasm and flaunting a huge diamond ring. The image he displayed was precisely what Jackie's attorneys hoped for. The first round, they believed, was theirs.

As is often the case in court battles, false confidence was riding high. Jackie was almost euphoric during the early days of the hearings, but time wore on—and, with time, the tide began to turn. Several weeks passed before Jackie began to realize that the case would not be as cut and dried as he and his lawyers supposed. Finally he was called into his attorneys' offices. Their message was: "Forget it, Jackie, they've got you."

"What do you mean, they've got me?" he wailed. "I made millions of dollars."

The attorneys patiently tried to explain that there was neither a California law to protect him, nor indeed one in the entire land. There was no precedent.

"Then you set a precedent," Jackie demanded.

To do so, they explained, Jackie would have to take the fall, and, since there was no money for them unless they won the court case, they could no longer work for him. Jackie stormed out, convinced the law firm was in collusion with the Bernsteins. He acquired another set of lawyers and proceeded.

Before the case ended, Jackie would have justification for any paranoia he might have suffered, but until the final countdown he retained blind trust that he would still win. Betty must have shared his confidence, because it was her bank account that was keeping them going.

While the case proceeded, Betty was kept busy at Paramount and was being publicized as "Betty Coed," a term that has since been adopted at large for the description of the typical college female. In *Give Me a Sailor,* both Grable and Bob Hope were upstaged by the mugging, loud-mouthed buffoonery of Martha Raye. Betty, as always, was appreciated by critic Bosley Crowther. *The New York Times* reviewer was never one to lavish praise on anyone, but over the years he was consistently kind to Betty. In this film, he felt that the slapstick of Martha Raye was a bit too much, and the farce a bit too farcical.

Betty's next start at Paramount saw her enter a new status level. In *Campus Confessions* she was given top billing for the first time in her career, but, unfortunately, the quality of the product served to negate the achievement, since there was really no one else of sufficient stature to be billed over her. When the movie was released, one of the reviewers said succinctly: *Campus Confessions* has little to confess." *The New York Times* went more into detail: "We have a confession to make: We don't see the relation between *Campus Confessions* and its title. We got the campus angle right enough—in fact Paramount has been subject to a sinister undergraduate influence for so long now that we sort of took that for granted; but frankly, we confess that the confessional angle has us stumped . . . and we should like to have seen it justified particularly since Betty Grable heads the cast." Once more, Bosley Crowther treated Betty well, while pinpricking the vehicle.

Betty seemed to be riding high at Paramount. She was becoming known to the world—thanks mostly to Jackie Coogan—and was receiving leading-lady assignments. After *Campus Confessions,* she segued into another co-starring role, and this one promised to turn the tide. Betty played opposite Jack Benny in *Man About Town,* which was a cut or two above the prestige of the previous film, and she was pleased as could be.

She and Jackie were clinging to their fairy tale, having ice cream sodas at C.C. Brown's ice cream parlor on Hollywood

Boulevard and attending champagne parties at Carole Lombard's house in Malibu. With everything so rosy, Betty was sure justice would prevail in her husband's court battle. But a curious incident occurred that should have been a foreboding of future events.

Betty answered a telephone call and was told Louis B. Mayer wished to speak with Jackie. Jackie had been avoiding telephone calls because of the court battle, but he would take this one. Louis B. Mayer? He took the instrument tentatively, wondering if someone were playing a practical joke, but there was no mistaking the imperious sound of the voice. The mogul greeted Jackie as amiably as he might have some dozen years earlier, when little Jackie was still the giant of the lot. The message was more amazing than the call itself. Mayer asked Jackie if he would like to return to the MGM fold and said that, if he were agreeable, there was a seven-year contract awaiting him.

Jackie, whose career had been in limbo for years nearly collapsed. Would he agree to a seven-year MGM contract? Would a starving wolf agree to a T-bone steak? "Of course, Mr. Mayer," Jackie said eagerly. "I'd love to come back to MGM."

So it was settled; Mayer invited Jackie to his office for lunch the next day, when the terms of the contract could be drawn up. Jackie started to hang up, eager to let out a cheer that would rival any Betty had mustered in her campus films, but L.B. wasn't quite finished. "Oh, by the way, Jackie," he added, "you won't mind dropping that law suit, will you?"

Jackie froze where he was standing. "The law suit?"

"Yes, you know what I mean."

"But I can't. Mr. Mayer," Jackie said weakly. "It's no longer in my hands . . . it's in the hands of the State of California."

There was an electric silence. "Jackie," said Mayer. "Are you telling me you won't drop the case?"

Jackie apologized profusely, but repeated what he had already said, adding that it wasn't the case itself, but the civil injustice involved.

"Are you saying you *refuse* to drop the law suit?"

"Yes, sir, I guess I am, Mr. Mayer."

"Very well," said Mayer grimly, "but remember what I say. You will never work in this town again."

End of call.

The warning was no idle threat. Jackie had already been signed for the second token role at Paramount in *Million Dollar Legs,* but this was to prove the last film performance for Jackie for six long years.

Jackie was never sure what motivated the Louis B. Mayer offer, or the resultant threat when he refused its conditions. In the forthcoming book, *Jackie Coogan—The Forgotten Prince,* his son, John Anthony Coogan, will present a series of hypotheses. He says it was known that Mayer and Bernstein were fast friends at the time, and it could have been Mayer's gesture to a friend to solve a messy problem. He thinks it might otherwise have been a reaction to Bernstein's fighting tactics during the case. According to young Coogan, Bernstein planted any number of anti-Semitic statements with columnists, attributing them erroneously to Jackie. Mayer may have wanted to put an end to the Jew-versus-gentile promulgations. Anti-Semitism was rampant during the Thirties, and Mayer may have seen such racial snipes as a threat to the industry. His motives will never be known, but Mayer made good his threat, or at least it proved prophetic, because Jackie was long unemployed.

At the beginning of 1939, when Betty was preparing for *Man About Town,* all was not well in paradise. There had been lover's spats, and the delicious making up afterward, but now matters had taken a more negative turn. With the diminishing chances of Jackie winning his legal case, the foundation of the marriage began to weaken. The quarrels became more strident and less soluble. There were squabbles about the charge accounts Jackie was running up, and discontent was brewing on Betty's part regarding Jackie's spirit of individualism. He had been spoiled since he was born and expected everyone to tolerate the residual idiocyncrasies. If he went to the corner for a magazine and came back the next afternoon, Jackie expected no flak upon his return. Such behavior was becoming more prevalent, and, while Betty would always be a paragon of patience, when it came to misbehaving lovers, she had her limits.

Riding on his continuing wave of publicity, Jackie formed a band, probably with Betty's financial aid. He took to the road at the time she reported on the set of *Man About Town.* She had finished several days of shooting when she began having abdominal pains. At first Betty attributed it to her growing nervousness, but ruled that out as the severity grew. She was finally taken to a doctor, who diagnosed the problem as acute appendicitis. Betty was prepped for immediate surgery.

United Press ran this bulletin: "Betty Grable, wife of Jackie Coogan, collapsed while doing a picture at Paramount studios today and was rushed to a Glendale hospital, where Dr. H.G. Westphal operated for appendicitis. The actress complained of a pain in her side for several days. Coogan, who is now on a personal appearance tour in Texas, took a plane to be at his wife's side."

Throughout most of her life, Betty Grable would be a child of fate. She would take two steps forward and three steps back; luck would snatch her from the jaws of despair, and, when she was repaired and on an even keel, once again the same gods would set her back. Now, because of an untimely illness, she was pushed several rungs back down the ladder of success. The producers waited a month, but the lead role was finally assigned to another Paramount newcomer, Dorothy Lamour. When she was well enough, Betty was given a consolation prize, an unbilled specialty number in the same film.

Ever since litigation was first underway, Coogan had been harassed by a pair of private detectives who popped up anywhere and everywhere. Their mission was to induce Jackie to sign a contract of settlement with the Bernsteins. He had always turned them down.

When Jackie flew back to see Betty through her appendectomy, something had modified his stand. His fighting spirit seemed to be waning. One night he parked his car in the stall beneath the apartment he and Betty shared and was once more approached by the detectives. He may have been drinking or simply weary of it all, but he signed the papers without a pause. The Bernstein accounting came up with the settlement figure of $250,000, which was supposed to be all that remained in the corporation account. Jackie would get half this amount, the rest would remain with the Bernsteins.

The settlement was far from satisfactory, but it was at least a settlement. Millions had gone down the drain, but Jackie was young and had every confidence he was capable of earning millions on his own. He had done it before—he could do it again. He started spending money as though the future millions were his. His first act was to lease a home on Montana Avenue in Westwood. He was in love with Betty and believed the home would mend any flaws in their marriage. The home *did* help. Betty was willing to give it the old college try.

Morey Amsterdam, a mutual friend, lived just around the corner from them, and Morey recalls that the couple spent more time at his home than at their own. "They had practically no furniture," says Amsterdam, "only a mattress and a sagging couch, and Ghengis, their hundred-and-eighty-five-pound Great Dane, slept on the couch. The kitchen cabinets were filled with nothing but dog food. They weren't broke at the time—they just didn't give a damn."

He said they bicycled each Sunday to the beach, ate hot dogs, and, after cycling back, collapsed at his home in utter fatigue. He said there was no getting drunk in those days, and certainly no marijuana. He said Betty used salty language, but took offense if anyone told a dirty joke that wasn't funny. Amsterdam recalls them both as fun-loving kids. He had known Jackie since he was twelve, and worked in vaudeville with him and his father. As for Betty, Morey recalls the necessity of having to tie her legs to the bed because of her sleepwalking habit, which was particularly acute at the time.

At about this time, Betty and Jackie both went to work in *Million Dollar Legs,* with top billing going to Betty. The legs in the title did not refer to Betty's, but to the athletes of the college rowing team in the picture. Buster Crabbe played the part of the coach. The film introduced Peter Lind Hayes, but did little for

Betty's career, and certainly failed to enhance her marriage to Jackie. He was misbehaving again, and Betty was losing interest in a lost cause.

Betty and Jackie were guest stars on the April 11, 1939, Bob Hope radio show, and were reviewed favorably. Their routine moved a *Hollywood Reporter* columnist to write: "It should be plenty good for a p.a. tour." There would be a road tour in the not distant future for Betty, but it would not include the radio routine—nor would it include Jackie.

When the Jack Benny program closed down for the summer, Betty went on tour with Phil Harris and Eddie "Rochester" Anderson. Her weekly pay was set at $1,500 a week, which was a thousand more than she was making at Paramount. But the Paramount salary was no longer of importance. Despite Betty's rising popularity with the fans, her rise hadn't been sufficient to satisfy her bosses. Her contract was dropped without ceremony. Once more Betty was confronted by rejection.

When Betty took to the road, Jackie entered an auto customizing venture with Sid Luft, who was then secretary-manager to Eleanor Powell and who would later marry Lynne Barry and Judy Garland. The business scheme failed, and Jackie's sudden wealth was rapidly diminished.

The Bernstein settlement had done little toward settling Jackie's financial problems. His debts remained unpaid, and at last Betty threw in the towel. She filed for separate maintenance on July 30, 1939, and began divorce proceedings.

Betty returned to Hollywood to free-lance at RKO with Joe Penner in *The Day the Bookies Wept.* When the work on her leading role was completed, Betty was off again, this time to San Francisco with Jack Haley for a two-week variety act at the Golden Gate Exposition.

Whenever hard luck befell Betty, she somehow managed to accept her adversity with equanimity, as though saying, "This time it's *really* the end." But it never was, and her mother refused to allow Betty the luxury of even slowing down. "You go to the World's Fair, Betty," said Lillian, "and everything will be all right." Betty went, and everything was, indeed, all right.

---

While Betty was performing in San Francisco, word came through that yet another studio was willing to take a gamble on her. But this wasn't *another* studio—it was the first one. She signed a contract with Twentieth Century-Fox, where it had all began nearly a decade earlier.

In 1935 Darryl F. Zanuck merged his successful Twentieth Century studios with the floundering Fox organization and assumed control. He wasn't pleased with most of the contract players he had inherited and was still making changes. He saw newspaper photos of Betty that were released from Paramount and liked what he saw. It was her face, however, and not her body that attracted him. It had been his cunning practice to keep reserve talent in his stable as a threat to the prevailing stars. Betty, blond, young, and cute as a coed, would be just what he needed to keep Alice Faye on her toes.

Although Betty was not aware of it for a time, another producer became interested in her after catching her performance in San Francisco. It was B.G. "Buddy" De Sylva, who was about to produce a Cole Porter musical for Broadway. De Sylva had been away from Broadway for six years and, ironically, had been running things at Paramount—the studio from which Betty had been so recently fired—in the interim. He thought Betty was perfect for the role of Alice Barton in the show that would be called *Du Barry Was a Lady.* He negotiated with Betty's new boss, Darryl Zanuck, who released her for the musical.

During the remainder of the summer, Coogan made a series of attempts to woo back his recalcitrant bride, but Betty was not to be wooed and rewon. She was moving onward and upward, and Jackie was spinning his wheels. Betty was growing up; Jackie was still a child.

Betty had several dates with eligible bachelors, which made Coogan jealous, but none of these were a threat. Unknown to almost everyone, Betty was falling hard for someone, who was intellectual, handsome, and quite famous. The current flame of her life was bandleader Artie Shaw.

After Betty's interlocutory decree was granted October 11, 1939, she was seen in the nightclubs with Shaw, and their photos cropped up in newspapers and fan magazines, with accompanying quotes. One of Shaw's comments didn't go over well at all with the composer of Betty's new Broadway show. Shaw said he was thinking of writing a song or two for Betty to sing in the show. Cole Porter let it be known that he didn't really need Shaw's help.

Betty appeared before Judge John Beardsley to ask that her marriage be dissolved on grounds of "extreme cruelty." She was, of course, accompanied by Lillian and, according to the United Press release, "wore a smart black dress, black hat set at a dangerous angle, and a cross fox fur."

Betty testified that Coogan was of quarrelsome disposition, that he frequently stayed away from home at night, and refused to say where he had been, and that he was not considerate of her welfare. "One morning," Betty was quoted, "I came downstairs to breakfast to find a man moving out our furniture. I said, 'How come?' Jackie said, 'I've got to sell this stuff to pay some bills.' I thought that was all right and consented for him to sell the furnishings, but he did not pay a bill with the money. Instead, he bought a new car and left town. If it hadn't been for my mother, I wouldn't have had any place to go."

Betty and Jackie had lived together for a year and eight months, which wasn't very long. This was particularly evident by comparison, because another divorce was concurrently in the works. Betty's mother and father were also calling it quits after thirty-one years.

# Chapter 6

There were gossip mongers who insisted Betty's acceptance of the featured role in *Du Barry Was a Lady* was due to her infatuation with Artie Shaw, who was playing in New York. The fact that Shaw would be nearby may have, indeed, been the icing, but the important role in a Cole Porter musical was certainly the cake. Betty was sensing, for the first time, the change of luck her mother insisted was at hand.

With her run of bad luck, it must have occurred to her that she was praying at the wrong altar. She had been in a topsy-turvy struggle for ten years now, and had thirty-one feature films behind her. Now, it seemed, she was back to square one. It was as if she were a perennial ingenue, for whom growing up meant the final curtain.

Finally, she had been given a second chance at the studio where it all began, and now, at the ripe old age of twenty-three, she would get a crack at a class Broadway musical. Betty had no intentions of letting the opportunity fail. As in all those campus scripts with which she had become so familiar, she would give it a good college try.

The play opened on November 9, 1939, on the road in New Haven, and the reviews were raves. "De Sylva has a strong contender for ace musical honors here," said *Variety*. "The Bert Lahr–Ethel Merman combo is socko from start to finish." It said of Betty: "Of the featured Betty Grable–Phil Regan pair, the former does the better job, pleasing with looks, and warmth from the acting angle, the last a somewhat pleasant revelation. Regan is of good voice, but lacks the volume to punch his numbers across."

The show played to equally receptive audiences in Boston and Philadelphia, but Regan, who was obviously not right for the role, was replaced before the New York opening night. The play opened at the Forty-sixth Street Theater on December 6, 1939.

After the New York opening *Variety* had this to say:

> B.G. (Buddy) De Sylva debuts as a producer with the second major musical of the Fall period. Despite over-touting from out-of-town, *Du Barry* looks to be definitely in the money.
>
> Ethel Merman and Bert Lahr are the main fun-makers, she with her manner of handling ditties, he with a type of low comedy antic which, though familiar through many seasons, has a new variation and is surefire as ever. They are rightly starred. Both have had their fling in Hollywood and the same goes for Betty Grable and Benny Baker, who are featured. De Sylva was a Coast fixture for a period that seems to have been too long. . . .
>
> Betty Grable is something of a revelation as a new soubrette. It is her first time on Broadway, but she performs like a thoroughbred. Not so blond as pictured, Miss Grable is a lovely little trick who knows her stuff in both songs and dances. Most of the hoofing is with Charles Walters, and they make a scoring team. Miss Grable has appeared in vaudeville units, but it is probably the careful training as a kid that stands her in good stead now.

In his *Hollywood Reporter* column, Irving Hoffman said:

> Betty Grable grabbed laudatory lines [from the critics], not only for the lines of her face and figure, but for the way she

> handled her singing, dancing and acting assignments. She came to *Life* with a big bang, appearing on that mag's cover Friday. Mr. Zanuck, the 20th Century-Fox, has already signed her to a contract, which makes it a certainty that she will 20th Century-fox-trot it back to Hollywood after *Du Barry*'s run.

Overnight, Betty became the toast of the town. A star was born; she was legitimatized. There is no place on earth that takes more chauvinistic pride in discovery than the New York theater crowd, and they happily affixed their seal of approval to Betty. She wore the honor with pride and aplomb.

A table was reserved for the cast at the Stork Club on a nightly basis, and Betty seldom missed an evening. Ethel Merman was also a regular, because she, at the time, was going with the nightclub's owner Sherman Billingsley. Betty invited sister Marjorie to New York to help her celebrate her new celebrity status, and the whirlwind fortnight was never forgotten. "I never saw daylight," Marjorie recalled. "Betty was going out with a very wealthy boy just then, Alex Thompason. He owned—oh Lord, everything—and after the show we'd go out on the town."

Betty had her choice of eligible males, but during the first month her free time was reserved for Artie Shaw. He would be winding up his nightclub performance when Betty was out of wardrobe and makeup and dressed for the street. They were discreet during this time for reasons not quite clear to Betty. She was strongly attracted to Shaw and didn't especially care who knew it. She was linked to a variety of males during the fall and early winter of 1939, including Buddy De Sylva and even Coogan, who camped on her New York doorstep with hopes of patching their differences. But it was only Artie who warmed her heart.

Betty was primed for a brief separation over the New Year's weekend. Artie gave advance notice that he had a playing date in Los Angeles. It was acceptable, of course, because who should know better than Betty that business was business. Artie left on schedule, but it turned out that his trip was not a hundred percent business—at least in a professional sense. He was keeping a long standing date with Lana Turner.

The newspapers of January 2 noted that Shaw had joined Turner at a birthday party for her mother. The couple had tickets to attend *The Man Who Came To Dinner,* but when the dinner carried them beyond curtain time they went for a long drive instead. The drive carried them into Nevada, where they prevailed upon a justice-of-the-peace to make them man and wife. Betty read about it in the newspapers along with the rest of the population. Whether or not it was a surprise to Shaw, it certainly came as a total surprise to her.

Betty must have been stunned at the news, but it wasn't evident in her behavior. She went on laughing, continued to be the life of everybody's party, and had plenty of dates. She closed the chapter on Artie Shaw.

During the run in *Du Barry,* Betty found still another musician to fill up her date book. He was the rising Cuban star, Desi Arnaz, who was appearing nearby in *Too Many Girls.* In his recent *A Book,* Desi refers to his fleeting relationship with Betty:

> That same year Betty Grable was a sensation in Ethel Merman's Broadway show *Du Barry Was a Lady.* She was gorgeous—what a figure and what legs! Her skin was magnificent and so smooth she looked like a peach all over.
>
> Our theaters were next to each other. We all had the same matinee days so we started having dinner together at Dinty Moore's between shows. She would join our table, and it was impossible to sit next to Betty and not want to know her a little better.

Arnaz was doubling at the La Conga at the time, and Betty would often catch his nightclub act after work. Then, afterward, they would go out bowling or to do whatever there was to do in the wee hours of the morning.

Lucille Ball visited New York at this time and called on Betty. She was to play opposite Desi a few months later in the movie version of *Too Many Girls,* and subsequently fell in love and married him, but that would all come later.

On this occasion, Lucille came backstage to check out her old pal from the RKO days and was impressed by everything she saw. "I watched from the wings," Lucy said. "I could hear the one-liners Betty was throwing at the gypsies. You couldn't hear it from the audience, but she was breaking everybody up on the stage. When she was upstage she would say these things from the corner of her mouth, and everybody was loving it."

When Betty was riding high, she loved sharing it with family and friends, and Betty's friends were embraced as warmly as if they were family. Her pal Paula Stone was a frequent companion during the New York days, and she recalls one of the Stork Club incidents. Betty was late in joining the table, because she had a commitment to a press photographer, but, when she made her tardy entrance, she did it with true Grable-ese flair. "You know what a gorgeous figure Betty had," said Paula. "Well, she comes in wearing this pink sweater that looked like headlights on a Pierce Arrow. She approaches us and aims her bazooms at everybody as though they were a pair of machine guns. 'Don't nobody move,' she says, 'I got you all covered.' Of course the place came down. Betty always had something planned for her entrances, and it was always funny."

What went on inside Betty Grable wasn't often revealed to those around her, because, as almost every close friend will attest, Betty was a very private person. She seldom revealed personal thoughts or volunteered details of her personal life. Paradoxically, she was more inclined to reveal her secret side in nationally published interviews. In an article published during the *Du Barry* run, she revealed something of her lack of inner security.

"Hollywood," she was quoted, "has a way of letting you down that is rather discouraging. I guess the only reason I'm in a Broadway show is that the films don't want me. It comes like something of a shock after you've worked in several studios and have been publicized around the country for years, suddenly to realize there are no new roles for you."

But there would be new roles for Betty, and coming up was the biggest role of Betty's career. Just as she was settling in for a long, secure run in *Du Barry,* she received a call from Hollywood. It was from Darryl Zanuck himself, who informed her that he wanted her to replace Alice Faye in a forthcoming musical. It would be a technicolor extravaganza with no expense spared and would surely establish Betty as a star.

Zanuck must have been taken aback at Betty's reticence, but she tried to explain it to him. Alice Faye was a star—a *real* star—and Betty couldn't presume to replace her in anything. Betty had heard that Alice had been stricken by appendicitis and, from her own experience, knew that the delay needn't be interminable. She also remembered that she had missed out on a key role at Paramount because of her own bout with the same illness. As much as she wanted the part, she simply could not accept it under the circumstances.

Betty had little choice in the matter. She was, after all, under contract, but in this confrontation Zanuck wasn't required to throw his executive weight. He had merely to explain that Faye's ailment was not appendicitis, as it had been reported to the press, but that she was actually suffering from hemorrhoids, which required a longer recuperation period following surgery. When Betty was convinced it would be impossible for Alice Faye to do the film, she accepted the offer with enthusiasm.

It was early June when Betty received the fateful telephone call from Darryl Zanuck. The operation was performed on Alice Faye June 7, and Betty was reporting for work at Twentieth on June 21 for the leading role in *Down Argentine Way.*

# Chapter 7

Betty played opposite Don Ameche in the film, and the casting of Ameche in the male lead indicated Zanuck's keen interest in the production. Ameche was one of the recruits Zanuck acquired when he began reorganizing the Twentieth Century-Fox roster and was a personal favorite of his.

Others in the cast included Carmen Miranda, Charlotte Greenwood and J. Carrol Naish. Cesar Romero had been set for the role of Tito, the ubiquitous male escort, but a case of paratyphoid put him into the same hospital as Alice Faye. His role went to Leonid Kinskey.

Through press releases, Zanuck expressed his great confidence in Betty's ability and said he was especially anxious to have her filmed in Technicolor. His interest, of course, was immensely aroused by her runaway success in *Du Barry,* but the motivation didn't matter to Betty, who was getting the role of her life and would be filmed in a color process that had gone through vast improvement over recent years. From where she stood, things looked pretty good.

*Down Argentine Way* was not only designed for the entertainment of domestic audiences. It was also specifically fashioned for Latin American consumption. The market south of the border was increasing steadily, and was more important than ever since Europe had been all but lost to Nazi expansion.

A record ten months were required to complete the picture, and 35,000 miles were covered by train, plane, and auto during its filming. Second units were transported to Buenos Aires for atmospheric shots of South America and remained there for a month. They returned home with 20,000 feet of technicolor footage, which measured out to a foot of film per mile traveled.

While this was in progress, another crew was dispatched to New York to film and record the performance of Carmen Miranda, whose contract with a nightclub precluded her appearance in Hollywood. It was the first time such a dispensation was made for a film personality.

This marked a return to musical comedy for Don Ameche, and was the first film in which he danced. His success in the art was attributed to the deft coaching of the movie's dance directors, Nick Castle and Geneva Sawyer.

Betty worked more than fourteen hours a day in the week before shooting—rehearsing, recording, and standing around wardroom salons for fittings. It was announced even before the film was officially underway that she would later team up with Alice Faye to play her sister in *Tin Pan Alley*. The studio wanted to make it clear that Betty was receiving star status from this point forward.

Rehearsal was long and arduous, but Betty was never one to shirk hard work. She was pleased for the opportunity to make such thorough preparation, and felt privileged to have a director for whom rehearsals were important. This would be the ninety first film to be directed by Irving Cummings, and his philosophy was: "Let 'em act." He believed that adequate preparation provided the actors with greater confidence, which resulted in looser, more uninhibited performances. It was his reputation to require seldom more than three takes on any one shot. There would be no retakes charged to Betty.

When the camera rolled, she was ready, and her vast experience paid off handsomely. Not only did the dailies reveal a bright and refreshing image of beauty, but her personality spark was clearly evident. In addition to all this, her performance was top drawer, and she worked quickly.

Zanuck must have sensed what he had stumbled upon in Betty, and no matter what disagreements later evolved over the years, he never had cause to discredit Betty for lack of industry. Even Zanuck had to agree that no one on the Twentieth Century lot worked harder than Betty Grable. Her films always met budget and came in on time.

The only time Betty would seem to succumb to weariness was when by doing so she could help out the crew. If quitting time was closing in, and it appeared they would wrap within the hour, Betty more than once feigned tiredness and retired for a few minutes respite in her dressing room. When it was obvious "the kids" would be in for some overtime pay, she would bound back and do her scenes. She never allowed the studio's profit to take precedence over the welfare of her workmates.

There were only a few times in Betty's life when she could have been described as unhappy, and then only a few of her most intimate friends would be allowed to know. For outward appearances, Betty maintained a facade of cheerfulness and high spirits, as though it were a case of noblesse oblige.

But there was no pretense required to appear happy at this juncture in Betty's life, because she was. During these early days at Twentieth, she was almost euphoric, and for good reason. Her career was blossoming, and she was earning a four figure weekly salary and having fun and laughing every day. Betty was the darling of every grip, gaffer, and prop man on the set. She was plain Betty to everyone and made the least prepossessing among them feel important.

Technicolor would become a kind of trademark for Betty, and she loved it as much as it loved her, but it was hot beneath the clusters of powerful Kleig lights and floods. To keep the lamps from exploding, special fans, known as blowers, were trained over them during the shots. After the wrap of one of Betty's scenes, the assistant director called out, "Kill the blowers!" Betty, never one to miss a straight line, answered pleadingly, "Oh no, please don't. . . . I'm too young to die!" Here was Betty's brand of humor, and it delighted the work crews.

Shortly after the completion of *Down Argentine Way,* Betty went into *Tin Pan Alley,* playing third lead under Alice Faye and Jack Oakie. The crew stood by nervously on the first day of shooting, anticipating the inevitable flare-up between Betty and Alice Faye. It never came. From the moment of their first meeting, Betty and Alice were soul mates and remained so for as long as Betty lived. The studio liked rivalry between its stars—it kept them on their toes—but Betty would never play their game.

By the time Betty finished her final shots in *Tin Pan Alley, Down Argentine Way* was being previewed in Westwood Village. The October 2, 1940, screening brought favorable response from both *Variety* and the *Hollywood Reporter.*

*Variety* thought Betty's "rhumba stepping is much more effective than her vocalizing," but liked the film overall. The review capsulized the plot line of this key Grable film, saying:

> It's another one about breeding and race horses. Ameche's father breeds thoroughbreds in the Argentine, and Miss Grable is the rich New York girl whose hobby is collecting blue-ribbon jumpers. Ameche brings a consignment to the United States for sale, but there's an old family feud the young folks are unaware of, so none of the horses can be sold to the girl. The romance starts there, and continues in the Argentine when Miss Grable follows him back home. Then the two lovers must convince the old man on two points—the feud was unnecessary, and his prize jumper is a champion flat racer.

The *Reporter* said, "This is easily the most alluring picture to come from Twentieth Century-Fox in many a day, so full of lilting brightness, romance, sparkling melody, and an all-pervading spirit of joyousness that it comes as a particularly welcome tonic to the somber-hued world of today."

The movie opened in New York October 18, and Bosley Crowther wrote:

Off hand, we can't think of anyone more abundantly qualified to serve as a ministress plenipotentiary to the Latin American lands than Betty Grable. So it is altogether likely that Twentieth Century-Fox's *Down Argentine Way,* in which Miss Grable appears and which opened yesterday at the Roxy, will excite a powerful lot of good neighborliness in the countries south of us. Yessir, we can just imagine how the boys down in Rio and B.A. will bubble with amity when they see Miss Grable up there on the screen. But why confine it to the boys down in Rio and B.A.? There are plenty of hometown fellows who will feel very neighborly to her too.

After the completion of *Tin Pan Alley,* Betty was given a break, in which to make a personal appearance and have a brief vacation. She boarded the Super Chief with her mother, dog, and a third travel companion who would add considerable publicity to her already heralded journey—leading man, Victor Mature, who just happened to be traveling on the same train.

Mature recalls having the time of his life on the trip with Betty, a fateful one for his lagging career. "I had made three movies by that time," says Mature, "and was going to New York to talk with some people about a stage play. Betty was leaving at the same time, so we went on the train together."

Mature had dated Betty prior to the trip, and, while columnists tried to blow the relationship into romantic proportions, he insists now, as Betty insisted then, that it wasn't true. "I was very fond of Betty," he says, "and for a time we saw quite a lot of each other, but it never went beyond that."

Whether or not he had had higher hopes for the relationship wasn't expressed, but both he and Betty remembered that trip. Though each of them was going for reasons of personal importance, they had a great time by joining forces.

Betty's first goal was Chicago, where she would appear at the Chicago Theatre with Ken Murray. On the night before her opening, she asked Mature to take her to the College Inn. There was a friend singing in the band there, a young crooner named

Dick Haymes. Mature agreed, and they made dinner reservations. After the show, Haymes joined their table and introduced both Mature and Betty to his boss, bandleader Harry James. It was the first time Betty had met James, and she said later that this first meeting had no effect on her, because she knew James was then a very married man.

While Betty did her week at the Chicago Theatre, Mature elected to use the time for a brief trip to his hometown of Louisville, Kentucky. "I left my grip in Betty's room until I got back," he said. "She had this dog—a Sealyham, I think it was called. It was a small dog, about the size of a cocker spaniel, but tough as hell. When I came back, I found out the dog tore open my suitcase and chewed up all my clothes. I wasn't in the bucks then, and I had to buy all new clothes to go on to New York."

But he did go on to New York, and it worked out well for him. He had fun with Betty and was introduced to many of her influential New York friends, including Ethel Merman, who was about to marry Bill Smith. They attended the wedding together. But Mature's mission was to meet with Ira Gershwin and Moss Hart, and to land the lead in their new play, *Lady in the Dark.* He remained with the play for a year and returned to Hollywood a bonafide star.

"Betty and I did almost the same thing," he said. "We both had made movies before and both went back to do Broadway shows. Then, boom, we went from practically zero to $5,000 a week."

Mature admits that being in New York with Betty Grable didn't hurt him in the least. While she didn't exactly open doors for him—he had made contact with Moss Hart previously, regarding the play—just being in her company enhanced his image. They were highly publicized, of course, and this could not have hurt his chances at all in the eyes of the play's producers.

"It was one of those things where you're in the right place at the right time in the right atmosphere, and in the right grouping," he says. "Betty was a much bigger star than I was at that time, and she commanded a lot of attention. I didn't."

Mature went into rehearsal, and Betty, complete with

mamma and luggage-eating-dog, returned to Hollywood. The month of November 1940 was a turning point for Victor Mature, but it was no less important for Betty. She met a husband-to-be during this sentinel month—and lost a husband. Her divorce from Coogan became final November 19.

# Part Two

# Chapter 8

After she was set for the lead in *Down Argentine Way,* Betty Grable made a statement in a newspaper interview that has been widely quoted throughout the years: "This is the first time I ever got a chance to do good parts in the movies. If I mess this up, I have only myself to blame."

The statement tells something of the inner frustration Betty must have been suffering in her upward climb and of the desperation she must have been feeling at this point in her erratic career. As it turned out, she found no reason to blame herself, because she emerged from the movie a star and remained one as long as she lived. Not that her stardom precluded future frustrations, because there would be many, but as far as her career was concerned she had found the path that would establish her as one of the greats in motion picture annals.

The timing of the release of *Tin Pan Alley* and its attendant favorable reviews came as a bonus twenty-third birthday present for Betty. The critics liked her and Alice Faye as a team and singled out Jack Oakie for praise in a role they considered well suited to his wise-cracking personality. The movie also established the career of leading man John Payne. Of Betty and Alice, the *Hollywood Reporter* said:

> The teaming of Alice Faye and Betty Grable was a dangerous piece of casting in that one might be reckoned to spoil the show for the other, but this was not the case. There was perfect balance to their assignments, each doing her top work in individual scenes, and when the two were together, you saw a knockout combination, both in performance and looks. Alice sang beautifully and little Grable grabbed sustaining looks in her song numbers and particularly in those cute little wiggles she put into most of her dances.

Betty played another sister act in her following film, which went into production early in 1941. She played Carole Landis's sibling in *Moon Over Miami,* a technicolor remake of the 1938 movie, *Three Blind Mice,* which had starred Loretta Young and David Niven. The plot was familiar: attractive young ladies in search of rich husbands. The first edition in the genre had been *Ladies In Love,* made in 1936 by Zanuck and starring Janet Gaynor, Simone Simon, Don Ameche and Tyrone Power.

*Moon Over Miami* found Betty, Carole, and Charlotte Greenwood zeroing in on Don Ameche, Robert Cummings, and Jack Haley. It would be done again as *Three Little Girls In Blue,* with June Haver, Vivian Blaine, and Vera Ellen portraying the gorgeous gold diggers. Betty would have yet another fling along these lines a dozen years later in *How To Marry a Millionaire.* Zanuck never found it easy to bury a winner.

With the huge success of *Down Argentine Way,* Zanuck pledged it would be nothing but Technicolor for Betty from that point forward. But he reneged after a single picture. *Tin Pan Alley* was in color, but her next two films, *A Yank In the RAF* and *I Wake Up Screaming,* were both black and white. Betty played straight dramatic roles in each of them, and even though she came across fairly well, she was far from happy. With the insulation of an adequate number of dance routines, Betty felt comfortable delivering lines, but she was convinced her acceptance on the screen depended on her specialized skills and not on her ability as an actress.

*Moon Over Miami* was received well, if only for the excellent quality of the color print. Charles Higham and Joel Greenberg, in their book *Hollywood In the Forties,* had this to say about the film:

> Perhaps the most striking feature of the film is how much it is ahead of its time, predating *On the Town,* which in many ways resembles it in its use of free dancing through its sets and locations. When the three women arrive in their Miami hotel, they dance right across their suite singing with delightful enthusiasm, "Oh Me, Oh Mi–ami." The songs flow naturally out of the action, expertly wedded to the dialogue, and the introduction of Miami is dazzling: shot with irridescent gaiety as director and cameraman create an exciting feeling of discovery, a plane flying across a beach past a luxurious hotel, a man swimming across a glowing emerald pool shot from far above, a row of flamingoes, horses spanking down a racetrack, accompanied by a male chorus exultantly singing "Miami, Here I Am!" A visit to an underwater aquarium, a motorboat race shot with great lightness and ease in overhead tracking shots through the everglades; this is a film of irresistible American energy and verve, orchestrated to perfection by Alfred Newman, electrifyingly recorded, especially in the "Conga To a Nursery Rhyme" number expertly danced by Betty Grable and the chorus in an hotel lounge.

Regarding Betty's work in *A Yank In the RAF,* Bosley Crowther, her champion at *The New York Times,* wrote, "Tyrone Power is a cleancut youngster who behaves and looks as you would think an American would under the circumstances, and for similar reasons. Miss Grable is plenty of a reason, too, and acts as though she knows what she is about. Both are as good as they have ever been in this. . . . There is good entertainment in the picture. Thumbs up for *A Yank In the RAF.*"

*I Wake Up Screaming,* which marked the return of Victor Mature to the screen after his year on Broadway, was either extolled or summarily dismissed by the reviewers. Bosley Crowther said, "Three of the principal roles are played with virtually no distinction by Betty Grable, Victor Mature and Carole Landis." But whether it was loved or hated, *I Wake Up Screaming* was a box-office winner. Victor Mature's recollection has Betty happy in the straight role. "The only one who got nervous about it," he says, "was Zanuck. He kept wanting to inject things into the script that he thought seemed like Betty. We are driving down the street, for example, and she asks what I'm smiling about, and I say, 'Oh, you wouldn't believe me.' She says, 'Well, tell me, honey,' and I say, 'Well, when I was a boy without money, I'd love to have gone swimming, but I couldn't. And now that I'm in the chips I go down to the park and go swimming a lot—and I was just thinking about it.' That's what I mean, bullshit like that in a retrospective murder mystery—that was Darryl. She says, 'Let's go.' So, we go in swimming. We get undressed and dive in. It was the only phony thing in the movie. Betty didn't want to do that either, but Zanuck did, and that was that. He just had to get Betty Grable out of her clothes."

Betty had a brief vacation in November of 1941 and spent the time in New York. By planned coincidence George Raft was there at the same time. Betty's friend Paula Stone was living in New York at the time and was lonely with her new husband away in England with the R.A.F. Raft squired both Betty and Paula to the posh New York night spots. "I felt like a third wheel," says Paula. "But George and Betty were sweet. They didn't want me sitting home worrying, so they would take me every place with them." (Paula's husband was shot down and killed over Germany the following year.)

Paula recalls that Betty and George had a bitter quarrel, which resulted in Betty cutting her vacation short. "She was in tears," Paula said, "and asked me to take her to Grand Central Station, where she would catch the Twentieth Century Limited for LA. When we reached her compartment, there was a huge bouquet of roses awaiting her. They were, of course, from George, and as she read the card a big smile broke through the tears. She was so in love."

During the visit to New York, Raft bought two additional race horses, which brought his stable to about ten. He also bought a Rex Beach story as a vehicle to star him with Betty. The property cost him $35,000, even though he had no commitment from Warners to cooperate on the venture. He was under studio suspension at the time and believed that if Warners refused to produce the film, Twentieth Century-Fox would.

"It's a great story for Betty," he said at the time, "but as for me, they got me right back in the old groove—sour-puss, woman-hating gangster. But we can rewrite that part of it."

There had been talk about starring the popular couple in a movie, but this was the first definitive move in that direction. The idea may have been a good one, but it failed to come to fruition. Twentieth certainly had Betty's date book filled, since she was rapidly becoming the hottest property on the lot, and they probably saw no need to bolster her popularity by pairing her with Raft. World War II had become a reality, but Betty Grable would not become one of its casualties.

Although Zanuck was always stubborn in his dictums, he had no choice but to listen when Betty spoke, because before 1941 came to an end, her fan mail was becoming prodigious. Little Betty, with her campy grin and wriggly nose was catching on in a big way. Men were being turned on, and the women seemed to be accepting her as a sister under the skin. Betty wasn't the mysterious femme fatale their husbands and boyfriends would run off with. She was "regular"—the girl down the street against whom they could compete. Whatever it was that Betty had, she seemed to be having it for everybody.

She certainly had it for George Raft, because he was already making moves to rekindle the sparks that had flamed and fizzled nearly a decade earlier. He was more diffident this time. He had been the one to put her on hold years before, but now the situation had changed dramatically. In the days when he had escorted Betty to the Six-Day Bicycle Races, it was he who was the superstar and she the aspirant. Now it was possible that the Betty Grable star could very well outshine his own.

When he finally mustered the courage to ask her out, Betty

accepted with great enthusiasm, but an unforeseen problem arose. On the day of their date, Betty came down with tonsillitis and had to cancel their evening out. She was afraid he might think she didn't want to see him, and he had his share of doubts. But he did ask her again, and the resultant date was a winner. It marked the beginning of something big—in both their lives.

The velvet-voiced, gangster type was excitement personified to Betty. He appeared strong and macho and mysterious, but Betty, remembering their previous relationship, knew there was another side to Raft. Although he certainly had his share of underworld connections, George was himself a pussycat to the core. He was kind and lavishly generous to Betty, her family, and her friends.

When he learned, for example, that Thursday was the maid's night off, George always included Betty's mother in their plans for that night of the week. Betty's friends were always welcome to come along on their nightclub visits, and George was a generous gift-giver. He remembered birthdays and anniversaries—as Betty always did—and would make sure the occasions were commemorated by something expensive.

When George and Betty weren't dining at their favorite bistros, they attended a wide variety of athletic events, with Betty cheering even more vigorously than her escort. Just as frequently, they had stay-at-home dates in Raft's Rossmore Manor penthouse. When it was race season in Caliente, Mexico, they would take off for weekends together. There, alone and unchaperoned, Betty and George could be themselves without fan magazine photographers peering at them from around corners.

The fan magazines billboarded the lovers during the early forties with traditional overkill. It was no secret that Raft was inexorably tied to an early marriage. He married Grayce Mulrooney in 1923, and her devout Catholicism precluded divorce. There were numerous gossip column hints that a divorce was imminent, that Grayce had agreed to a settlement, but it never came to pass.

It was probably a residual effect of quarrels on this subject that occasionally resulted in emotional flare-ups in public. On most occasions Betty had eyes only for George, but sometimes she was observed table-hopping and giving handsome actors affectionate hugs and kisses in the process. George, admittedly possessive of his women, would sit alone at their table following Betty's antics with his most villainous glares. Betty confided to pals that George sometimes retaliated with an angry slap or two, but it is generally believed that her accounts of Raft's abuse were exaggerated.

Betty's sister was one of many who remembered Raft as a gentle man. "He was awfully good to us," said Marjorie. "We were like poor relations. He took us out to dinner all the time. He was kind to mother, he was kind to daddy, he was kind to everybody. But I'm sure there was a lot of frustration on Betty's part, especially when it became clear the romance had no place to go."

# Chapter 9

The declaration of war, in December of 1941, sobered Hollywood as well as the rest of the nation, but no time was lost retooling the movie industry for war. Many male stars signed up for military service—Victor Mature included—and those remaining behind contributed heavily to war causes.

Existing production plans were scuttled in most studios, and war schedules were adopted. The stars and crews had to arise earlier because blackouts eliminated night shooting. Distant film locations became past history due to fuel conservation. Cameras could no longer film military installation, dams, or war plants; even the railroads were off-limits for location shots. For the duration, the back lots of the studios had to serve for locations exotic and domestic.

Heavier emphasis was placed on war films with no apologies for their propagandizing content, and studio contract players were asked to work overtime hours to produce war related movie shorts. Stars entertained military troops at home and abroad, and spent much of their leisure time as volunteers in USO clubs and canteens. There were severe shortages of materials but the troops and civilian defense workers needed entertainment, so the industry was designated "essential."

Millions were raised by War Bond rallies, and Betty Grable took part in many of them. After the Hollywood Canteen opened its doors in October of 1942, Betty was among the many stars who appeared regularly to entertain, serve, talk to, and dance with lonely GIs. Betty felt an honest affinity for the boys in uniform, and hundreds of them would carry lifetime memories of their encounters with this warm and down-to-earth movie queen. Many of them had little time to contemplate their dances-of-a-lifetime, because this was often the last stop before going overseas—and not all of them would come home.

For those who weren't lucky enough to have Betty, Lana, or Hedy as a dancing partner at the Canteen, there was a substitute phenomenon about to be born. Soon military men around the world would have likenesses of their favorite movie stars readily available. Cheesecake and pinup photos would adorn barracks walls, smile from foot lockers, and, in pocket size, be carried into battle. Hand-painted reproductions of the same popular photos would decorate bombers, boats, and Jeeps. The stars in most demand were Lana Turner, Rita Hayworth, Dorothy Lamour, Veronica Lake, Marie MacDonald—and, of course, Betty Grable. Betty was the winner of the GI popularity contest hands down, probably because of the single chance photo made of her by a Twentieth Century-Fox still photographer. The photo is regarded as second only to the flag raising shot at Iwo Jima in wartime popularity. It was the picture of Betty looking impishly over her shoulder, with her hands on her hips and wearing a skintight, white bathing suit.

The photo came to life in early 1943, but 1942 was a busy year for Betty. She made *Song of the Islands* with Victor Mature and Jack Oakie. While this Technicolor musical had little to relate to the prevailing war climate, it was a huge box-office smash and made Betty's face and body that much more familiar to her fans. Her fan mail was increasing dramatically, and exhibitors were demanding more films starring this cute and sexy young blonde.

Betty then teamed up with Mature again in *Footlight Serenade.* The movie won no artistic awards, but was once more a winner in the provinces. Betty's third movie of the year gave her the opportunity to become better acquainted with the man she would marry within a year. It was *Springtime in the Rockies.*

*The New York Times* was no more impressed with this offering than it was with Betty's other 1942 films. This review followed the November opening at New York's Roxy Theatre:

> Pretty as a lollipop and just as common, *Springtime in the Rockies* is a smooth job with faded material. Here and there Miss Miranda, who believes that charm should be emphatic, brightens the proceedings with a turbulent ditty. And for the record it should be mentioned that each appearance of the bandleader Harry James on the screen was a signal for frenzied applause yesterday, a totally mysterious phenomenon as far as this corner was concerned. For all its lavish trimmings, *Springtime in the Rockies* is just a second rate song and dance.

At about the time of *Springtime in the Rockies,* Harry James's wife, Mary Louise Tobin, was making rumbles about divorce, which, for Betty, probably added to the attractions of the handsome, horn-playing Gabriel. Betty sang "I Had the Craziest Dream" for the first time in this film, but her own craziest dream was still George Raft. Betty was flattered by the interest James demonstrated during the shooting, but she wasn't quite ready to expand her romantic horizons. She and Raft weren't married, but they were certainly going steady. If studio publicity dates were a source of George's fits of jealousy, what combustion would result from meanderings of her own design? She maintained her cool.

Before starting work on *Coney Island* with George Montgomery and Cesar Romero, Betty participated in a War Bond junket throughout most of the western states. While the film was in progress, she took time to captain the Comedians' football team, which played for war charities at the Los Angeles Coliseum against the Leading Men captained by Rita Hayworth. This was in October of 1942, and Betty's love affair with Raft was becoming tenuous. She was pressing hard for marriage, and he was stuck with his status quo.

When asked what happened to his plans for the Grable–Raft film project, George told a columnist, "I don't want to make a picture with Betty for Fox or any other studio because I'm too much in love with her—and working together might lead to an argument somewhere along the line." The columnist commented: "Does that mean they never have any?"

By the end of the year, Betty was ranked eighth among Hollywood's most popular stars; it was the first time she had broken the top-ten barrier. She would remain in that upper echelon for the following decade and more. In November it was announced that Betty ranked first in photo requests by military personnel, with Teresa Wright second, and Rita Hayworth third.

A giant Christmas Eve party was held for servicemen at the Hollywood Canteen, and Betty was an eager volunteer to share hostess duties. There were also three name bands, among whom was the Harry James congregation. Betty didn't shrug her responsibilities with the servicemen, but during her breaks she found herself drawn to the backstage area, where Harry was. In one of their visits Betty casually mentioned she was without a ride home, and Harry was quick to offer his services.

When the Canteen closed down at midnight, Betty left with Harry through the Ivar Street stage door. He asked if she was hungry. At her affirmative nod, Harry drove less than half a block to a drive-in restaurant at the corner of Cahuenga and Sunset. Harry parked, and an astonished car-hop stumbled toward them with menus. Their simultaneous order was a hamburger with raw onions. It was immediately apparent that, aside from music, they had other tastes in common.

The drive-in experience may have been an awakening for

Harry; although he was a star in his own right, he could enjoy a reasonable degree of privacy. On this occasion, hardly a bite of their hamburgers was consumed before clusters of fans began collecting to stare at them and giggle. Harry was a star; Betty was a star—together they were traffic stoppers. After this incident, there would be few drive-in restaurants in their future. But there would be a great deal of each other.

Betty was a fourteen-year-old chorus girl at Fox Studios at the time of this photo. Her contract was cancelled when her true age was revealed.

Betty was trying to look especially sophisticated in this early studio portrait because she was pretending to be sixteen, at least two years older than her actual age.

(Above) Fred Astaire looks on as Betty does her first featured dancing number with Edward Everett Horton in the 1934 musical, *The Gay Divorcee.* Betty also sang the Cole Porter song, "Let's K-nock K-nees."

Lucille Ball joins Betty in a lap or two around the racing track at Gilmore Field in Hollywood.

Betty shows she can hold her own on a pair of roller skates for this Paramount publicity shot about 1935.

In late 1935, Jackie Coogan and Betty Grable posed for a Kansas City photographer during their coast-to-coast tour as M.C.s for a Franchon and Markle show, "Hollywood Secrets."

Betty signs her name to the marriage license just prior to the November 1937 wedding to Jackie Coogan. She was warned by Jackie's mother that she was marrying a pauper, but love was Betty's only motive.

(Above) Conn Grable wasn't too happy with his daughter's attraction to Jackie Coogan, but he smiles after the wedding ceremony at St. Brendan's Church in Los Angeles.

The bridesmaid on the right is older sister, Marjorie, whose lack of talent left it up to Betty to make the Grable name famous.

One of many hundreds of publicity stills for which Betty posed.

Betty and another Paramount employee show how costumes are designed. The photo was taken in 1937.

The title of this 1939 production was *Million Dollar Legs,* but it had nothing to do with the legs so amply displayed in the photo. Betty's admirers are (left to right) Buster Crabbe, Richard Denning, Jackie Coogan and Tom Brown.

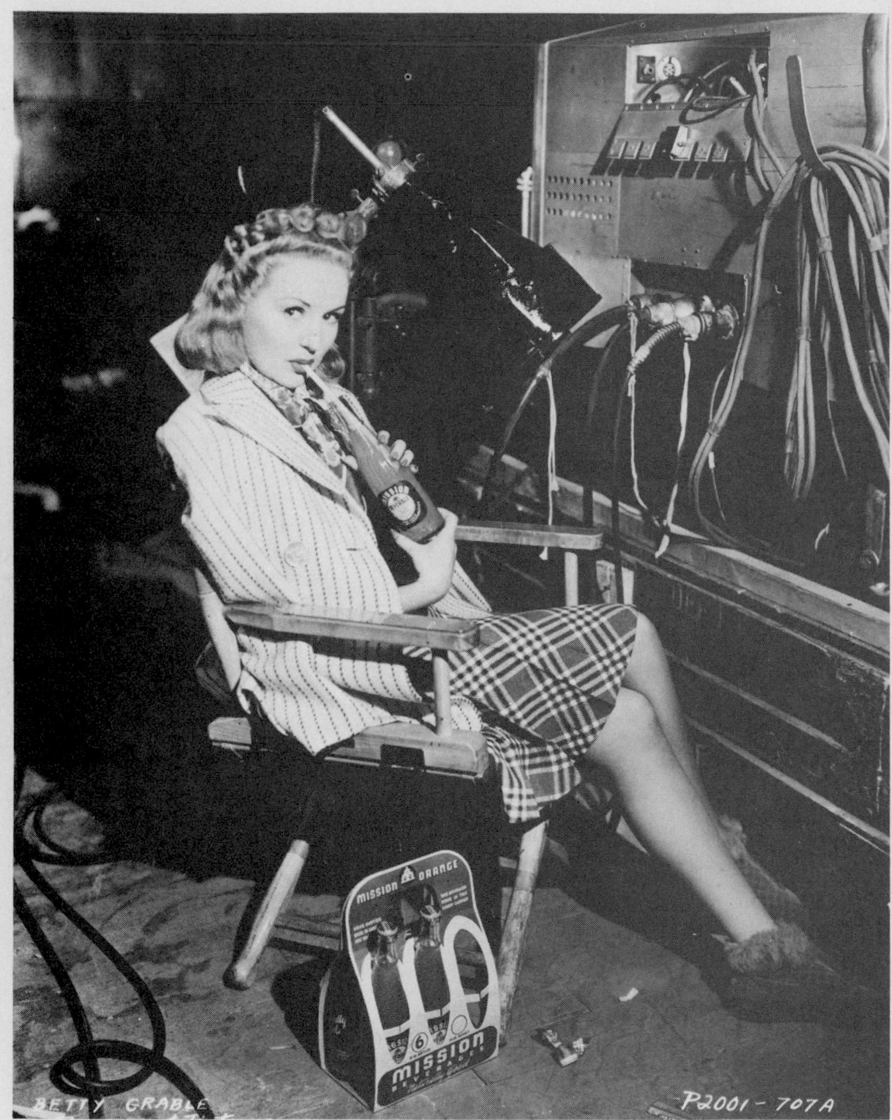


Was Betty caught stealing the electrician's private stock of orange soda, or was she hinting to the Mission Beverage company that she would like a lifetime supply delivered to her door? The candid photo came from the Paramount era, about 1939.

Betty is seen snipping one of the thousands of publicity clippings that began to come her way after the 1940 20th Century-Fox film *Down Argentine Way.*

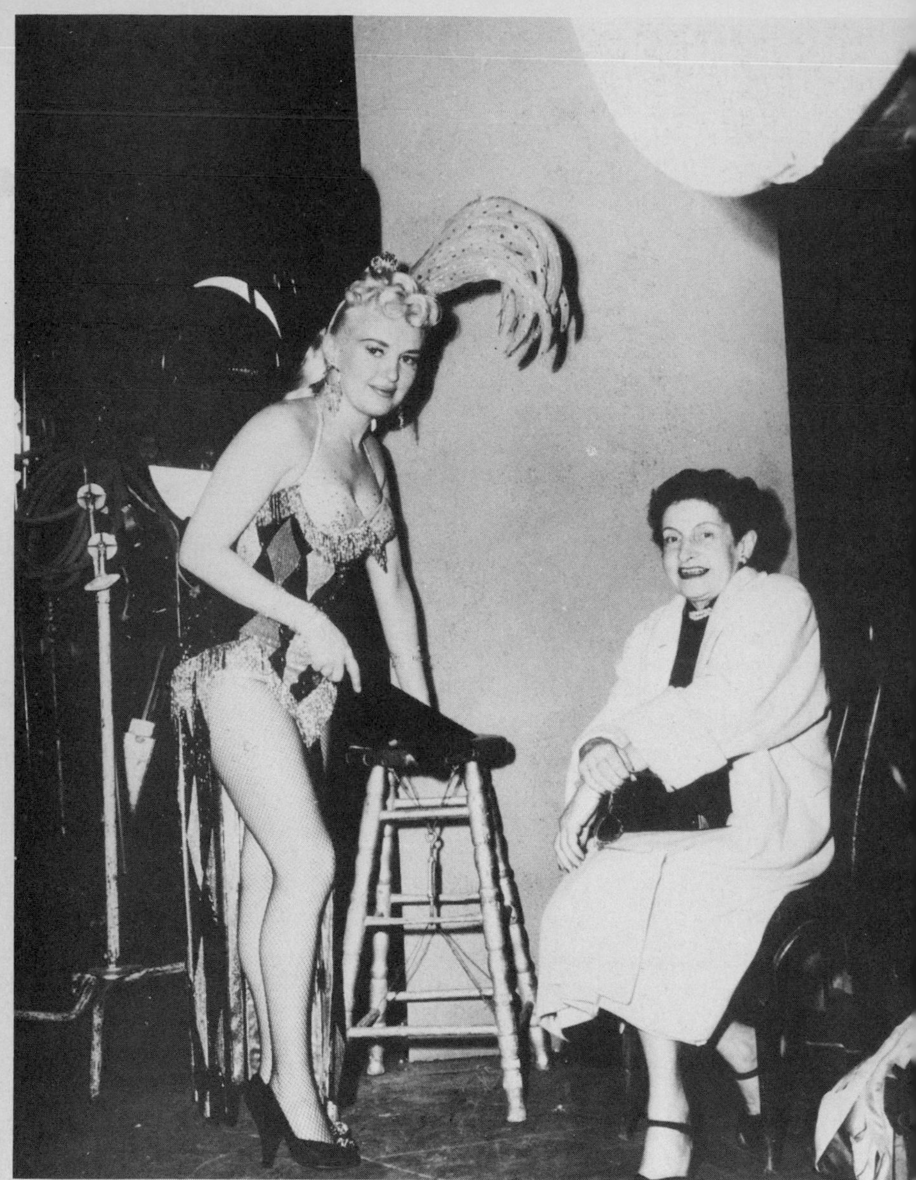

Betty is caught on a 20th Century-Fox sound stage with her mother, Lillian. Small and crippled, Lillian was strong in her determination to make her daughter a star.

(Above) Just one of Betty's Christmas shopping expeditions in December of 1942. There must be something nice for George Raft among the gaily wrapped presents.

(Right) Betty and one-time love, George Raft, dancing together in 1941.

Harry and Betty invite the press to get acquainted with their firstborn daughter, Victoria, just after her birth in March 1944.

# Chapter 10

The pinup picture of Betty Grable that decorated barracks' walls and locker doors the world over—"the picture that launched a million dreams," as it was dubbed by the publicity department—was made by Fox stillman Frank Powolney. And that is about all the concrete truth there is regarding its creation. Betty herself has been attributed with several versions, some on-the-level, others obviously in jest or misunderstood. One of her simpler explanations was that she was pregnant at the time with her first daughter, an obvious reason for turning her back to the camera. If this were true, it would mean Victoria was born at least six months before her parent's marriage, perhaps before they were even alone together. That version is untrue no matter what its origin.

Betty also said that her tummy was a bit flabby at the time, so she refused to be photographed from the front. Actually, Betty's tummy was a bit flabby more often than not, and, while she may not have enjoyed being photographed from the front, it didn't stop other frontal cheesecake pictures from being taken. Once more, Betty was simply making conversation.

Other erroneous accounts:

The wardrobe people on *Sweet Rosie O'Grady* needed photos for the designers to use in their creation of period costumes for the film. The prints turned up in wardrobe, where an employee who liked the over-the-shoulder shot called it to the attention of the people in publicity.

Betty, posing for Powolney, was surprised by a visit from none other than Darryl Zanuck. He said "Hi" to Betty, who turned around in surprise—just as the picture was being snapped.

Magazine writer Ron Alexander quoted Betty: "It was just a fluke. I had been posing in period hair-do for a studio artist who was doing some *Police Gazette*-like artwork. A big hat and fancy garter were later air-brushed out, and the photo was sent to the servicemen. I would never have posed like *that.*" Another Grable fantasy.

Powolney, a gentle and low-key man, insists that all the above are untrue, whether attributed to Betty or anyone else. He admits having made some shots for the wardrobe department that day, but they were all front shots. From there he proceeded to pose Betty for a wide variety of publicity shots.

"She tried several bathing suits in different colors," he says, "and they weren't exactly right. Finally, she put on the white one, and we made a couple of shots. She started to walk away and glanced back over her shoulder. It looked pretty good, so I asked if she would come back and do it again. She struck the pose, and said, 'Is this what you want?' I shot it, and that was that."

Powolney explained that Betty was very impatient during photo sessions, and she always requested him because he worked fast. "She didn't like the usual tactic of photographers who shoot things over and over again to be safe. I would always try to break it up into a lot of different poses, and then I would make only one or two shots of each pose. That way, she wouldn't get restless."

In those days there was no such thing as strobe lighting, and for stills they never used thirty-five millimeter cameras. They stayed with eight-by-ten view cameras with that size negative and would shoot as many as forty or fifty at a sitting. The exposure, with the view cameras, could not have been faster than about one fiftieth of a second, which made the story about Zanuck's surprise visit a total impossibility.

Studio estimates place about five million copies of the famous pose in GI hands during the war, and the over-the-shoulder pose was the only one that was used for this purpose. Powolney believes the term "pinup" was born with this Betty Grable photo.

Betty was a representation of the girl-back-home for thousands of homesick young lads. For some, she may have been their only infatuation, the last girl they had ever lusted for, loved, or adored. She was company on a cold night, comfort at times of pain. Betty had an idea she was admired by the GIs, but had no way of knowing exactly how much. It was more than the sexy picture that enamored them of her; there was a magical wholesomeness and substance they saw beyond the curves of her figure. It was her very essence that was loved.

When the studio finally awakened to what they had, their publicists gave her the full-star treatment. They enlisted a podiatrist to assure the world that Betty had not only perfect legs but also the most perfect feet. Lloyds of London were paid to insure her legs for a cool million, and Betty was honored in concrete at Graumann's Chinese Theatre.

The *Hollywood Reporter* of February 16, 1943, acknowledged the Graumann ceremonies as follows: "Prints of Betty Grable's feet, and one of her right leg, from a point slightly above the knee, were preserved for posterity yesterday in the forecourt of the Chinese Theatre. There, these features of the star of Twentieth's *Sweet Rosie O'Grady* joined the profile of John Barrymore, the nose of Bob Hope, and the skate marks of Sonja Henie. Betty took off her shoes before stepping into the cement—having shoe rationing in mind."

Betty was variously described as the "gal with the gorgeous gams," "the girl with the million-dollar legs," or, the girl with "the limbs that launched a thousand sighs." She didn't mind at all. Betty, as with most of her wartime contemporaries, took her role quite seriously. "A lot of guys don't have any girl friends to fight for," she was quoted. "I guess you could call us pinup girls kind of an inspiration."

The war years were great times for labels in Hollywood. Other glamour queens became known as "The Girl With the Peek-a-Boo Bangs" (Veronica Lake), "The Sweater Girl" (Lana Turner), "The Oomph Girl" (Ann Sheridan), "The Body" (Marie MacDonald), "The Sarong" (Dorothy Lamour). Even the men were issued monikers. Victor Mature, for example, was tagged "The Hunk," which pleased him not at all.

It was George Raft's age that exempted him from military service, but he contributed in his own way. Sportsman that he was, Raft hired a group of top-notch boxers to stage exhibition bouts at military bases. Betty joined him on many of these tours, which were said to have cost him more than $50,000.

Raft wasn't at all secure in his romance with Betty, especially after Harry James came into the picture. In early 1943 he presented Betty with an exquisite diamond watch, but she was well aware of George's generosity by now. It was what George didn't give her that bothered her most—a proposal of marriage.

In March the Hollywood Palladium organized a promotion that involved bandleaders in a jitterbug contest. By some coincidence—not recognized as such by George Raft—Harry James drew Betty Grable as his dance partner. This information was published in the March 5 newspapers. There was another item on March 8, the day following the event, that Harry James had won the contest hands down—but with actress Nan Wynn as his partner. Raft must have influenced the sudden change in partners for James, because Betty didn't even show up. It was obvious by now that the Grable-Raft love boat was listing badly, and many of the columnists hinted it was about to sink.

There had been many breakups and make-ups in the past for Betty and George, but by this time Betty was cool and detached in her reaction. If she reacted emotionally to the current lover's quarrel, the entire cycle could very well start all over again. There would be the usual agonies during the breakup period, and, inevitably, the ecstasies enjoyed later on with all the kisses in making up. Not this time—Betty was as certain this affair was over as she was at the end of her marriage to Coogan. No power on earth could change her mind.

She called Raft and gave him the news: their current quarrel would be their last. She was walking away and would be grateful if he did not follow. He wanted to hear it from her in person, but Betty refused. It was all over—period.

Raft had been up to dirty tricks during the latter weeks of their relationship, like sending pals to spy on Betty. Once Ben Platt climbed a tree to peer into a bedroom where he expected to spot Betty making love to Harry James. Platt saw nothing, but Betty and Harry saw Platt—when he plunged, with arms flailing, from the tree branches.

After Betty's terminal phone call, there were some loose ends to attend to in the Raft household, one of which was a stone marten coat. The fur had been ordered for Betty some days earlier and had now been delivered to Raft's home. It isn't clear whether Raft wanted Betty to have the coat out of pure generosity, or if it was a last ditch effort toward reconciliation, but he enlisted another good pal, Mack Grey, to take it to the person for whom it was ordered. His orders were to hand it over to Betty, or to leave on her doorstep. When Betty refused to appear at the door, Grey draped the expensive coat over the welcome mat. Raft believes today that Betty eventually rescued the coat from the elements. At least he never saw it again. Unless her gardener or paperboy ended up better dressed than his peers, Betty had a final lavish gift from one of the world's most generous ex-boyfriends.

The coat was probably a trivial part of the hundreds of gifts Raft bestowed upon Betty over the two-and-a-half-year romance. There were gold watches, bracelets, diamond necklaces, and at least one race horse. By George's own estimate, Betty's gifts represented an investment of more than $50,000, a pretty penny for those days. But he loved her, and in his old-fashioned chivalry the gifts were integral to the courtship.

Betty told Louella Parsons: "I would have married George a week after I met him. I was so deeply in love with him. But when you wait two-and-a-half years, there doesn't seem a future in a romance with a married man."

Parsons, who was interviewing Betty on the set of *Sweet Rosie O'Grady*, pointed out that Raft was bitter about her tactics in calling off the affair, that she could at least have faced him directly. Betty skirted the issue, by saying she was sure Raft had no ill feelings toward her. She said she was sure he still loved her, and that she loved him. "You can't see a person every day, and have them do all the little thoughtful, attentive things George did, and break off without feeling lonely. I don't expect to get over George today, tomorrow, or next week. But I do know there is no turning back."

Louella confronted Betty with the rumors about her and Harry James, but Betty denied everything. At this stage, she was probably a bit gun-shy about involvements with married men, and even though she was thoroughly involved with Harry, and although it was fairly well established that a divorce was imminent, Betty was taking no chances. Yes, she was seeing Harry—they did have a common interest in music—but no, they weren't romantically involved.

Lucille Ball remembers this pivotal period of Betty's life very well: "The only time I saw Betty when her spirits weren't up, was when George Raft couldn't be persuaded to get married. Then she fell in love with Harry James, and she was very much in love with Harry. I remember I'd go to see her, and she'd lie on the floor with her radio right to her ear, when Harry was playing in Chicago or someplace. Everything else would stop when he was on the radio. It would be blaring, and she'd be listening to that horn."

In the spring of 1943, before Harry went on his eastern tour, he and Betty were dining in a Sunset Strip restaurant. George Raft, who had never been known to ingest anything stronger than 7-Up, made an exception on this occasion. He approached their table, and insisted on talking with Betty. She asked him to leave but Raft persisted. The result was a scuffle between Harry and George, in which James was named winner. It was a distasteful scene for Betty, but the assertiveness displayed by Harry obviously endeared him to her even more.

George traipsed off with his tail between his legs, knowing full well that the romance was dead now, even if it hadn't been before. He was probably also giving some thought to his $50,000 investment, because no matter how lightly he spoke of the matter in later years, he was surely aware of value received for dollars spent. According to sources close to the scene, George Raft received precious little for his money—or little of what might be considered precious in a male-female relationship. There were kisses, hugs, laughter, and good times—but sex? Maybe not.

Love affairs are usually thought of as sexual affairs, at least today, but in those years, and with Betty Grable, nothing of this kind can be taken for granted. Despite Betty's good-natured lasciviousness, she possessed high intrinsic morality; she was more show than go.

# Chapter 11

Betty made a quantum leap in popularity in 1943—from number eight to first place. She was now the top female star in Hollywood and was drawing thousands of fan letters each week. Her mother, who was always around anyway, was put on the Twentieth payroll to oversee the fan-mail processing. The more interesting letters were answered by Betty, via Lillian, who imitated her signature to perfection. Betty's movies were never regarded as masterpieces and seldom received even mild praise from the critics, but they were selling tickets by the millions. It wasn't the movies that sold the tickets, actually. It was Betty. She was rewarded by steep salary boosts, which would peak a few years later.

Betty's good friend Dorothy Lamour became Mrs. William Howard in April, and Betty could attend the ceremony without too much personal envy, because conditions were beginning to look excellent for a not-too-distant marriage of her own.

It had been almost a year since Harry's wife had filed for $1,155 a month separate maintenance. This was to support her and their two children, until a divorce could be finalized. Harry paid the monthly tab, but no further word was forthcoming about the divorce. Now he was pressing for a quickie divorce in Mexico, and it appeared the former band singer would agree.

When Harry was in New York in May, he paid Benny Goodman $20,000 for the King of Swing's investment in the Harry James band. Considering the original loan was for $4,500, the payoff seemed handsome enough, but Goodman, consummate business man that he was, promised to sue for much more.

A Hollywood gossip columnist took note that, on May 17 Betty spoke long distance with Harry for two hours and ten minutes, but that was only one of the calls. If a tally were kept over the next few years, the cost of the Betty–Harry romance in absentia would probably add up to fairly a good salary for the average American worker. By the end of May, Betty had some time and prepared for a train trip to New York—one that wouldn't cost much more than the nightly calls and would be infinitely more rewarding.

While Betty was in New York, *Coney Island* opened, and Bosley Crowther of *The Times* liked it:

> This one has Betty Grable exercising her vocal chords and limbs to no inconsiderable advantage as a song bird of the 1900 school. It has George Montgomery and Cesar Romero as a couple of rising carnival men constantly crossing each other with their conniving tricks to win her hand. And it has a fair amount of old tunes, as well as several lively new ones, which thump very nicely on the eardrums and background some colorful displays.
>
> Among the enjoyable ditties which Miss Grable cozily sings are "Cuddle Up a Little Closer," and "Everybody Loves a Baby." She also puts a mean and snakey wiggle into her dancing.

It was Betty's first trip to New York in a couple of years, and the first ever under such circumstances. Previously she was able to move about in relative anonymity, but no longer. New York fans, far more demonstrative than those in Los Angeles, allowed not a moment's rest. She was now a major star and for the first time was made stridently aware of it.

When Betty wasn't with Harry, she spent most of her time with good friend Paula Stone, who was by then producing plays on Broadway. One evening she asked Paula to come with her to see one of her earliest pictures, *The Kid From Spain.* Betty had never seen it, and, since it was playing at the Gaiety, only a block or so from the Astor Hotel where she and Harry were staying, it seemed like an ideal opportunity. Paula agreed, and met Betty at the hotel, from where they could walk the short distance to the movie house. They made it to the theater without incident.

They sat through about an hour of the second bill and all the shorts, and finally *Kid From Spain* started. Betty had been a chorus girl in the film along with Paulette Goddard, but Betty was rewarded with lines. "Her big scene was practically the first one in the movie," said Paula. "The girls were all lined up in rows of beds, and Betty sat up and said, 'We are the girls of the dormitory.' I was just settling back to watch the rest of the movie, but Betty was gathering her things together. 'That's my part,' she said. 'That's it. I'm not interested in the rest of the movie.' So out we go.

"Now if you can imagine—this is Times Square. We walk out on the street, and soon you can hear a murmur run up and down Broadway, 'BETTY GRABLE!' With that, a wall of humanity starts toward us. Betty grabbed my hand so hard her nails sunk into my palm. She was absolutely terrified.

"I looked at her with her gorgeous figure, the tight dress, and her cotton-candy hair piled high on her head, and said, 'Even if you weren't Betty Grable, people would look, Betty.' But she wasn't mollified. She was almost in a state of shock.

"I don't know what made me think of it, but I turned to her and started talking gibberish. Betty caught on and started talking gibberish of her own. Then somebody behind us said, 'That ain't Betty Grable,' and the crowd let us through, convinced they had made a mistake. 'My God, it works!' Betty said. Every time we would be approached, Betty and I would go into our foreign language act, and it did the job.

"Betty was absolutely delighted. With such success behind us, Betty suggested we venture into Walgreen's Drug Store for a chocolate soda, something she had been unable to do for a long time. We did it and used our diversion whenever anybody would come up to us.

"Now Betty was really feeling brave and became irrepressible. We got up to the Astor Roof, where Harry was playing, and were walking along the corridor. Suddenly, with no warning at all, she bangs on a door. 'GET THAT MAN OUT OF YOUR ROOM!' she yells. Then she runs off leaving me standing there. I, of course, ran for my life, and when we were safely around the corner, we could hear somebody opening their door, bellowing in rage."

Most newsworthy events in Betty's life leave a variety of accounts from which to choose. There are the newspaper or wire service versions of the incident, the studio publicity department's concept, and then, rarely in confirmation of any of these, there is Betty's own story. Such a bouquet of choices surround her marriage to Harry James. The only absolute truth is that they were really married, and the correct date of the event is Monday, July 5, 1943, in the early dawn hours.

On July 2, Harry's wife went to Juarez, Mexico, where she attained a mutual-consent decree from Judge Xavier Caballas. Two days later, Betty and her mother were on a train wheeling their way through the desert to Las Vegas. They expected to be met by Harry at 2:20 A.M., when his train was scheduled to arrive from New York. He wasn't on time.

A wire service account:

> The trumpet tootler with the elastic lip was due at 2:20 A.M. but his train was an hour and a half late. During the wait Miss Grable, flanked by her mother and by two publicity men, who were there to see she got as little publicity as possible, smoked cigarets in a limousine parked by the station.
>
> When James finally arrived, the couple dashed to the Little Church of the West in the Last Frontier Hotel, where the knot was tied by the Rev. C.S. Sloan, Baptist minister.
>
> James gave his age as 27; Miss Grable as 26.

> They gobbled down a quick honeymoon breakfast and then hit the road for their Beverly Hills cottage and sleep.
>
> Betty could use plenty of it—she had been up since 5:00 A.M. Sunday to get to her man.
>
> Miss Grable, remarking that she was very happy but a bit nervous, wore a "something new" hat at a dangerous angle atop her curly hairdo, and twisted a "something borrowed" handkerchief given her by Alice Faye.
>
> The bandleader slipped a plain gold band on the left hand of his bride. She wore no engagement ring.

In her own account, given later to *Photoplay,* Betty apologized for closing herself off from the fans who surrounded her limousine while she awaited Harry's arrival. She said she was too sick even to eat after the desert train ride in an un-air-conditioned car and did nothing but smoke cigarettes while she sat in the car waiting for Harry. She said he was four hours late rather than an hour-and-a-half and described the time of day as "dusk" when he finally showed up. She said they sped off to the church and found it lit up like a Christmas tree.

"People were lined up for blocks," she said. "A spotlight picked up our car, and a loudspeaker boomed: 'Here they come folks!' I saw Harry's face turn white—we got out the wrong side of the car, took hands and ran to the hotel. The minister, in answer to our pleading, performed the ceremony there.

"We don't care much for mob scenes—mostly because crowds are our business, and getting away from them is our relaxation. Both of us have worked since we were kids—the noise and excitement began earlier for Harry than for me, because both his parents were professionals. His dad led the circus band, and his mother did an "iron jaw act" right up until a month before his birth."

The morning following their marriage, Betty had to report for work on *Pin-Up Girl* and Harry rehearsed for his tri-weekly radio show. They stayed briefly in Betty's home, which she shared with her mother in Stone Canyon. Sister Marjorie and her husband moved to make room for Harry. Later Betty bought her mother a trim little home on Rodeo Drive in the heart of

Beverly Hills. Betty sold her house and lived in a rented one until she and Harry could find exactly the place they both wanted. Harry liked modern furniture in desert hues; Betty's love was for antiques. The antiques went to Lillian's home, and Harry's choice prevailed.

The press was unhappy about the sneak marriage and were especially miffed when the only wedding pictures were taken by studio photographers. To make amends, Harry distributed photo layouts to the magazines and newspapers through his own press agent.

Defending her need for privacy, Betty was quoted: "I didn't get married as a publicity stunt. I married Harry because I loved him and not to bring people around to look at us or to get a lot of pictures of us kissing each other. It's not that I don't appreciate people being interested in us. I do. I like people, and I want them to like me. I wish sometimes I could let them know how much I appreciate their greetings. Some girls can hop off a train and wave a big greeting to everyone, but sometimes crowds get me all nervous inside.

"Some people just naturally have a hail-fellow spirit. I'd like to have it, but I haven't. Maybe I'm bashful or something, I don't know."

Whenever Harry was in town, he and the band played regularly on Monday nights at the Hollywood Canteen. After their marriage, Betty never failed to come along as band singer. The GIs loved it, but probably weren't aware that it was also the Harry James trumpet that awakened them each morning. One of Harry's contributions to the war effort was to record all bugle calls, which were played exclusively when live buglers were unavailable.

*Sweet Rosie O'Grady* opened in the Fall of 1943 to long lines of waiting fans. The script had kicked around town for five years with no takers until Zanuck saw its value as a Betty Grable vehicle. As so often would be the case, his judgment was right.

Betty's childhood friend, Emelyn Pique, returned to Hollywood to work on a movie at Twentieth, but this time she was known as Mitzie Mayfair. She starred with Kay Francis, Carole

Landis, and Martha Raye in the true-to-life story, *Four Jills in a Jeep.* Betty, Carmen Miranda, and Alice Faye all did cameo roles in the movie.

This assignment closed out the year for Betty. She had traded a boyfriend for a husband, jumped from number eight in popularity to number one, and was on her way to becoming one of the most highly paid actresses in the world. She was also on her way—about six months worth—to becoming a mother.

To cap off the greatest year of her life, Betty threw a big party at the Palladium for Harry's December 28 opening. It was in commemoration also for their happy early evenings there, when their love song was just being written.

About this same time, George Raft was trying to drown his memories with another young actress. He was dating twenty-year-old Bonita Granville, much to her mother's dismay; when she was grounded Raft visited a favorite piano bar where he would cry in his 7-Up to *I Saw You Last Night and Got That Old Feeling.* Nobody in the bar was aware that this was the secret love song for him and a very special blonde he had loved—a very special, *expensive* blonde that he hadn't really stopped loving at all.

# Chapter 12

It was apparent from the outset that the Grable–James combination would be a winner. Although Harry was far more introverted than Betty, he laughed at the same things, seemed to like most of her friends, and, in his laid-back way, liked the same activities as his lovely bride. Certainly no complaints were heard coming from their nuptial chamber—Harry was always rumored to be eminently gifted in that area.

In October of 1943 the Jameses purchased the home of Bert Lahr on the corner of Coldwater Canyon and Heather in Beverly Hills, where they would remain for several years. Both daughters were born there, with Victoria Elizabeth arriving March 3, 1944. The birth was by caesarian section, and Betty was taken off salary for the long period of pregnancy and recuperation.

In a later fan-magazine interview, Betty suggested that her prognosis after the birth was questionable, but that energy surged back into her body when Harry came into the room bearing an armful of crossword puzzle books. "You can't let a man like that down," she said, "which is probably why I'm still around, and I'm still unable to resist a crossword puzzle.

"After I was home again, he joked about how cooperative I was to have the baby on a Friday instead of on Tuesday or Thursday which would have interfered with his radio broadcasts."

The brown-out was lifted by this time, but the Hollywood glamour had not exactly returned. There were neon-lighted storefronts, and the general feeling that the war might indeed be survived, but the weekend invasions of furloughed servicemen made the presence of war almost palpable. Their throngs drove away all the stars they hoped to glimpse. Honky-tonk bars cropped up, and Cahuenga Boulevard became the mecca for military visitors. Almost every door led to a photo booth, a sleazy bar, or a penny arcade. The USO and the Hollywood Canteen were within a block of each other on Cahuenga, and the men would wander back and forth between the two from early morning to late at night. The heart of Hollywood had already begun the descent from being the glamour crossroads of the world; the tarnish of the war years would be impossible to erase.

A favorite GI catch phrase of the time was "In like Flynn," but among others coming along was, "I want a girl just like the girl that married Harry James." Betty's marriage didn't diminish her popularity in the least. In fact, it seemed to enhance it. Maybe the girls liked her better now that Harry had taken her out of circulation, and the bobby-soxers idolized Harry James. To the men, Betty Grable was still Betty Grable, no matter whom she married.

One of Betty's least favorite films was *Pin-Up Girl,* and her opinion was shared by most critics when it was released in the spring of 1944. Starring with her were Joe E. Brown and Martha Raye, about whom one critic said, "They opened their big mouths often, but nothing amusing came out." The movie was an artistic flop, but at the box office it might as well have been an Academy Award candidate. It was a financial smash.

Most celebrities receive more barbs than accolades, and, in the spirit of sour grapes, those around them tend to propagate the negative and forget the positive. Betty was one of the lucky ones who seemed to have more champions than she did detractors. She was generally well-liked, and some of her friends would fight a duel to protect her good name. Others, however, while in a minority, want it known that Betty Grable was not all sugar and spice and everything nice.

She could be difficult—complaining, snippy, captious. When she was growing up in Hollywood, she was known to be rather spoiled and querulous. The complaints turned toward a prima donna syndrome after her new stardom of the forties, especially after she married Harry and figuratively divorced Lillian.

At this point she began to be charged with a near compulsion for privacy and aggressive demand for respect. Betty was no longer a flouncy chorus girl. She was now a movie star and a dignified wife and mother. She must have thought it time she was treated that way.

Betty was confused, actually. She wanted deference, yet also wanted to be one of the gang. This dichotomy, in various guises, would follow Betty throughout her life. She would never really be sure what she wanted or who she was.

Lillian didn't abdicate her position of power, of course; it was Betty who deposed her, at least for a time. Slowly, Lillian would regain her throne, though with somewhat diluted authority. Betty needed her mother's guidance, even though she now had Harry with whom to talk things over.

Betty may have been a bit shaky when she returned to the lot after nearly a year of enforced domesticity. It could have been insecurity or simply a reluctance to crawl back into the old harness again, but she was not happy in late August of 1944 when she started work on *Billy Rose's Diamond Horseshoe.*

This was George Seaton's first directorial assignment for one thing, and Betty felt that somebody of lesser stature should serve as his guinea pig; the costumes weren't right, nothing pleased her. She went to Zanuck with her complaints, and he tossed it all right back into her lap. He called a production meeting, to allow Betty to voice her grievances directly. This wasn't exactly what she had in mind, but she was stuck with it.

All the production heads were corralled into Zanuck's office, including the producer William Perlberg. Charles Le Maire, Broadway designer, had been added to the Twentieth roster, and *Diamond Horseshoe* was one of his first costume assignments. He was on hand at the meeting.

"Zanuck gave me carte blanche for all pictures," says Le Maire. "I had agreed to open and close this picture personally and would delegate staff members for the rest. Betty complained that I was on another set and wasn't paying attention to her.

"She stood there like a little school girl with her finger in her mouth, pouting. She said that nobody said good morning to her, that she didn't like the direction, and that she wasn't being treated any better than an extra. She looked at me and said she didn't like her costumes and that her fitter had been taken away."

Le Maire explained that the fitter had been promoted to head of wardrobe, but that she was still overseeing everything. Betty said she knew this, but that it wasn't the same thing. She then charged that her costumes were being altered overnight, because they didn't fit around the waist. She suggested that somebody might have pressed them with a too-hot iron, or something.

"I assured her," said Le Maire, "that nothing had been done to her costumes and that she was suffering from bloat. I said she had puffed up because she sat around all night playing poker, sipping bourbon with beer chasers. I pointed out that I had dressed some of the most beautiful people on Broadway for twenty-five years, and never had a complaint. I also told her it was no wonder none of the girls wanted to fit her, because she was unprofessional in the way she treated her co-workers. I said that my name would appear on the screen as well as hers, and that nothing would be changed."

Le Maire doubts if Betty had ever been spoken to in that way before, and his speech had its desired effect. She backed off sheepishly. Zanuck closed the meeting, and, when everyone had left, Le Maire said Zanuck turned to him. "Charlie, you were wonderful. That was the God-damndest waste of time I've ever been through."

Le Maire said that he never had trouble with Betty after this, but insists she was not very well liked on the set. "If she got up feeling bad," he said, "she would be mean—slam doors, try to snap everyone to attention, that sort of thing. She always had to be handled with kid gloves."

He thinks part of Betty's behavior was the result of running scared. "There was always a new girl rehearsing with Hermes Pan," he said. "Zanuck always had a replacement in the wings, and she knew it."

Even though Le Maire had his problems with Betty, he concedes she was often sweet and generous. On a later picture, she presented him with a very expensive cigarette lighter, with an engraving of the costume he designed for her.

When Betty got into one of her snits, Marie Brasselle was often called upon to act as liaison. Marie was not only Betty's longtime hairdresser, she was family. Betty's daughters addressed her as Aunt Marie, and it was she who accompanied Betty on trips when Lillian was unavailable.

"Anyone who conned Betty was out," says Marie. "I never did that, so I always got along with her—but we had our differences. If she asked me about somebody, and I didn't say what she expected to hear, she would say, 'Oh, you're like Jesus Christ—you love everyone.' She would be real mad about it. Then I'd say, 'Why the heck did you ask me then?' "

When someone suggested that Marie wasn't as good a friend as Betty thought she was, Betty retorted, "As long as she treats me as rotten as she does I'll stick with her." Marie stood up to her, and Betty always respected that.

Betty's forebodings about *Billy Rose's Diamond Horseshoe* were groundless, because it came out another winner. Dick Haymes made his film debut in the picture and scored heavily in vocal renditions of "I Wish I Knew," and "The More I See You." The movie made Haymes a star and helped Betty hold on as number one box-office champ.

By the end of 1944, it was asserted (probably by the Twentieth Century-Fox publicity department) that one out of every fifteen men in the Armed Forces belonged to a camp, regiment, company, or other unit that had elected Betty Grable mascot, dream girl, honorary commander or some other coveted position. It was also suggested that half of the other GIs kept her picture around without bothering to elect her anything. They just liked to gaze at her sweet face, her ample figure, and, most of all, her gorgeous gams.

Betty defended her pinup image: "People talk about my legs as if I were a centipede, but my legs wouldn't have taken me anyplace without years of training in dancing."

Her legs were certainly significant enough to break all records in a nationwide bond drive staged in Pulaski, Virginia. It wasn't her legs exactly, but, more accurately, a pair of nylons which had once adorned them. The stockings, accompanied by a signed document confirming their authenticity, were sold for the high bid of $110,000.

# Chapter 13

When World War II entered its final year, Betty Grable was drawing an average of 10,000 fan letters a week. During one month in 1944 an avalanche of 90,000 letters were trucked to the Twentieth Century-Fox studios. Betty was the studio's top money-maker for 1945 and would remain so for two more years. Her salary topped out at $208,000, which made her the highest paid star in Hollywood.

Betty's physical measurements were listed in various articles that appeared during the war years. She was five-feet-four inches tall, and weighed a hundred fourteen pounds. Her thighs measured nineteen and a half inches, her calves thirteen inches, and ankles seven. From lap to floor she measured thirty-eight inches.

The measurements modified somewhat after her marriage, though the increases weren't reflected in the publicity releases. But Betty knew, even though it required word from Harry to prompt her to attack the problem. Betty said his tactful message was, "Hey, kid, you're getting fat."

A more gallant gentleman might have regarded her extra

weight as all the more to love, but not Harry. He preferred his women svelte and didn't mind telling her so. Since Harry wasn't all that loquacious, Betty listened when he spoke, and, since her mother had been demoted in rank, she relied upon Harry to give her the nudges she always needed. It was carrots and celery until the bulges faded away.

She said that Harry was really quite gentle in criticism and did most of his talking to soften the impact of negative messages. He couldn't bear to fire anyone, according to Betty, and would leave the job to someone else, or would simply keep the person on the payroll.

She credits Harry's low-key methods with making her a better person. "There was a time," she said in an interview, "when I would pout or yell when something didn't please me, but I've learned to be more patient."

She said how lucky they both were to have found each other, because there was perfect mental attunement between them. "We get an idea," she said, "and, bang, something has to happen. We decided we liked horseback riding, and that it was fun and healthy, so we bought two saddle horses right away. That's how it started, and now we have sixty-two acres of land, and plan to build a racing and breeding business."

Betty insisted that she and Harry never quarreled. "This may seem unbelievable when you consider my picky disposition my mother always said I had, but it's true. You can't fight with Harry. He can't stand dissension, and on those rare occasions when he does get mad, he turns white and says nothing."

Harry also influenced Betty to ease off on all the heavy makeup she was accustomed to wearing. "I don't wear all those rats in my hair anymore either," she said, "because Harry said I look better without all that, and he's right."

Domesticity took its toll on Harry as well as Betty when it came to weight. He gained twenty pounds over their first year of marriage, but he was better able to absorb it. It certainly wasn't the result of Betty's culinary capabilities. Neither she nor any other member of her family considered themselves competition to Betty Crocker; they liked to eat, but not to cook. The mutual chubbiness was more the result of contentment and happy times in the home. She and Harry loved each other, and both of them adored their young daughter. As for movies? It was what kept the beans in the pan. Since Harry's income at the time was estimated to be about $100,000 a year, the beans were abundant.

One of the blondes standing in wait for Betty came into clear focus when shooting began on *The Dolly Sisters.* It was almost as if Darryl Zanuck had held a national Betty Grable look-alike contest and June Haver was the winner. She was blonde, she was compact, and her curves were all in the right places. Betty almost always fooled everyone by becoming friends with her competition—almost, but not always. The single exception was June Haver. Betty did not like her, and that was that. She always regarded Haver as hypocritical, with biblical quotations always at hand. Betty was baptised an Episcopalian, but that was probably the last church service she attended. She believed in God, but hated to be proselytized.

Whether she liked June Haver or not, they worked well together in this first production by George Jessel, and the movie was Betty's smash hit of 1945. In it, she sang the song "I Can't Begin To Tell You," and it too became a hit.

The movie was completed in the spring, but wasn't released until late fall. In the interim, many monumental happenings occurred: President Roosevelt died in April; Germany surrendered May 7; the atom bombs were dropped over Japan August 6 and 9: and the Japanese surrendered August 14. The lights came on again all over the world, and Hollywood quickly re-geared for postwar production.

As for Betty, her image was still very much alive in the hearts of the war-oriented public, and her popularity lasted long after the more than fifteen million GIs returned home to begin their baby boom.

Darryl Zanuck, in his own way, appreciated the millions Betty had earned for the studio over the war years and was giving considerable thought to what measures should be taken to insure Betty's future. He invited her to lunch not long after VJ Day, and made what he considered the proposition of a lifetime.

He had decided to give her a crack at the role of Sophie in his movie version of the great Somerset Maugham novel, *The Razor's Edge.* Betty was a star, but this would make her great. It would prove she was more than songs and dances and silly romances. He gloated as he handed out the good news and then sat back awaiting Betty's screams of joy. He waited and waited and waited.

Betty stared blankly, wondering what was happening. Was he serious? She had never known him to joke before, not Darryl Zanuck, and he seemed very serious. It isn't known what Betty's exact response was, but the sentiment was, "No thanks!"

As his fury began to mount, Betty tried to explain. She was a song-and-dance gal, nothing less, nothing more. "That's the limit of my talents," she told him. "If I have a good enough director, he can usually pull me through the tight places. I'm no Bette Davis. I just want to make pictures people will like.

"If I play Sophie—that scene where she jumps off the bridge into the Seine to commit suicide—my audience would never accept that. They would expect me to coming bouncing back up out of the water doing a back stroke with feathers in my hair singing 'I'm yours for a song.' "

Needless to say, the luncheon date came to a sudden close, and Betty was once more suspended. With the exception of a gag appearance in the Harry James movie, *Do You Love Me,* Betty would be off the screen for almost a year.

Betty's appearance in *Do You Love Me* was without lines or billing. In the story, Harry James loses Maureen O'Hara to Dick Haymes and walks off by himself. He is alone until he comes across a waiting fan. The fan is Betty Grable, and off they walk into the sunset.

The movie had been delayed twice, which disappointed Betty and Harry, since they hoped to take an extended vacation upon the completion of both their films. Now, since Betty was on suspension, it didn't make that much difference.

Sheilah Graham interviewed Harry while the picture was in progress and commented on his attentiveness to Betty when they lunched in the studio commissary. Two years had passed since their early morning marriage, and they appeared to remain very much in love. Harry confirmed this, said they were buying a ranch in Calbasas, and that he was happy to settle down for the first time in his life.

When asked how it felt to make love to Maureen O'Hara in the picture, Harry replied, "It's strictly an experiment." He said if it worked out he might go in for the romantic stuff. "But only if it doesn't interfere with the band. I'll never make a picture without the band."

When the picture was over, the Grable family moved to a rented apartment in the Sherry Netherland Hotel. Harry had an extended band engagement in New York, and nothing stood in the way of Betty going along.

# Chapter 14

According to Paula Stone, stardom was something Betty could never quite comprehend, at least in terms of her own stardom. Betty once told her "You know, Lana Turner and Joan Crawford, they really deserve to be stars. I don't."

"What are you talking about?" Paula protested. "You're bigger than either of them."

Betty shook her head. "No, they know how to act the part. When they go out, they're all dressed up, and I hate to dress up. I've seen Lana at parties with little diamonds in her hair—and Crawford always looks so beautiful. I just feel uncomfortable. I don't like all the attention, and I don't deserve it."

Betty always insisted she was simply lucky, and perhaps she was. She knew she was nobody special and, in her pure, middle-class honesty, was unable to pretend to be something she was not. There were times, certainly, when she could accept her status for what it was, but there were other times when she had to shake her head and wonder about it. New York was always a place where the most head shaking would occur, because there was no place where her super-stardom was more readily apparent.

To avoid the crowds, Betty and Harry spent as much time as possible at the Forest Hills home of Paula's father, but most of the time Betty had to contend with the Manhattan throngs.

"When people would push up for an autograph," said Paula, "you could just see Betty retreat into a shell. It wasn't that she was ungracious, she was simply very uncomfortable with people she didn't know.

"Once Betty asked me to go shopping with her on Fifty-seventh Street. I met her at the Sherry Netherland, and we took a taxi to the stores. These were very elegant shops, and, although the clerks and customers stared at her, they didn't bother her. But when we went back out on the street, a group of people began to grow. Betty clutched my hand in fear. 'Let go of my hand,' I told her, 'so I can go out and hail a taxi.' She begged me not to leave her. I finally propped her beside a mailbox and told her to hang on. She was like a little child. It was only a minute or two, but by the time I returned to her she was surrounded by people demanding autographs. I took over and apologized for her, telling the people we had to leave. I let them glare at me instead of her."

The studio was constantly trying to call Betty during her suspension period, and, when their efforts proved fruitless, they tried to enlist Paula's help. "I asked them not to make me the go-between," said Paula. "I said that one of the reasons Betty and I were such good friends was because I didn't butt into her life."

Eventually the studio hatched a scheme that would get Betty to the phone. She told the switchboard operator that Paula Stone was calling. Betty spoke with them on that occasion, but it didn't work again. From then on Betty and Paula devised a foolproof code. The handy cover name was "Fonge Donge."

Very early in Betty's relationship with Harry, she frequently traveled on band gigs and occasionally sat in for a song set or two. She loved it, and Harry seemed to like it too, but that all changed. Whether it was a matter of being upstaged, or whether

Harry wanted breathing room, isn't clear. It was simply agreed that he would go and do his work and Betty would remain at home. Betty missed the groupie activity and was known on occasion to disguise herself and sit far in the back of the hall, just to listen to the sound of the trumpet that so pleased her.

In 1946, when the tally was made for the previous year, Betty earned enough money to make her the highest paid star in Hollywood at $299,333. About this time a reporter asked Lillian Grable what her daughter was really like. "She's just like any other little girl who earns three hundred thousand dollars a year," Lillian told him.

When Betty returned to work in 1946, she starred in her only Twentieth film that was a box-office dud, *The Shocking Miss Pilgrim.* The Gershwin score did little to stimulate interest for a Grable film in which not a glimpse of stocking was shown. The Victorian era film served only to inspire nearly 100,000 letters of complaint from Betty's fans. Dick Haymes suffered through the experience with Betty, but he came out with a song hit, his rendition of "For You, For Me, Forevermore." When the film was released, *The New York Times* said, "There is no more voltage in *The Shocking Miss Pilgrim* than in a badly used dry cell."

With the end of the war came the reopening of the local race tracks, and Betty's interest was quickly renewed. Harry was soon sharing her zeal in the sport of kings, and their annual exodus to Del Mar began. On these early occasions their bets were on other people's horses, but it was not long before they were backing horses from their own stable, which became one of the largest at the track.

With their preoccupation with horses, the Jameses entered their "Western" era. Harry would send Betty thoughtful gifts from stops along the way on his road tours: riding jackets, spurs, fancy boots. She would reciprocate with gifts of silver-inlaid saddles, custom-made tack. Their interests for the time being were perfectly attuned, and the most important common interest was their beloved daughter.

"There couldn't be a story about Harry and me," she said in a 1946 magazine interview, "unless it listed the number-one reason for our happiness. Vickie is a two-year-old replica of her daddy. I really don't know how I rated two such dispositions in one family. We haven't any special plans for her—just want her to be healthy and normal, and we'll be content to let her find her own happiness, the way we've found ours."

By the time Betty's next picture was in preproduction, she was into a preproduction program of her own. She was pregnant with their second child.

Despite occasional bouts with morning sickness, Betty trouped as never before in *Mother Wore Tights.* Much of her zeal came from the special chemistry brought forth in her teaming up with Dan Dailey. It was more than mere chemistry; it touched upon alchemy, as she and Dailey camped their way through their routines in this top money maker of all Betty Grable musicals.

The movie was delayed because the studio was negotiating with Warner Brothers for the services of James Cagney in the role of Frank Burt. This failed, as did a bid for Fred Astaire, so the new Twentieth contractee, Dan Dailey, was assigned the role. There must have been a sigh or two of disappointment on Betty's part when a virtual unknown was cast in the role where the studio had set such high goals, but all possible misgivings were soon dispelled. Betty would never find a co-star as finely keyed to her own personality, and an affinity was forged in this grand encounter that lasted all her life.

The plot was narrated from the point of view of the Burt's younger daughter played by thirteen-year-old Connie Marshall. The off-camera voice that represented the grown up daughter, belonged to Anne Baxter, who, ironically, would win the 1946 Oscar for her portrayal of Sophie in *Razor's Edge,* the role rejected so emphatically by Betty.

The film was an adaptation of a novel by Miriam Young, in which a vaudeville team returns to work after bearing two children. In order to be free to go on tour, the couple trundles the kids off to grandmother's house. Although Betty did not identify closely with the story at the time, she played the role as though she owned it. While her previous film had measured lowest in box-office receipts, this one topped all of Betty's previous records. It was considered her ultimate screen acting accomplishment.

Despite Betty's stardom, it would consistently be others who benefited and profited from the songs she helped introduce. Dick Haymes made a separate career of recording his songs from Twentieth Century-Fox musicals. Betty's contract forbade similar activities, which limited her recording to studio soundtracks. She did, however, manage to slip in one recording for Columbia Records. The song was "I Can't Begin To Tell You," from *The Dolly Sisters.* She recorded it with the Harry James orchestra under the name Ruth Haag—Ruth, her unused first name, and Haag, Harry's middle name. If the studio knew about it, they chose to turn their heads.

Harry scheduled his band dates to coincide with the projected birthdate of his second child, but higher powers prevailed. He was in the middle of a one-nighter in Atlanta on May 20, 1947, when six-pound-twelve-ounce Jessica came into being; this birth also was a caesarian. The James family would be complete at four.

If Betty had had her way, she would have had half a dozen children, but, as with her mother before her, births were not easy to negotiate. Although Betty was the epitome of healthy young motherhood, a third caesarian birth would be far too risky. Harry had hoped for a boy in his second siring and had the name Jesse already selected. But, when it turned out to be a girl, the name was altered to Jessica, which was a shade less villainous in tone.

Betty was ready to begin a new picture when *Mother Wore Tights* opened in late August. "This is a pretty good song and dance show," *The New York Times* review said of it. "It displays the shapely gams of Betty Grable whenever it gets the chance, and it must be said that Miss Grable in Technicolor is balm for the eyes. For the greater part of its nearly two hour length, the film wanders all over the place as it chronicles the steady rise to fame of a loving couple—the most devoted stage people the movies have ever displayed—and their two sparkling daughters. . . . Dan Dailey puts a good deal of personality into the tired dance numbers. . . . Mona Freeman is attractive. . . . Connie Marshall is altogether winning as the uninhibited kid sister."

Betty wasn't too keen on her next assignment, *That Lady in Ermine,* but came around when she learned Ernst Lubitsch would direct and that her co-star would be the suave Douglas Fairbanks, Jr. The movie had only begun, however, when Lubitsch succumbed to heart failure. He was replaced by Otto Preminger to whom Betty took an immediate dislike. Her illusions about Doug Fairbanks also were quickly dispelled. His affected accent and apparent snobbery started almost at once to rub against the earthy grain of Betty Grable. She criticized both director and leading man for showing more interest in socializing than in the business at hand. One morning Fairbanks affronted Betty by suggesting that she looked tired. He said: "Did you party last night, dear?"

"Uh huh," she responded. "I guess I went to the potty a couple of times."

As it turned out, the film was a critical failure, with a surprising exception—*The New York Times* loved it. Their complimentary review followed the film's August opening in New York, and another surprise came with the August 23, 1948, edition of *Time* magazine. Betty was on the cover in color, wearing her ermine cap, and an extensive layout was carried inside.

The interest of *Time* may have been stimulated by Betty herself, rather than by her most current film attraction, because it was at this time that Betty was named the highest paid female in the United States with a 1947 salary of $325,000. Her salary exceeded even that of her ultimatum-issuing boss, Darryl F. Zanuck.

# Chapter 15

When Betty Grable was a gossip item with George Raft, she neither smoked nor drank, which were characteristics Raft found particularly endearing. Soon, a few cigarettes each day became a couple of packs, and sips of wine turned into belts of hard booze. Betty was always surrounded by heavy drinkers: her mother, her father, and finally Harry James. Many of those around her succumbed to the habit, but not Betty. She never became a problem drinker, but she did love to imbibe.

On the set, Betty frequently invited gypsies or crew members into her dressing room between set-ups for a belt or two of vodka. Although her mother was a fifth-a-day Bourbon drinker, she was highly critical of Betty's imbibing, which caused Betty to take it easy when Lillian was around. Due to her mother's limp, Betty could tell when she approached the dressing room, by the *clop-clip-clop* of the thick sole and cane. On one such occasion, she was swapping small talk with the gang when the telltale sounds were heard. Betty scooped up the paper cups and hid the bottle in her dressing-table drawer. "If I've told her once, I've told her a hundred times," Betty said to her pals, "there'll be no dancing in the hallways."

Betty rarely criticized her mother, but there were a number of idiosyncrasies that plainly annoyed her. When she showed up at Betty's house, she always wanted a drink. "What would you like?" Betty would ask, ritualistically.

"Oh, the usual," Lillian would say. "Just a drop of Bourbon and some water."

Betty always wondered why her mother asked for a drop when what she really wanted was a healthy belt. Or why she would ask for just a sliver of cake when she wanted a big hunk. One time Betty was careful to pour a single drop of Bourbon in a glass and hand it to her. Lillian sent her a withering glare. "Don't you be smart with your mother, Betty Grable!"

Lillian was as hooked on the horses as the rest of the family, and when Betty and Harry departed for the race meet at Del Mar each summer, Lillian would be there too. But she didn't join them. She enlisted someone to drive her there—usually one of Betty's friends—and moved into a small apartment of her own. Her travel costume was a long, black coat, and she brought two cases of Bourbon. She refused to visit the James's box and avoided the Turf Club, where their paths would surely cross. There was no evidence that a previous family crisis resulted in this degree of isolation, but that was how it was.

Lillian was continually entreating Betty to invest her money in real estate, which was excellent advice, but Betty prefered horses. The stable originated in part, as a tax write-off. Since she and Harry were in the ninety-five-percent tax bracket, write-offs were needed, but real estate would have been the practical way to go.

The Jameses, with little in the way of business acumen, relied heavily on their business manager. He devised a plan where the stable would show a profit every five years, and permit write-offs in the interim years. This resulted in their paying minimal taxes over several years, but the scheme eventually caught up with them. In the meantime they believed they were living in the best of all worlds.

Conn Grable was proficient in operating the ranch and was content in the small house he had on the land. After his divorce from Lillian, the two became good friends and saw each other often. If Conn had business in the Los Angeles area, the night would be spent in Lillian's spare bedroom. They had never been as compatible as spouses.

The house provided by Betty for her mother was small but very comfortable and was crammed with the expensive antiques eschewed by Harry. Lillian regarded the furniture as her rightful possession. As such, she offered to will it all to daughter Marjorie.

"I told her not to bother," said Marjorie. "I reminded her that Betty bought the house and everything in it, and if she did leave it to me, I would just have to sign it back over to Betty. Mother considered all these things her own and thought she could dispose of them as she saw fit, but I didn't feel that way—although there were some things I would have adored having."

While it is true Betty gave everything to her mother, it is also true that Lillian had something due her. Had it not been for Lillian's tugs and pushes, Betty couldn't have bought a tarpaper shack and fruit crates. But the disagreement was between Lillian and Marjorie, and Betty knew nothing about it. Besides, Betty would more than likely have accepted whatever decision Lillian reached. She was never regarded by anyone as niggardly and made a habit of taking care of her own, without condition.

The Grable standard of living improved measurably after Betty began earning big money, but none of the clan, before or after Harry James came along, lived lavishly. Betty was simple by nature and had no predisposition for luxury. Her extravagances were limited to the horses and gambling—but these indulgences would prove more devastating than any others imaginable.

Over all the years, Betty's close friends could be counted, perhaps, on the fingers of both hands. She had acquaintances by the hundreds, of course, and was able to strike transitory friendships at work, but when it came to close personal relationships, there were few.

Even Lucille Ball, who adored Betty, said, "You know, it just dawned on me. I never knew where I stood with Betty. She never said how she felt about me, or anyone else that I can remember. I only know how I felt about her."

Betty was able to express fondness to certain of her friends, among them a Betty Grable fan whom she accepted as a near-family member, and there were pals like Alice Faye, Paula Stone, and a few others. None, however, was closer to Betty than Betty Ritz.

Betty Ritz was the wife of Harry Ritz, the member of the Ritz Brothers comedy team with the spinning eyeballs. Harry Ritz was a longtime pal of Harry James, which brought the two couples together. And after a rather tenuous beginning, the two Bettys became closer than sisters.

Many attribute Betty Grable's ribaldry to her association with Harry Ritz, who was known for his outspoken profanity. Betty would usually hedge in her dirty phrases by adding verbal disclaimers, such as, "Oh, fuck it, *said the lady to the sailor,*" or "Bull shit, *she cooed.*" Betty enjoyed her bawdy language, perhaps for the resultant stunned expressions on certain staid faces, or because it made her feel like one of the guys. But, whether she picked it up from Ritz or not, they felt comfortable in each other's company. And Betty Ritz had a sense of humor that matched Betty's and both Harrys', but Betty Grable was not aware of it on their first meeting at Del Mar race track.

The two couples had enjoyed a winning day with their bets and went together to the bar of the Hotel Del Mar to have drinks in celebration. The two Bettys excused themselves to visit the ladies room, where Ritz asked Grable if she would mind lending her her comb. Grable frowned but finally handed it over. "You be careful with that comb," Grable admonished. "It's my very favorite."

When Grable entered the stall, Ritz examined the prize comb, wondering if Grable had been joking. "It was one of those big combs," said Ritz, "with big teeth at one end and fine teeth at the other—but most of the teeth at both ends were gone. It was a terrible comb. I used it as best I could, and as luck would have it, I dropped the darn thing and it broke in half."

Betty emerged at that moment, and stared in disbelief. "Why, you've broken my comb!"

"It was already broken."

"Oh, no, I've had that comb for years, and it was fine—and I'm very superstitious about that comb. I just know I'm going to have bad luck now for the rest of the meet."

"Well, I'm sorry."

"That doesn't help."

That was how the dialogue went, and Betty Ritz says Betty Grable was dead serious about it, and quite angry. "When we returned to the table and sat down," said Ritz, "the first thing she said to Harry James was, 'She broke my comb.'

"The following morning everyone went to the beach except me. I went to the corner drugstore and bought every comb they had in stock, big ones, little ones, all sizes, shapes, and forms. I had the clerk gift wrap all of them in a cigar box with a red bow. Later on at the track, I had someone deliver the package to the James box. Betty opened it up and read the card, on which I had written, 'I hope you can use these.' Everyone in the stands could hear when she yelped, 'Oh My God!' She looked around until she spotted me and ran over to give me a big hug. 'You're too much!' she said. From then on we became best friends."

Betty Ritz provided close companionship for Grable over nearly a dozen years of Harry James road tours. They would chat over the telephone, shop, and have lunch, and frequently have dinner together, but the latter could be problematical. Betty's evenings were subject to conditions. Had her call come in from Harry? Had she called her mother for their daily visit? But, it was usually Harry's call that worried Betty most.

"We might be having a good time," said Betty Ritz. "We could be at the Encore Restaurant, for instance, where Bobby Troupe played, and maybe we happened into John Payne or Dan Dailey. Just when we were all relaxed and having fun, Betty would say, 'Oh my God, what time is it? I've got to get home for Harry's call.' She would be very upset and nervous if she missed being at home at the appointed hour, because Harry expected her to be there. And Betty never told Harry about our good times together, because she was afraid it would upset him to learn she was having fun while he was working."

On the subject of Betty Grable's language among friends, it was, according to Betty Ritz, a far different scene from her demeanor at home. She was a remarkably protective mother, and Betty shielded her daughters from everything suggestive or earthy. She was a nervous wreck whenever Harry Ritz was a guest in the home, fearing he would expose her children to his gross language. "In those days," said Betty Ritz, "such language was practically unheard of in mixed company. My children were immune to it, having been brought up in that atmosphere, but Betty's kids were something else."

Although there were falling outs between the two Bettys, they were closest friends for years. "We loved to go shopping," said Ritz, "even though we seldom bought anything. We'd go to Saks and try on hats like a couple of nuts. We would sit and giggle, putting them on the wrong way. When the sales lady would try to put them on straight, we would say, 'Oh no, we don't like it that way.' Then, we'd be so embarrassed we would end up buying something we really didn't want."

They would often dress up in cocktail dresses and go out to nightclub openings together. This, of course, was when the husbands were both on tour. On one occasion, they attended the opening of Bobby Darin at the Mocambo, and Betty Grable got into such a laughing fit, she had her inevitable accident, and it required great care to keep the evidence from public scrutiny.

"Betty loved it when I would imitate her," said Ritz. She would say, 'Oh, do me singing such and such.' I'd do it, and Betty would clap her hands, and practically fall on the floor. 'Oh, that's me,' she'd say, 'that's *really* me!' She was such a great audience. I don't think I ever laughed as much with anyone else, and that includes my ex-husband, who was a very funny man."

Betty Grable is remembered as being extremely generous

with her friends and family, and she also enjoyed receiving gifts, but, according to Betty Ritz, she did not like receiving gifts from her fans. It depressed Betty, because she wondered always if they could afford sending things to her, and she could never understand their reason for doing it. "The only things she kept," said Ritz, "were handkerchiefs. I don't know why, because she never used them, but she had drawers full of them. Once I mentioned the need to buy some, and Betty said, 'You want handkerchiefs? I'll give you handkerchiefs.' She came out with about two hundred of them, and they were beautiful, and of course they were monogrammed with a *B.* I still have most of them."

These were the halcyon days for Betty Grable, the late forties and early fifties. It would not always be this way, but in the days when her marriage was strong, her career was thriving, and her children were young and dependent, Betty was in the middle of one of the happiest periods of her life. There would always be conflict, however, and jutting into the heart of these happy days came a slice of strife that put Betty's marriage to the acid test.

# Chapter 16

At this time in Betty's career, her hit movies seemed to be sandwiched between relative failures. To guard against this occurrence in her next assignment, Darryl Zanuck reverted to his fail-safe formula—if at first the film succeeds, do it again and again. He pulled the script of *Burlesque* out of mothballs, assigned a contract screenwriter to make the necessary alterations, and had Mack Gordon and Josef Myrow add some tunes. The result was *When My Baby Smiles At Me.* It turned out very well indeed.

The first version of the play adaptation was called *Dance of Life,* filmed in 1929 and starring Nancy Carroll. It was done again in 1937 as *Swing High, Swing Low,* with Carole Lombard and Fred MacMurray. The previous renditions were filmed by Paramount, but this time it was Twentieth's turn, and it worked.

Many said Betty did her finest acting in this picture. Betty and her co-star Dan Dailey once more played vaudevillians, but were brought forward in time to the 1930s. The plot had Betty rising to the Broadway heights, while Dan was left behind, but when Academy Award time approached, he was nominated for an Oscar as Best Actor.

If Betty and Dan were friends before, they now became closer than ever. He was in the midst of a failing and miserable marriage and spent many evenings in the James home to keep out of firing range. Betty couldn't ignore his warmth and outgoing good nature, and no one was more attuned than Dan to the Grable brand of humor. They were like brother and sister, with perhaps just a shade of incest. Betty couldn't empathize with his unhappy marriage, since she was lucky with a solid marriage and thriving family, but she could certainly sympathize, and she did.

There were, of course, rumors regarding her own marriage; there always were, but Betty simply shrugged the gossip off and went on with what she was doing. Even Louella Parsons regarded the Grable–James union as the most substantial in Hollywood—and who should know better?

The most persistent stories centered around Harry's road behavior. Was it true he was like a sailor with a girl in every port? Betty refused to believe the stories, even though many of the sources were generally reliable. It could have been that Betty chose to reject the charges because, with her concept of marriage, there would be only one recourse open to her. She wasn't proud of the previous failure at marriage, even though she had been little more than a child at the time. This time, she was an adult, and would have to handle any upheavals as the mature person she had become. At least once she asked Harry if the prevailing gossip had any basis in truth, and he closed her out in angry silence. She avoided such confrontations from then on, allowing Harry the benefit of doubt whenever the tales came under her door. She really didn't believe Harry was cheating, so it wasn't even a matter of turning the other cheek.

Her greatest marital crisis would arise in 1950, during the filming of *My Blue Heaven*, but meanwhile she played the role of the perfect little wife with the perfect little family. In a Louella Parsons article of October 10, 1949, it was pointed out that the Jameses had few close friends, that they rarely frequented night spots, and that they were the picture of family devotion when they all summered at Del Mar. "She and Harry were together constantly," said Parsons, "and if some of the gossips who have reported their separation could have seen them they would have known the reports were completely erroneous."

The article recounted the progress of the Baby J Ranch and how it had grown from two saddle horses to eight thoroughbreds, and Betty said her greatest thrill was watching their own foal grow into a winning racehorse. When asked if the hobby was expensive, Betty told her, "Of course it's expensive to start with, but our horses have pretty well paid for their keep. I can't say they have made any money yet, but that doesn't worry us. Harry has a good job and so have I."

Regarding her state of happiness, Betty said, "I have everything in the world I want. The only cloud appeared when I made *The Beautiful Blonde From Bashful Bend.* I didn't want to do it, but I have never interfered with my studio. I never read a script until it's ready, and I always leave the selection of the story, direction, and cast to Darryl Zanuck, for whom I have great respect.

"But if he ever gives me Preston Sturges again, you'll hear Grable's voice. However, I don't think Mr. Zanuck will ever make me do a picture again that I am as much opposed to as I was the Sturges atrocity. In fact, I have the studio's promise that I can do the things that my fans like best, and that is musical comedy."

If Zanuck did indeed make the attributed promise to Betty, he would break it before much time had passed, and as far as her criticism of *Beautiful Blonde From Bashful Bend* was concerned, she wasn't alone. The publicity department gave notice that Betty's legs would not be featured in this production, and it made it provocatively clear which part of her anatomy would be accented. The ad campaign carried the catch phrase: "She's Got the Biggest Six-Shooters in the West!"

Betty's least favorite role had her cast as a saloon B-girl who is mistaken by the local gentry as the schoolmarm they have been expecting to arrive in town. Betty assumes the teaching tasks and maintains classroom discipline by shooting inkwells off pupil's heads.

Betty referred to Preston Sturges, whose career was waning at this point, as "low man on the totem pole," and considered it an affront to have him assigned as her director. Sturges was panned by the critics along with the product itself. Betty was well supported by a cast that included Cesar Romero, Rudy Vallee, and Olga San Juan, but none of them faired well in the reviews. *The New York Times* said, "Preston Sturges's latest production, which came to the Roxy yesterday, has little more comic distinction than a flat-handed whack on the rump."

Betty maintained the high esteem of her fans, and Zanuck must have panicked at the sour results of *Bashful Blonde,* because he scurried back to formula. This time he decided on a rehash of Betty's own past success, *Coney Island.* With this in progress, it was announced that Betty had again topped the Hollywood salary list with a previous year's earnings of $325,000. Bing Crosby was up there with her, but, as for females, Betty was recognized as the highest paid woman in America. Her status was commented upon in a United Press release of June 12, 1949:

> Betty Grable, the nation's highest paid woman, said today that after she pays about 80 percent in taxes, she spends her money on horses. She and Harry James own eight horses in a breeding farm in Calabasas, California. Riding and playing the horses are the only extravagances the couple have. They, and their two daughters, live in a relatively modest home of 12 rooms and no swimming pool. They seldom give parties or go to nightclubs. Miss Grable's wardrobe is simple. James collects about $100,000 as a bandleader. It is estimated that about $50,000 remains after taxes.

Betty became the only actress to remake a picture in which she had starred previously when *Wabash Avenue* was whittled out of *Coney Island.* For this go-around, the amusement park was set in Chicago, and it was Victor Mature rather than George Montgomery who was cast as the smooth-talking promoter who shapes the girl's destiny. Betty's friend Phil Harris was added to the cast, which helped the film's comic aspects, and brought Betty back into close contact with Alice Faye.

Alice had retired five years earlier and made it stick. Her

last performance for Twentieth or anybody else was in the 1945 film *Fallen Angel.* She moved into the desert climes of Palm Springs with her family and dropped out of the limelight entirely. For a time, she and Harris continued their Fitch Bandwagon radio show, but there were no more films.

Betty enjoyed telling the story about her first meeting with Alice Faye on the set of *Tin Pan Alley.* Betty was as much in awe of the Hollywood superstars as any fan in the world. Alice was one of her favorite screen idols, and Betty was like a child in anticipation of meeting her. "I just didn't know what to say," said Betty. "I always admired her so, and here I was face to face with her. I just looked at her and said, 'Alice, you've got eyes just like a cow's.' She gave me kind of a strange look, and said, 'That will get you a cup of coffee, and a piece of stale bread.' I felt like a fool and was sure that would be as far as our friendship would go." It wasn't as far as the friendship went, of course, since they became very close friends.

Even though Betty continued to cling to the top rung of the popularity ladder, Zanuck was growing nervous. Despite the success of her films, Zanuck believed her day of reckoning was rapidly approaching. She refused to edge gracefully into dramatic roles, and how long could she play song-and-dance parts? Betty was in her thirty-fifth year, and glamour had a habit of fading fast. It was also a fact that, with the passage of time, Betty was becoming more and more difficult for Zanuck to manipulate. Just to be on the safe side, Zanuck always had a cute blonde or two standing by.

In *My Blue Heaven* Betty co-starred with her favorite leading man, Dan Dailey, but joining them both was a bright-eyed newcomer, facile of foot, abundant in curves, and very, very young. Dancing with them beat-for-beat was nineteen-year-old Mitzie Gerber, who, for marquee purposes, would become known as Mitzi Gaynor.

Once more the jaded crew primed themselves for conflict between the reigning queen and the aspiring starlet, but they were again disappointed. Betty welcomed the blonde-standing-in-the-wings with warmth and cordiality.

To everyone's surprise, Betty went to Zanuck in Mitzie's

regard, not in complaint but in applause. She thought the youngster was great, and worthy of more important tasks than had been assigned her in the picture. Betty suggested that Mitzie be given a production number of her own. Zanuck complied with the request and saw to it that the part was expanded. Betty then spent many hours with the pretty and talented newcomer, teaching her professional secrets that had taken Betty a decade or two to acquire.

*Saturday Evening Post* photographer Gene Lester says he visited the set several times during the filming of *My Blue Heaven,* and each time found Betty huddled with Mitzie along the perimeter of the set, coaching the newcomer in her role. Betty and Mitzie would become lasting friends.

But in Betty's list of friends, few would rank higher than Dan Dailey, and here they were thrust together once more. When a couple as compatible as Dan and Betty are drawn together in a common artistic pursuit, there are often suspicions that the parties are more than just pals. Such suspicions prevailed on this occasion, yet no one knew for sure. If Betty did cross the fine line between friendship and intimacy, it could have been through commiseration for Dan's unhappiness, or possibly Betty was retaliating against Harry James's philandering. But no one can be sure if it really happened.

Rumors at the time were as varied as accounts of the over-the-shoulder pinup shot. Some say Harry paid a visit to the set and walked into Betty's dressing room, to catch her and Dan in the act. A fist fight ostensibly ensued, in which Harry was the overwhelming victor. But it is all rumor. The only certainty is that Betty somehow came up with a black eye that halted shooting for several days. Her explanation was that she was riding in the passenger seat of the car when Harry stopped too suddenly and her face was slammed against the windshield. Rumors persist even today about an affair between Betty and Dan. If it really happened, it must have seriously jeopardized one of Hollywood's most solid marriages.

Shooting finally resumed when makeup could obscure the black eye. It was a story involving stars of a radio variety show, who, unable to conceive a baby of their own, adopt one. Then, inevitably, they do have their own baby, and attendant problems evolve. Grable and Dailey made the movie another box-office hit, but it was newcomer Mitzie Gaynor who garnered the most studio publicity.

Mitzie didn't achieve stardom this time around, but it wasn't because Zanuck didn't try. Despite the fact that Betty was the draw that made so many mediocre movies successful, Zanuck persisted in developing new faces to push Betty into the background. By this time, it may have developed into a personal vendetta on Zanuck's part. He liked obedience from his underlings, and Betty failed to play his game. The fact that Betty was still the top moneymaker at the studio, and that she remained the darling of the stockholders, didn't seem to satisfy Zanuck. When Betty's popularity began to cool somewhat, Zanuck became ruthless in his machinations. Any other star would have been setting fire to the sets at such blatant affronts, but Betty, for a long while, rolled with Zanuck's punches.

For the first time, Grable and Dailey made back-to-back pictures. From *My Blue Heaven* they segued into *Call Me Mister.* In this heavily rewritten Broadway musical, Betty played a USO performer who turns up at her ex-husband's Army base overseas. In the ex-husband's attempts to win back his former bride, he misses his homeward bound ship and is declared AWOL. The setting was originally World War II, but by this time the Korean War was in full stride, so the story was updated accordingly.

Betty and Dan gave their usual upbeat performances, with no outward suggestion that Dan was ailing within. He was, however. Beneath the happy Dan Dailey facade seethed a volcano of tangled emotions. The inevitable eruption was only one film assignment away, and the ultimate breakdown resulted in a four-month confinement in a psychiatric hospital.

# Chapter 17

The teaming of Dan Dailey with Betty Grable was a stroke of genius—or luck—on the part of Darryl Zanuck. Dan had been previously under contract to MGM, where he played mostly heavies. Cognizant of Dailey's burlesque background, Zanuck experimented by slipping Dan into *Mother Wore Tights* as a song-and-dance man. The result is show business history. From then on it would be the Grable–Dailey team efforts that earned the most money of all the Betty Grable movies.

It is possible that Betty's teaming with Dailey extended her term of popularity beyond its normal limits. There were four films in which Betty and Dan worked together, and all of them were hits. When Dan was removed from the bill, Betty's career began to slide. She eventually lost her berth among Hollywood's top-ten stars, and her wavering career found itself beset with nothing but problems.

With Betty and Dan so successful together, it would have made sense for Zanuck to bring them together again, but he never did. Perhaps he derived sadistic pleasure in watching

Betty's downward slide. He never appreciated contractees who stood up to him, and was, for whatever reason, particularly contemptuous of Betty. He could have rustled up another property for the team, even if it meant reverting to a remake of a remake of a remake, but when Dan came out of the Menninger Clinic, he was channeled in other directions, and Betty was left to founder.

Immediately following *Call Me Mister,* Dan Dailey was assigned the lead opposite Susan Hayward in *I Can Get It For You Wholesale.* It was on completion of this film that he lost control of his emotions. He had broken up with his wife, which he knew was inevitable, but it also meant separation from his adored three-year-old son. This, along with his chronic problems, sent him over the edge. The compelling symptom was depression, so severe he wished he were dead. To compensate for the depression, Dan began to drink heavily, and the drinking made the depression worse.

In a United Press interview, he said his basic problem was too involved and personal to explain. "It was a series of circumstances over a number of years," he said. "They added up and I got a little confused. It would be the same if you'd driven a car all your life and done it competently. Then you find yourself going sixty on a mountain road and forget how to drive. You panic. All you can do is yell for help."

Dailey's marital problems had been compounded by a four-year separation when he was in the service, but there was more than the marriage itself to concern him. He had a series of more personal problems to deal with, including transvestism—the compulsion to dress in clothing of the opposite sex. Whether this aberration was extended to include homosexuality is conjectural. In any case, there is no question that Dan was attracted to women.

He entered the clinic November 27, 1950, and was released March 3, 1951, a better adjusted man. During his confinement he sent Betty a leather wallet he had crafted during therapy. The accompanying note said, "Hey, Queenie, I'm getting better." Betty was delighted with the gift and would always treasure it.

Dan's wife filed for divorce after his return from Menninger's, and he later married Gwenn O'Connor, who had been married previously to Donald O'Connor. It was during this marriage that a widely circulated Hollywood story came to life. The incident occurred at a house party hosted by the Daileys. One of the guests was an up-and-coming young comedian, who was well known as a poor drinker. He asked the hostess where to find the bathroom and was directed down a hallway and to the left. He made a right turn by mistake and ended up in Gwenn Dailey's closet. He took a fall, pulling down evening gowns and a fur coat on top of him. Dan, followed by several of the guests, investigated the commotion and found the comedian examining the feminine apparel over and around him. He looked up at Dailey. "Well, Dan," he said. "I found your closet—now can I see Gwenn's?"

When Dan was pulling himself together after his stay in the hospital, Betty was working in *Meet Me After the Show.* Jack Cole staged some spectacular dance numbers for the musical, and Betty never worked harder. She performed one number with Gwenn Verdon, who was Cole's assistant at the time. Gwenn would later marry choreographer Bob Fosse and was the real-life model for the female character in Fosse's *All That Jazz.*

Betty performed the strenuous dances with fine humor, and made a good showing. Verdon wasn't trying to out-dance Betty. She was simply performing to the level of her energies and talents, but Betty had to strain to keep up. She did keep up, however, and matched the young redhead step for step. For a thirty-five-year-old mother of two, it was not bad, but there was Betty, once again having to compete with youth—raw, inspired, and gifted.

*The New York Times* liked Betty's work. "There's no denying that the sight of this curvacious, platinum-topped dynamo, sprayed in Technicolor and singing and hoofing as though she were having the time of her life, is still something for anybody's sore eyes."

The conflict between Zanuck and Grable was in full swing by now. He would take an executive swing at Betty, and she would retaliate with a star-property poke in return. The only problem was that Zanuck had an advantage over Betty—he could control her income. Upon completion of *Meet Me After the Show,* which, by the way, Betty often referred to as, *Eat Me After the Show,* Zanuck assigned her to another musical, *The Girl Next Door.*

Without even a week of rest, Betty was ordered to jump into another musical. That would have been difficult enough, but the strenuous dance numbers of *Meet Me After the Show* had come at the end of the shooting schedule. The dance routines in her new assignment were scheduled to go in the front.

Betty protested and with justification. She needed rest and deserved a little time to spend with her family. She thought her case was reasonable, but Zanuck didn't. He ordered her to work. She refused to report. She was put on suspension.

This was fine with Betty. She had plenty of money, and a several-month rest was just what she wanted—even if it proved costly. She spent much of the time at the race track, where the James horses were running in the money. Big Noise, one of the Baby J thoroughbreds, would earn $80,000 over the 1951 season. Betty enjoyed her vacation, fully convinced that she would be welcomed with open arms once her suspension ended.

Zanuck, at the same time, was probably plotting ways of settling the Betty Grable enigma. It was costing the studio $5,000 a week to nurture an aging and petulant prima donna, when for a few hundred dollars he could call in the services of any number of eager youngsters. He had been faced with a similar situation in 1935, when he had assumed control of Fox Studios. He could see no reason at all to pay a huge salary to Janet Gaynor, when so many pretty young things were available for peanuts. It was with this reasoning that Betty Grable was signed in 1939. Zanuck managed to drop Janet Gaynor without too much difficulty, and now he would go full circle with Betty. To his way of thinking, she had reached the end of her crest in popularity and was no longer a valuable asset to the studio. It was time she made room for others.

It was almost a year before Betty was called back to work,

and, while she didn't care much for the assignment, she reported for work in yet another Zanuck remake. This time it was a musical version of *The Farmer Takes a Wife,* which had been a Janet Gaynor picture in 1935.

Betty couldn't really see herself as a cook on an Erie Canal barge, but she didn't protest. She knew it would mean another extended suspension if she did, and she was ready to return to work. Zanuck spent money on production, and cast the popular Dale Robertson as Betty's leading man, but the reviews were negative. *The New York Times* said, "It takes more than good music to make a musical show, and the thing that is lacking in this picture is symbolized by Miss Grable's shrouded legs. The whole thing is just a bit too genteel, too quaintly and self-consciously costumed, too calculatedly folksy, too primly respectable."

To illustrate her feelings for the film, Betty was quick to give it a slightly modified title. She would always refer to the picture as *The Farmer Takes a Dump.* She hated it, but was particularly docile at the time. It may have been because she was about to ask a favor of the studio for the first time in many years. She wanted desperately to play the role of Lorelei in *Gentlemen Prefer Blondes.*

She confronted Zanuck with her request and felt confident he would comply. It wasn't as if she were asking a favor, actually. She had earned $100 million for the studio over the years, and she was perfect for the part. She would have preferred that Zanuck come to her, but, since he didn't, she made her services available.

He seemed cordial to Betty and suggested that she had already been in contention for the coveted role. He said he would soon give her the word. But it is doubtful that he ever considered Betty. His sights were centered on another blonde at the time, a different kind of blonde, sexy and seductive—her name: Marilyn Monroe.

It seemed as though Zanuck were rubbing salt into her wounds when, in September of 1952, he assigned Betty to a dramatic role in *Blaze of Noon* opposite Richard Widmark. She had only to hear the story line to turn the job down firmly. The plot revolved around secret agents and communists, with Betty's role that of a hard-boiled go-between. If she had turned down Sophie in *Razor's Edge,* it wasn't likely she would sign on for this. The film was eventually made as *Pickup on South Street,* with Jean Peters in the role planned for Betty. It was not a terrible film, but would have been laughable with Betty in the role. When it came out, Betty was still on suspension, and this suspension cost her an admitted $200,000 in lost salary.

When December arrived, Betty was on suspension. As she passed her thirty-sixth birthday, she could look back twenty years to the December day she joined Frank Fay and Barbara Stanwyck in San Francisco with *Tattle Tales.* It must have seemed like a hundred years and a million miles of tortuous highway. Then her career was well ahead of her, but now? Where would she go from here?

# Chapter 18

Betty's suspension ended March 6, 1953, three days after daughter Vicki's ninth birthday. On this day, Betty reported on the set for the role of Locao in the nonmusical, *How To Marry a Millionaire.* She wasn't informed that she would be subordinate to Marilyn Monroe in all promotion and advertising. It was in her contract that she would receive top billing in all her films, and she did in this one, *on the screen.* But everywhere else it was "MARILYN MONROE IN . . ."

Marilyn had been nudged into the Golden Girl slot at Twentieth, and nothing could change that. She was a hit from the recently released *Niagara,* and her star was rising. Betty saw the eclipse coming, but was philosophical about it by this time. There had always been a blonde standing by, and this time it appeared the standby was a winner.

The crew was again charged with anticipation when Grable and Monroe had their first eyeball encounter on the sound stage. Betty, fully prepared for this, chose a moment when the stage was silent, so everyone would hear her words clearly. "Honey," said Betty warmly. "I've had mine—go get yours."

Betty and Lauren Bacall, the other lead in the film, were always on time, made up, and ready to go at the appointed hour. Marilyn never was. She would show up an hour or two late, and everybody would have to sit around and wilt while she was being donned with fresh makeup. It was Bacall who suggested that she and Betty do their waiting before makeup, and they could all go in together. This was done.

There was one scene in which Marilyn was to be shot from head to toe, barefooted. Betty took one look at Marilyn's scruffy feet, and said, "You can't go before the cameras like that." Marilyn had no idea what Betty was talking about, but submitted gratefully when Betty ushered her into her dressing room to scrub and paint Marilyn's feet and toenails. Betty Grable, superstar, gave Marilyn Monroe, fledgling actress, a complete pedicure.

As with Mitzie Gaynor, Betty shared the tricks of the trade with Marilyn with great generosity and pleasure. She was even accredited by many with suggesting the Marilyn Monroe trademark: her walk. Marilyn is said to have asked Betty how to walk properly—or improperly, perhaps. Betty told her to do exactly what she was doing but to exaggerate it about a hundred times.

Marilyn was involved with Joe DiMaggio at the time, and, when he and Harry James were out of town, Betty and Marilyn would have bachelorette dinners together at Betty's home. On other occasions they went out together, like the time Betty acted as chauffeur and escort for a studio banquet. Betty told Marilyn the party was an hour earlier than its actual time, to compensate for her new friend's chronic tardiness. Still Betty had to wait while Marilyn labored over the long white gloves she was skinning on for the formal event. When they arrived and dinner was in progress, Marilyn couldn't be bothered with the annoyance of removing the tight gloves. It was noted by everyone—including newspaper reporters—that Marilyn partook of the feast—including corn on the cob—with long white gloves in place.

During the shooting of *How to Marry a Millionaire,* Betty's younger daughter, Jessica, took a spill while riding. Betty left the set in a rush to be at her daughter's side. Jessie survived with only minor injuries, but Betty never forgot that it was Marilyn who called that evening to find out if her daughter was all right—and she was the *only* person to call.

Betty loved to make subtle jokes at Marilyn's expense, probably because Marilyn was so exceedingly serious about everything. For example, when Marilyn would make a telephone call to Betty, the unmistakeable whispery voice would say, "Hello, Betty? This is Marilyn."

"Marilyn who?" Betty would always ask. Marilyn never caught on that she was being kidded.

The movie was successful, and it was Monroe who benefited most from its success. For Betty, it served only as a rather glorious swan song. The fact that she was lauded in her role didn't open further studio doors. Zanuck, in fact, scheduled Betty for loan-out to Columbia for a film called *The Pleasure Is All Mine.* Betty sensed it was all over at Twentieth, and she turned down the assignment on principle. She had absorbed all the Zanuck insults her system could bear. A stalemate had been reached, and for a moment at least Betty prepared herself for an extended waiting game.

Her refusal to accept the Columbia loan-out resulted in Betty's third suspension in two years. She was no fool, and she could read clearly the handwriting on the wall. She considered herself the scapegoat for every studio loss over the past ten years. If a picture went over budget, many of the exceptional costs would be tacked on to Betty Grable budgets, since her films were always in on time and under budget. If other films did poorly at the box-office, some of the profits from Betty's pictures would find themselves entered into the loser's books to make the ledgers more acceptable. These were Betty's suspicions, at least, and her suspicions were shared by many of those knowledgable in Betty Grable financial matters.

Quarrels between star and studio have been publicized since the star system began; victories marked up in the star's columns have been few, but rarely if ever has a star capitulated in the height of battle. They usually hang on like bulldogs, and then lose. Not Betty—she decided to back off. Although she was counseled to hang in and make Zanuck's life miserable for the remaining five years of her contract, she simply could not. It was a matter of pride. It wasn't in her nature to stay where she felt she wasn't wanted.

Betty, who was certainly one of the greatest movie stars of all time, never asked for special treatment. If a meal was complimentary, she would end up spending more in tips than the meal would have cost. If she went to a movie, she would never call the box office to see that she was met at the door. She would queue up with all the others and wait her turn.

One time Betty joined the long line in front of New York's Basin Street East in a driving snow storm. Her mission was to catch the show inside, but she didn't want to ask favors. Finally she was recognized by the management and escorted inside to a table. She was embarrassed when tables had to be rearranged to fit her in, but there was no reason to be—especially since the show was Harry James and his orchestra.

During Betty's tenure at Twentieth Century-Fox, there is no question that she had her bitchy moments, but she was engaged in warfare. She may not have been difficult at all had she been treated more respectfully. Perhaps typical of Betty's behavior during the time was that demonstrated in the incident of the ejected bookie.

It was during the filming of one of Betty's more extravagant musicals, where hundreds of actors and chorus and orchestra members were on hand. Betty's friend Bill Smith, whose earlier marriage to Ethel Merman was attended by Betty and Victor Mature in New York, was connected with the Twentieth publicity department and was a fellow horse player. On this occasion, Betty called his office and asked him to hurry down to the sound stage. When he arrived, Betty showed him a telegram that contained a hot tip on a horse.

"We had a bookie that hung around the casting office," said Smith. "For Betty's bets mostly. She asked me to go and bet a thousand dollars on this horse for her, and I said okay. I go to the casting office to find out the bookie has been thrown off the lot. When I get back to the set, Betty says, 'Let's hope the nag wins.' I say it won't make any difference, because I couldn't place the bet, that they threw the bookie out. She says, 'You're kidding.' I say, 'No, I'm not.' Betty storms off the set and goes to her dressing room. While I'm standing there, she gets out of her costume, and puts on her street clothes. She takes off—goes home. Here are all these extras costing thirty or forty thousand dollars a day, and she takes off.

"I'm back in my office, and the phone rings. It's Zanuck, and he wants to see me in his office right away. I go there, and he says, 'Where is that goddamned Grable?' I tell him, and he calls casting. He gives them Hell and tells them to go out and find the bookie. Then he tells me to call Betty to try to get her back. I tried, but Betty said she wouldn't come back. I tell her they're looking for the bookie to bring him back, and she says fine—to call her back when he gets there.

"The bookie couldn't be found until the following day, and Betty showed up for work. When I saw her, I said, 'You know, after all that, the horse ran out of the money.' She said, 'But what if it had won?' "

It was on July 1, 1953, that Betty Grable entered the office of Darryl F. Zanuck. "Here's five years," she said, waving her contract before him. She carefully tore it into small pieces and handed them to him. "Merry Christmas or Happy Chanukah, or whatever. . . . I'm leaving."

# Chapter 19

It is doubtful that Betty expected Zanuck to come running after her, but even if he had, Betty's close friends are convinced that she would never have changed her mind. Her gesture was just about the only face-saving device remaining.

It was after Betty's departure that Marilyn Monroe's name was put above hers in billing for *How To Marry a Millionaire.* It was the first time Betty had received second billing since she was billed second to Alice Faye in *Tin Pan Alley.*

The Hollywood premiere of the film was held November 4, 1953. Mike Connolly, columnist for *The Hollywood Reporter,* had this to say about it:

> Nothing like it [Marilyn Monroe's entrance] since Gloria Swanson at her most glittering . . . Lauren Bacall was there too. Pics third star, Betty Grable, wasn't. Fox flacks explained, "Betty's out of town." But Betty wasn't out of town at all. She was sitting home chewing her nails. We phoned her to tell her it's

her best performance yet . . . Betty said, "I wanted to go but I've never been to a premiere, and just thinking of going to one of my own gives me the panics."

The year came to an end with Betty hiring dancer-choreographer Billy Daniels to stage a show in which she would star a few months later. It was to play at the Chicago Theatre, where she had made a personal appearance fourteen years earlier and met Harry James one night after the show. There was a break for Christmas, and Betty was surprised and delighted with Harry's gift, a brand new 1954 Cadillac convertible. Perhaps it was his way of assuring Betty that they weren't in the poorhouse yet, even though for the first time in nearly a decade and a half she was without employment.

Betty always insisted she was lazy and would purr like a kitten if she had only to run a home, get in some time at the track, and play regular rounds of golf. Now she could do these things and seemed content in doing them. She did, however, state publicly that she wasn't necessarily retiring from films. If a good role came around, she would be interested. She left the door open, but curiously few offers would come her way.

Columbia came to her directly with the proposal to do the film she had refused on loan-out, and she agreed to the terms. She would work opposite Jack Lemmon in the film retitled *Three For the Show,* with Marge and Gower Champion as second leads.

For five years the Grables lived in a sprawling home in the 600 block of Doheny Drive, but just prior to leaving Twentieth, Betty purchased a home on Beverly Drive that had originally been part of the giant Hearst estate. Much of Betty's free time was spent supervising the renovation of the new home, but this came to a halt, along with every other activity, in January of 1955. Her father, Conn, died then, quite suddenly, six months before his seventieth birthday. Betty was deeply grieved at the loss.

She found herself looking back to examine her relationship with her father. Had she been a good daughter? Had she been kind enough toward him? Had he known she loved him? Betty found herself haunted by words unsaid.

A few months later, rumors began to hurdle the gates of Fox studios. Rumors suggested that the previously docile Marilyn Monroe was beginning to establish a high profile on the lot, that she was driving Zanuck to the depths of depression with her demands. Betty Grable, people were saying, was Snow White compared to her platinum-topped replacement. Zanuck had created a monster.

Marilyn's demands diverged almost 180 degrees from Betty's. Betty had asked only that she be allowed to do what she could do best. Marilyn, conversely, was insisting that she do things for which she had no established track record. She didn't want musicals and comedy roles; she was convinced her forte was serious drama.

Marilyn was influenced a great deal by drama coach Natasha Lytess, who said she didn't want Marilyn to follow in Betty Grable's footsteps. "I want Marilyn to do dramatic roles from now on," she said.

But Lytess was only one of Marilyn's advisers; Marilyn had a retinue of "wise men" ranging from Los Angeles to New York, who had an assortment of directions designed for her blossoming career. Everyone but Marilyn herself seemed to know what was best for her.

Although Betty was free from Twentieth and Darryl Zanuck, she wasn't free from movie remakes. *Three For the Show* was originally adapted from the Somerset Maugham play, *Too Many Husbands,* and was made as a straight comedy in 1940 starring Jean Arthur. Its plot finds a Broadway actress married to one man, when her former husband, thought dead, returns on the scene.

Most of the dancing was left to the Champions, with Betty called upon to sing a series of long-established standards. The dance numbers were suspiciously similar to many done at Twentieth, and the sameness of everything didn't please Betty at all. But there were other matters in the shooting of the film that disturbed her. Status was one of them. A trade paper quip tells the story: "Voice over Columbia P.A. system: 'Will Betty Grable please report to the set immediately.' Remember at Twentieth when a chauffeur used to drive her from her dressing room to the sound stage?"

There were also reports of friction between Betty and the dancing stars of the film, Marge and Gower Champion. The couple were stars in their own right by this time and could well have resented being subordinate to Betty in billing.

When the film was released the reviews were spotty, and no box-office records were broken, yet Sam Goldwyn liked what he saw well enough to consider Betty for the Adelaide role in *Guys and Dolls,* which he had just acquired with a bid of $650,000.

A preliminary meeting was set up with Betty in July of 1955, only a few days after her eleventh wedding anniversary. Goldwyn told her he wanted her for the role, but it was necessary that he call her back one more time before the terms of the contract could be set. Betty was elated and assured Goldwyn she would be available for the final interview.

Betty wanted the role. It would bring her back to the status she had enjoyed a few years earlier, and it could launch an entirely new career. Every song and dance gal in Hollywood was salivating for this plum role, and she realized how lucky she was to be considered.

The day came for the final interview, and Betty was primed for the occasion. She would have been at the studio early, full of her old verve and enthusiasm. As it turned out, however, she was unable to keep the appointment. What she hadn't counted on was a family crisis that made the visit impossible—her fourteen-year-old poodle, Punky, managed to get a foxtail burr imbedded in his paw. He had to be rushed to the nearest pet hospital, and Betty was the only one available for the emergency. She didn't exactly stand Goldwyn up; she had her housekeeper call his office to explain that she could not keep her appointment.

When Goldwyn learned that the appointment was cancelled because of an ailing dog, he was furious. His frail ego couldn't handle such an affront. When Betty called back for a subsequent appointment, she was told Goldwyn had no interest in seeing her. The role of Adelaide went to Vivian Blaine, who had played the role on Broadway.

When asked at the time what her plans were for the future, Betty said her sights were set toward the next meet at Del Mar, and after that she would look for work if there were any jobs for her. "Otherwise," she said, "I can sing with a band. Have pierced ears—will travel."

At this time Betty insisted she had neither the time nor the inclination for television. She said she had made a picture a year for the past three years and would like to maintain that schedule. But television came into Betty's life almost before her words were out, and it was not necessarily by choice.

All during the glory years, Betty and Harry lived a life virtually free from financial woes. They were so solvent, Betty often said she could live the rest of her life without working. This might have been true for almost anyone else, but not for this couple with their mania for gambling. Still, they might have managed to stay ahead of the broken-kneecap collectors if another kind of collector hadn't breached the tranquility. This time it was the collector from the Internal Revenue who began banging on their door.

For fourteen income-padded years they paid only minimal taxes and bragged over the slick maneuvers of their genius accountant. It turned out the tax man was no genius at all; he was, in fact, totally inept. The IRS wanted half a million dollars in back taxes, and wanted it posthaste. To make sure it was forthcoming, the Baby J Ranch was attached.

Betty came out of semiretirement so fast it looked like she was racing Big Noise to the wire at Del Mar. Television was available, so television was where she turned. She and Harry did two Chrysler "Shower of Stars" shows at CBS. The first was aired October 4, 1954, the second came six weeks later. The paycheck for the two shows was $80,000, not nearly enough to square things with the government. Then, a third Chrysler shot was offered them and was set for later in the year. Betty and Harry were considering other means of income beyond what was scheduled when a fat and juicy plum was dropped in Betty's lap, or at least it must have seemed like it at the time. Betty would get another crack at movies, and it was none other than Twentieth Century-Fox who was calling her back.

Betty might have felt rather smug about her recruitment from the old lot. Most actresses would have seen it as crawling back with tail between legs, but Betty was no fool. She knew she was offered the part only by default, but she could certainly use the money.

Marilyn Monroe refused to do *How To Be Very Very Popular* and had dashed off to New York to establish Marilyn Monroe Productions, Inc. Darryl Zanuck, probably between antiacid tablets, called Betty's agent to see if she could return "home" to play Stormy in the musical. The answer was, "Yes, for a price." Betty's terms were met, and she was handed her script.

Marilyn Monroe wasn't around to upstage Betty, but—as she might have known—somebody else was. This time it was the statuesque starlet Sheree North the studio was pushing. It was all right with Betty, and again she was more than willing to lend a helping hand when it was needed. But Betty must have been somewhat slighted to discover how little she would have to do. The big dance number was "Shake, Rattle and Roll," and it was all Sheree's. It was the newcomer who also received the big play in the ads and lobby posters. On the screen it was, "Betty Grable in *HOW TO BE VERY VERY POPULAR*—starring Sheree North."

If Betty had been difficult to handle on previous occasions, she was as docile as a lamb on this outing. Perhaps she saw the wry humor in all of it, or maybe she simply didn't give a damn. She may not have had the last laugh on Darryl Zanuck, but she certainly earned a chuckle or two. Darryl was on the spot, and he came to Betty to bail him out; that in itself was fuel for satisfaction. Betty completed the film on April 11, grabbed her money, and ran.

Although the monetary transfusion from Twentieth was helpful, it was far from enough. The James' property on Ventura Boulevard in the San Fernando Valley had to be put on the real estate market. It was listed in late May and was finally sold in August for $300,000. The newspapers announced the sale price as $1,000,000, but that had been the asking price. They realized one-third or less of the actual value of the land. Sometime later Betty mentioned to a friend what a weird feeling it was to write out a check for half a million dollars; it was even more weird to hand it over to the IRS.

When *How To Be Very Very Popular* premiered in New York, it was Sheree North who was sent back East on the promotional tour. *The New York Times* reviewer thought little of the film in general but was kind both to Betty and Sheree. It didn't matter; the movie proved a box-office dud that did little to further Sheree North's career and served only as an inauspicious final effort for Betty. As far as Betty Grable was concerned, it was the end to a grand and glorious career in movies.

# Part Three

# Chapter 20

It was fortunate for the Jameses that they still had earning power when the tax man came to call. Their combined salaries plus the receipts from their property sale put them back into the government's good graces—at least for the time being.

It was curious that, all through their liquidation proceedings, no thought was given to selling off the horse stock. By then, they had seventeen thoroughbreds and additional foals and brood mares. Four or five of their horses were stakes winners. Betty would always swear that the horses paid for themselves, which nobody actually believed. But, even if they did break even in purses, they certainly failed to pay for the family bets on those and other horses.

Betty Grable and Harry James could have become one of the wealthiest couples in the world of entertainment. If they had only listened to Lillian when she urged them to invest in real estate instead of horses, it would have happened. But neither Betty nor Harry had the slightest talent for business matters, or the good sense to listen to others. Dan Dailey, notoriously frugal, would end up a millionaire, and so would Victor Mature, who wasn't known to be frugal at all. But the gambling instincts of the Jameses always kept them running to catch up.

When asked years later about handing over five years of contract to Darryl F. Zanuck, Betty agreed it was insane, but that was with hindsight. At the time, Betty had every reason to believe she was solvent, and that nothing but prosperity lay ahead.

The future could have been saved for Betty had she landed the lead in *Guys and Dolls,* because that was at a turning point in her professional pursuits. Her stature would have risen measurably with that solid role behind her, just when a boost was sorely needed. But Betty had chosen Punky, the ailing poodle, over Goldwyn, the feisty mogul, and the rest is history. Years later Betty would prove how right she was for the role of Adelaide, but that would come too late to advance her film career. It would, however, serve to open her second career—in theater.

Betty did several television shows in the fifties. On June 5, 1955, she did a "Shower of Stars" with Edgar Bergen and Dan Dailey. She was a guest on this show several more times, but one time she was unable to carry out her commitment due to a severely sprained ankle. The sprain was not caused by a fall in rehearsals, or anything that dramatic; it was, instead, the result of another of her sleepwalking miscues.

The producers panicked, wondering what they would do for a replacement, but Betty had the answer. "That girl in the chorus is great," she told them. "Let her do it." They took a closer look at the "girl in the chorus" and agreed. It was Shirley MacLaine, and she got the job. This was the second time MacLaine got a break through a sprained ankle. The first time was when she was understudying Carol Haney in *Pajama Game* and went on when Carol sprained her ankle.

Betty once more proved her unselfishness, but the gesture wasn't purely altruistic. Betty was a trouper, and as such she had an eye for talent. She knew Shirley was a gifted performer and it made sense to put her abilities to use. Betty shrugged off any credit for MacLaine's success. If it hadn't been that day, it would have been the next—talent would out.

In March of 1956 Betty starred in the NBC Star Stage production of "Cleopatra Jones," which was televised from the El Rancho Inn in Las Vegas. NBC picked up the tab for an expensive press junket to attend the show, but it didn't help. The show was panned. However, if little else was accomplished in the production, Betty did meet the man who later shared a milestone in her career. It was Casey Adams, who would later be known by his real name, Max Showalter. Under that name, Max would play opposite Betty in the stage production of *Hello Dolly.*

In June, Betty was one of the guests on the Bob Hope special, "The Road To Hollywood." Other stars included Dorothy Lamour, Marilyn Maxwell, and Jane Russell. The show was in color, which meant they would work under broiling lights, necessary at that stage of the new process. Bob Hope was credited for pulling the show out of its scripted mediocrity.

The same year, Betty played opposite Orson Welles in the Ford Star Jubilee production of "Twentieth Century." The TV adaptation wasn't considered very special, despite the expertise of Welles, and Betty was becoming demoralized. She wondered if she would ever be given a good review in a television show. But she determined then that she wouldn't wait to find out. Instead, she limited her television work to game shows or guest shots on variety shows. She believed that the dramatic shows during the early days of television tended to make everyone look worse than they were, and her ego wasn't hearty enough for that.

After 1956 Betty eased off somewhat, once more referring to herself as "semiretired." She reiterated: "I never had any great drive for a career. It was my mother who wanted it. She's mad at me right now for not working. My agent calls me now and then, but I just couldn't care less."

Betty and Harry worked together intermittently at the El Rancho Vegas for a snappy $12,750 a week, and Betty was a contestant on CBS's panel show, "Do You Trust Your Wife." She then joined Bob Hope for a guest shot on his "Chevy Show." It was also at about this time that Betty made an appearance on the live Dinah Shore Show. Director Tony Charmoli remembers it well. "It was a big number with Betty playing Helen of Troy," he said. "She came out on a Trojan horse and sang 'Let Me Entertain You.' It was a big production with dancers and about half a dozen muscle men, à la Mae West.

"During rehearsals everything went perfectly. There came a point in the routine where the muscle men form a circle with Betty in the middle. The men bend over to let Betty sit on the back of one of them, with her toe resting on the back of the next man. It was like a lotus, with Betty in the center.

"The muscle men didn't say anything to anyone, but, as with all muscle men, they oiled their bodies, to better display their muscles on camera. So then we're doing the number live on camera, and Betty takes her position on the back of one of the guys. None of us can figure out what went wrong, but there is Betty trying to sing, and she's sliding down into this mass of muscle and flesh.

"She carried it off beautifully, as if the bit were written into the script, and the audience was none the wiser. But I wish you could have seen Betty laughing offstage when the number ended. Most stars would have been furious that their big number was ruined, but not Betty. Dinah came back on camera laughing, but there wasn't time to explain what happened, so the audience must have thought that something funny had happened backstage."

The following New Year's Eve Betty did her own act at the Desert Inn and was well received. She did a spot on the Jerry Lewis Show on NBC and, with Harry, was a guest star in an "I Love Lucy" segment. This all came during the early months of 1958, which left plenty of time for Betty to devote to race track and family. Betty loved doing the Lucille Ball show, and Lucy always said how good Betty was, but it was the only time Betty was invited as guest star. She would often wonder why she wasn't asked back.

Betty's only other major effort during the year was a remembrance program presented at Hollywood's Moulin Rouge Theatre. Her fans showed up in great numbers to enjoy reprises of her many movie songs and dance numbers. The show was repeated with equal success the following year at the Latin Quarter in New York. By this time, Betty was preparing for her move to Las Vegas. That was where Harry did most of his band appearances, and it made sense to move there with the family. It would afford more family time and would also give Betty ample opportunity to play daily rounds of golf, which had become a passion with her. The time had also come to give up the race-horse business. The stable was sold, and Betty showed no further interest in the horses. The gaming tables of Las Vegas were there, however, to fill the gambling void.

Betty Grable and Betty Ritz had been pals from the beginning, but there were many occasions when their personality likenesses led to conflict. They were both strong and stubborn, but on most occasions their senses of humor saved the day. They especially enjoyed going out on the town as singles, studying the people around them.

Betty could usually predict which bar patrons would be coming around for an autograph, and she and Betty Ritz would make small bets on it. "See that guy over there at the corner of the bar," Betty would say. "Within three minutes he'll be over here asking for an autograph. It will be for his niece or somebody, definitely not for himself."

Betty would herald his, or any such intruder's, arrival by saying, "Here comes Willie off the pickle barge." The Grable brand of caustic humor was also illustrated by her greeting to Betty Ritz on one occasion that she visited a Twentieth set. Ritz was dressed in an elegantly embroidered Chinese dress of fine silk. Betty looked her over and said sarcastically, "Well, look who's here—the one and only Chiang Khe Schmuck."

There were frequent quarrels between the two Bettys, and one very nearly terminated their relationship. It occurred after Betty Ritz had become enamored of Mexican bullfighter, Raphael Baez, whom she would later marry. At the time, Ritz was flying back and forth to Mexico to be with Baez, even though she was still married to Harry Ritz. This provoked Betty Grable, who was increasingly sullen when the matter arose in conversation. Some say she was simply jealous of her friend's uninhibited happiness. It was in the late fifties when Grable's own dream boat was slowly beaching itself, so it could have brought her own discontent into sharper focus. Whatever the reason, she didn't approve.

Betty Grable was in a restaurant one night having dinner with choreographer Billy Daniels and Steve Preston when Betty Ritz came in to join them. She was carrying a Berlitz record course in Spanish and was outfitted in typically Mexican garb. She started spouting phrases in Spanish, and Daniels joined in. Grable became furious. "If everyone's going to sit here and speak Spanish," she snarled. "I may as well go home."

Betty Ritz made a joke of it, not convinced Betty was actually angry.

Grable countered: "I just think you're making a big fool out of yourself with all this Spanish shit. You can't even speak the language!"

Betty Ritz gathered her things together and stormed out of the restaurant.

Grable felt remorseful afterward and asked Daniels to give Betty Ritz a call and ask her to return. He made the call, but the invitation was emphatically refused. Later Ritz would admit to friends that she was as sorry as anyone, but just couldn't give in. She blamed this on her "Taurean temper" and her stubborn streak.

Months passed with each of them missing the other, but neither of them doing anything about it. Finally, when it came time to organize the James household for the move to Las Vegas, Betty found an opportunity to try and mend fences. She found a pair of Pyrex pie plates she was sure belonged to Ritz. She sent them to the Ritz residence with a friend, who presented them at the door. But Betty Ritz assured the caller that the plates were not hers and refused the suggestion that she call Grable to tell her so. She sent them back with the same intermediary with the message that the plates must belong to someone else.

Betty and Harry made the move as planned, but when the

Christmas holidays came along, Betty Grable sent a box of carefully selected gifts for each member of the Ritz family. Betty Ritz had to relent at last. She called Betty in Las Vegas, and the friendship was resumed once more. Betty Grable said, "You should have been my sister. You are my very dearest friend."

"That was something for Betty," said Ritz. "I think she had great difficulty expressing love, to come out and actually say, 'Hey, I dig you.' Betty was also very possessive in all her relationships. When she knew I was going to marry Raphael and move to Mexico, she was very upset. I was going to abandon her."

Betty Ritz says that Betty was an extremely strict mother and was determined not to allow the children to become part of the Hollywood scene. She was probably overprotective of her daughters, a fact which would come back to haunt her later. Ritz recalls a single incident that typifies Betty's austerity as a mother.

Victoria, the elder daughter, was an adolescent at the time and certainly the more manageable of the two children. Betty found a note Vicki had written to a school chum in which she used one or more vulgar words. "She came right over to ask my advice," said Betty Ritz. "I told her to forget it. Of course, my kids were weaned on words like that and thought nothing of it. But I suppose Betty was particularly concerned because it was Vicki, the perfect little lady. Betty went to Vicki's school and spoke with the sisters [Betty enrolled the girls in a Catholic school because of the promise of tighter discipline]. Vicki was severely punished. She was grounded for more than a month."

It was the incongruity that made such incidents unbelievable to Betty's friends. She set a double standard for her personal behavior and for that of her children. Despite her frequent complaints regarding the heavy-handedness of her own mother, Betty proceeded to administer the same kind of discipline over her children. They were left very little room to breathe.

Lillian Grable often said to Betty, as she was growing up, "You know why I walk this way, don't you?" It was Lillian's way of reminding Betty continually of the sacrifices she had made.

Betty was not beneath similar ploys of her own. For one thing, she later reiterated how she had maintained an unhappy marriage because of the children, as though it were all their fault.

It was Betty's hope that the move to Las Vegas would improve family harmony, but it didn't—not for long. After the passage of a little time, the very foundation of the marriage crumbled, and the lives of every family member went through a series of traumatic changes. Among the four members of the James family, it was Victoria who emerged the most stable, the least affected.

# Chapter 21

Betty made a grand effort toward domesticity after moving to Las Vegas. She had a hundred thousand dollar home to live in along the fairways of the Desert Inn Golf Course, and golf became her daily diversion. But cooking became her obsession. She studied cookbooks and even took a course in gourmet cookery; she was determined to become the first member of the Grable clan to be proficient in culinary arts.

Betty called her sister the morning after their first Thanksgiving in the new home to report on the happenings of the big day. She entertained a dozen guests. They were invited for an eight o'clock dinner, and Betty promised she would do everything herself. She bought a huge turkey and put it in the oven early enough so it would be ready in plenty of time. She had read the label instructions thoroughly, but overlooked one significant detail. The cooking time was prescribed for the turkey *after* it was thawed.

"We ended up having dinner about one-thirty in the morning," Betty told Marjorie. "All the booze had disappeared by that time, and we weren't even sure if we were hungry anymore."

Marjorie insisted that, despite this cooking disaster, Betty did turn into an excellent cook, that meals at the James home were always a delight.

Betty drove a station wagon, became friendly with her neighbors, and was playing the role of Mrs. Joe Average. Since she no longer followed Harry around to attend his concerts, the James home was bursting at the seams with record albums. Betty wasn't as directly involved in music any more, but she listened to it—all kinds from swing to rock. Her favorite songs were the old standards, but she enjoyed everything but country and western.

Betty was always big on games, from Perquacky to crosswords, and, from the time she was very young, Betty had spent myriad hours in poker games with close friends. Now her penchant for games extended to the gaming tables at the Vegas casinos. She became involved in a very big way. If possible, Harry was even more hooked on the table than Betty, and his friends say he has played more than one extended engagement in a club to pay off his gambling markers.

No one in the James family was ever in want of food, but from the time they moved to Las Vegas the family fortune began to dwindle dangerously. Between the tables and the tax man, there was never a time they were free of debt.

Dan Dailey had been playing a variety act around the country, and when he played Las Vegas, he and Betty spent some time together. When the subject of finances came up, it was Dan who suggested Betty try her hand at theater. She was certainly qualified, and she could probably work as frequently as she desired, right there in Las Vegas. The idea appealed to her, especially when Dan agreed to work in a show with her. Through Dan's agent, details were worked out for them to open at the Dunes Hotel in *Guys and Dolls.*

The trail had been circuitous, but at last Betty would play Adelaide, and, when the musical opened in December 1962, the response was outstanding. The show played to packed houses well into mid-summer of the following year. Betty was one of the biggest attractions to play at The Dunes, and her show was said to have kept the hotel flourishing during a period of hard times. Betty camped through the show with such obvious delight, one might believe she were figuratively thumbing her nose at Sam Goldwyn.

As Betty's career was beginning to come alive again, her marriage was entering its terminal stages. Harry was carrying on an affair—not that this was something new—but this time it was close to home. Throughout the years, Betty had been insulated by space from Harry's peccadillos, but this time it was right under her nose, and it was more than a mere one-nighter. Betty knew, her friends knew, and everybody was embarrassed. Yet, the thought of tossing twenty years to the wind was more easily said than done. On July 5, 1963, Betty and Harry had their twentieth wedding anniversary. Victoria was in her nineteenth year, but Jessica was only sixteen. Betty made up her mind to hold off on any actions against Harry until Jessie turned eighteen.

Aside from marital problems, there were personality quirks in the James home that made Betty worry. It was a mystery how two children of the same parents could be so completely different. Victoria was always sweet, studious, and obedient. With rare exceptions, the elder child never required discipline. With Jessica, it was another matter.

Today, Jessica recalls her childhood with mixed emotions. There is no bitterness remaining, but there were problems she found difficult to handle at the time. She says she has few clear recollections of her father during her younger years, because he was so often away. It was her mother she had to deal with on a daily basis, and, as a result of Betty's unyielding strictness, the time came when rebellion was Jessica's only choice.

"My mother was very strict," she says, "but she was at least consistent. I really believe that everything she did was for us. She made sure Vicki and I became self-sufficient, that we learned how to work and did not expect things to be handed to us. I had a job in a record store when I was fifteen and sewed my own dresses for dances. Because my mother was so strong, she made us strong. I'm sure she loved both of us in her own way. I believe she was trying to be the perfect mother, who never did anything wrong. Sex, for instance, was never discussed at home. The subject could never be brought up. Anything to do with feelings was something she kept very private. I never even knew my grandparents were divorced until I read about it in an old article my mother had saved. Nothing personal in the family was ever discussed.

"I couldn't say anything to my mother. She used to wonder why I didn't talk to her, but, whenever I did, it was always misinterpreted. I got real adept at lying, because she would believe a lie before she would believe the truth. That is simply how it was. She thought I was real bad, but I wasn't. There was no such thing as wondering what might happen if I came home late, for instance—I didn't come home late period. I knew I'd get smacked around if I did, and I was scared enough never to do it.

"The people my mother loved the most, the ones she was closest to, were the ones she abused most. I suppose it was because she had to vent her frustrations on somebody. She had so much pain, so much hurt—and so much naivété. Even though she had been an actress and everything, she didn't know how to express herself. I'm sure she never intended to hurt anybody; it was just the way it turned out. I think if she had someone to talk to—a psychiatrist or someone—she might have been able to sort out her feelings. Her mother did nothing at all for her. Mother was just a meal ticket, and her life wasn't real. She was never allowed to be a little girl."

Jessica suspects it was impossible for her mother to give loving strokes to her children. She said Betty had never received demonstrative love from Lillian Grable, so had never learned to receive or give it. "Maybe she was taught that affection was a weakness," she said, "that it makes you vulnerable or something."

Jessica said her older sister did all the things nice little girls were supposed to do: she was obedient, polite, an honor student throughout grammar and high school, and she continued in her academic excellence throughout college. Then she met a promising young man in college, William Bivens, and married him

August 15, 1964, when she turned twenty-one. Jessie was a problem child who was lucky to make it through high school, and, when she did, her father failed to attend the commencement ceremonies.

"Vicki did all the right things," Jessie admits, "and I took all the opposite turns—in rebellion, I guess. It was a result of insecurity. Actually, I think I was a lot like my mother when she was my age. She may have seen something of herself in me and couldn't deal with it. I think that was why she reacted so heavily to a lot of the things I did."

Victoria's wedding was a happy highlight of 1964, but it was not a good year for Betty otherwise. Her mother died of a heart attack December 4 at age seventy-four, two weeks before Betty's forty-eighth birthday. It was also twenty-five years after Betty's triumphant opening on Broadway in *Du Barry Was a Lady*. It was one of Betty's saddest Christmas holidays. Despite what may have been lacking in the relationship with her mother, Betty loved her dearly. The death came as a grievous loss.

To those on the periphery, Lillian Grable seemed something of a villain, because it was clear how relentlessly she pushed Betty in her career. Nevertheless, almost everyone who met Lillian personally liked her. She had the reputation of being friendly and cordial.

As for Betty, she was never heard to issue an abusive charge against her mother. Some of her remarks may have been construed in that way, but they were misunderstood. Betty took potshots at Lillian, but they were either in jest, or were simple statements of truth—but without rancor. Lillian pushed Betty and did it with evangelical fury, but that doesn't mean Betty was reluctant to comply. Through Lillian's tough management, Betty became one of the world's greatest movie stars and one of the highest paid women in the world. There were quarrels between them, but in general Betty was an obedient, loving daughter, and Lillian was, in many ways, a caring mother. Lillian Grable did what she felt compelled to do, and Betty followed along without very much resistance.

It is possible that Lillian had a detached attitude regarding

Betty Grable the performer. When she watched her sensuous wiggles in the dance number, "Wish I Could Shimmy Like My Sister Kate," Lillian saw what she wanted to see. "Isn't she absolutely adorable," she said to the person next to her. "That's my little girl."

Lillian's scoldings weren't limited to Betty's movie career. If she had something to say, it would be said if her lips were sewn shut. Lillian hadn't relented by 1962 when Betty was playing opposite Hugh O'Brien in *Guys and Dolls* near Disneyland. It was a dinner theater, and in such establishments it is often expected that the stars will pop out after curtain and greet the audience. Betty never did this, mostly out of shyness, and on this occasion it was her suggestion that the management bestow curtain speech honors on Hugh O'Brien. When he was asked, he agreed readily.

On one of the nights, Lillian entered the house to see this young man standing there taking all the bows. She limped double-time backstage to confront Betty on the issue.

"What are you doing?" Lillian asked.

"I'm getting ready to go out and have some drinks and dinner," was Betty's reply.

"But that man out there–what's his name?–he's doing a speech. You should be there. You're the star of the show."

"But I don't want to do it," said Betty, now applying lipstick. "And he loves it. By the time he's finished, I'll have had two martinis and half my dinner."

Lillian pounded her cane in perplexity. "Betty Grable," she said, "that's exactly why you'll never get anywhere in show business!"

Betty usually saw humor in her mother's nagging, though there were times when she screeched in rebellion. Yet there were certain edicts handed down by Lillian that Betty quietly accepted. The daily telephone call was one of them. Betty called her mother at least once a day, no matter where she was or what she might be doing. This daily process became so much a part of Betty's life that the sight of the telephone became a constant reminder of the void created by Lillian's death.

This early 1940s publicity still finds Betty in trim dancing form, though she was frequently on the losing end of her battle of the bulge.

With the addition of Jessica (right) the Harry James family is complete. This family portrait was taken in 1950.

One of the girls would wake up to discover that Santa had delivered the latest in electric trains.

This unusually pensive expression suggests that this photo represented one of the few serious roles Betty played at 20th Century-Fox.

A scene with Charlotte Greenwood from the 1942 film *Springtime In the Rockies.* Husband Harry James and his orchestra were also featured in the production.

Dick Haymes, Betty, and Gene Lockhart in a scene from *The Shocking Miss Pilgrim*—1947.

The laughter suggests that Marilyn Monroe didn't keep them waiting this day on the set of *How To Marry a Millionaire.* Relaxing in a dressing room between takes are Marilyn, Betty, and Lauren Bacall.

Carol Channing and Betty pose for photographers in Carol's Broadway dressing room. At the time, Betty was in rehearsal for the first national company of *Hello Dolly*.

Betty poses next to her World War II pin-up photo a quarter of a century later: "Look at the old girl now!"

The dolls, wearing costumes from all of Betty's movie hits, were made by super-fan Leonard Scumacci. His Chicago apartment is a shrine to the memory of his lifetime favorite movie queen.

(Above left) Betty Grable and Dick Haymes were presenters at the 44th annual Academy Awards on April 10, 1972. On this night, symptoms of her fatal illness became painfully evident. It would be her final appearance before a national audience. (Above right) No man was more devoted to Betty than Bob Remick, the last of her four great loves. The twenty seven year difference in their ages was far less important to Remick than it was to Betty.

Cortisone treatment was considered the cause for the added puffiness to the famous Grable figure when she made her final dinner theater appearance in early 1973 in *Born Yesterday*.

This snapshot was taken of Betty in Jacksonville, Florida, by a fellow cast member of *Born Yesterday*. It would be only a matter of weeks before Betty would enter St. John's Hospital in Santa Monica, California for the last time.

# Chapter 22

During the early sixties, Betty had her share of offers from theatrical producers to go on tour, but she wasn't interested. She was contacted once as a possible replacement for Carol Channing in the New York company of *Hello Dolly* but turned it down. She made the pledge to remain at home until both children were on their own, and at that time Jessica still remained in the family fold.

When 1965 came, Betty faced a year of decision. She had already written off the marriage and had been marking time. It hadn't been a smooth period of time to "mark" however, because Jessica had begun to rebel in earnest, seeking escape from the clasp of her overprotective mother. She was associating with friends Betty labeled unredemptive, hippies, dopers. Betty didn't really know Jessie's friends at all, but no amount of reasoning on Jessie's part could change her mind about them. Betty was unyielding, and it finally came down to ultimatums: "As long as you're under my roof, you'll do as I say."

While Betty awaited the proper time to divorce Harry, her

daughter was waiting for the time she could legally break free. She finally passed her eighteenth birthday May 20, and, when she graduated from high school the following month, she made good her own pledge. She moved out of the house.

Within a month or two Jessica had become Mrs. Ron Yahner and had a baby on the way. She had freed herself from one set of strictures, but her freedom was spare. In her confusion, she had ensnared herself in another web of limitation.

It would take time for Betty to admit it—even to herself—but she had literally driven her daughter from the home by imposing her double-standard morality on someone who needed to learn things for herself.

When she was young, Betty had submitted to authority and suppressed many of her deep urgings. Since she had known no other way, she imposed the same authority on her children, then was unable to understand Jessie's lack of loyalty. Jessie had a strong will and refused to accept coercion. It would require some growing up on her part, and some maturity on the part of her mother, before mutual respect was realized.

While all the domestic strife was taking place, more and more of the Grable–James income was being funneled into the gambling casino cash drawers. When Betty was given a second chance to take on the role of Dolly Levi, she was infinitely more interested. She needed the money, and the timing was perfect. She would tour in the first national company of the show, which was especially attractive to her, because the greater part of the run would be spent at home in Las Vegas.

The actual nailing down of the *Dolly* assignment came about by chance. Several stars were in the running for the role, once David Merrick announced the formation of the road company, and Betty was only one of them. But one evening when she was taken to see Eddie Fisher at the Riviera by her daughter and son-in-law, she had a stroke of luck. Fisher introduced her to the audience and then asked, "How would you people like to see Betty Grable right here in *Hello Dolly?*" In response, Betty was given a standing ovation, which impressed the management. When the time of selection arrived, they cast their vote for Betty. She got the job.

It had been a long, hot summer, but the air was beginning to clear for Betty. With the *Hello Dolly* contract in hand, she started to formulate a plan. The family situation at this time found Victoria securely married, and Jessica—if not exactly secure—was married and no longer Betty's responsibility. And Harry? Well, he was still going his independent route, less married now than ever before. At this time he was flagrantly involved with a girl half his age.

Betty was scheduled to join the *Dolly* tour in Chattanooga, where she would inherit the chorus of the Mary Martin company that was returning from Vietnam in early November. First, though, she was to go to New York to rehearse with the principals.

Betty engineered it so all the legal details would be complete before her October departure for the East. On October 7, 1965, in Las Vegas, she sued for divorce. The papers were presented to Harry after her departure.

As in her marriage to Coogan, when it was over, it was indeed over. The only difference was that it required twenty extra years for it to be over with Harry James. Her method of handling the breakup paralleled the telephone exit she used with Raft. In this instance, she didn't think even a phone call was necessary to explain things to Harry. She flew out of his life on an eastbound airliner.

In New York, Betty worked long, tedious hours with her leading man Max Showalter, under the direction of Gower Champion's assistant, Lucia Victor. She would have been happier had Champion shown enough interest to assume his own directorial duties and, from that moment forward, had a feeling Champion wasn't too excited about her in the role.

Max Showalter says Betty may have had some justification for her attitude regarding Champion, but it wasn't that the director thought her poorly cast in the role. "When he called me to play Vandergelder," said Showalter, "he said the show would be seen honestly for the first time, because Betty would play it that way, and I was given carte blanche in my interpretation of Vandergelder. It was a fantastic opportunity for both of us."

Showalter said that Betty was remarkably adept in rehearsals considering she had to learn the lines and all the complicated stage business within three weeks. "She carried it off beautifully," he said, "except in the eating scene. It was a scene where I was at her mercy, where no ad-libbing was possible. It was comprised of nonsequiturs, where nothing that was said led to anything else. Gower told me Carol Channing didn't get it for about two months. Dolly had to eat seven dumplings and throw food on my plate, and I was unable to cue her. She needed some prompting from the wings, but she got it finally."

In retrospect Showalter is convinced Betty Grable was the best Dolly in the lot, and Betty's manager at the time, Kevin Pines, agrees. "She was the best," says Pines, "because she was a natural comedian and not a mugger like Channing, and Ginger Rogers came over like Groucho Marx in drag. Mary Martin had the most talent, but, when Betty Grable came down that staircase and sang "Hello Dolly," nobody could touch her. She was scared, she was nervous—but she was great."

After having worked eight to ten hours a day in New York, Betty and the others reached a point where they could not absorb any more. They traveled to Chattanooga and, after the travel break, began rehearsals again in the time left before the November 3 opening. These rehearsals took place in Betty's hotel room.

Amid all the chaos, there were other problems. The woman who was to play Mrs. Malloy remained in New York, because her husband—who also had the lesser part of Ambrose—fell ill. The actress was expected to catch up with them before the opening, but this was impossible because her husband didn't recover. Replacements were required for both parts. When the entire cast, including the chorus of the Mary Martin company, finally merged for final rehearsals, it was almost laughable. It was backstage pandemonium—or would have been had there been a backstage.

"The Tivoli Theatre was a converted movie house," said Showalter, "and there was no room at all backstage. The dressing rooms were holes in the wall, and to manage scenery changes it was necessary to back trucks up to the stage doors, and move the furniture out of the theater and into the trucks."

All superstitious rituals were closely observed on opening night, and rabbit feet would have been at a premium. Disaster seemed inevitable, but that was not the way the show turned out. Betty had her usual problems in the eating scene, but the audience wasn't aware of them. The show played to a thoroughly appreciative audience, and the next day's reviews were glowing.

The reviews were almost unanimously favorable throughout the tour, but they were also consistent in criticism of Betty's vocal raspiness. She never fully overcame her voice problems, but this deficiency didn't detract from her performance. It did lessen praise for her work, since she was criticized for her voice's raspiness. She wore a microphone in her cleavage to help project her voice, and on at least one occasion the amplification system picked up not only Betty's voice but local police calls as well.

The show's itinerary carried them from Chattanooga to Knoxville in Tennessee; to Louisville, Kentucky; Columbus, Ohio; St. Paul, Minnesota; Omaha, Nebraska; and Denver, Colorado. During the five-night run in Denver, the days were used to rehearse the truncated version of the show that would run on a more permanent basis in Las Vegas. In the shorter version all of Betty's and Showalter's songs remained, but about thirty minutes of ballads and dialogue were eliminated. The show opened at the Riviera Hotel December 23, and two shows a night would follow—without an off-day—for the following eleven months.

For Max Showalter, the two-shows-a-night regimen was so exhausting he was taking daily B-12 shots, and nightly sleeping pills to assure sufficient rest. Not Betty—she did her performances each night and the town afterward. She was unable to unwind after performing and stayed up most of the night.

Showalter suggested that Betty have herself checked by a doctor to be sure she was fit enough to handle the physical strain, but Betty only laughed. "I haven't been to a doctor in twenty years," she told him. "I don't believe in them."

Betty was almost euphoric while she was playing in Las Vegas. It was as though her troubles were dissolved by her sweat and toil. When not on stage at the Riviera, she was lost in the cacophonous merriment of the Strip casinos. She had reached forty-nine by now, but had the energy of a teenager. Most people who live by night sleep away the days, but this wasn't true with Betty. She was a day person by nature, and even when she got to sleep at dawn, she rarely slept past noon. Often, while unemployed, she would drowse off at 9:00 P.M. while the television went on blaring into the night. That had changed now, and Betty had no complaints.

For doing fourteen shows a week, Betty's salary was only $5,000 a week, which, for a star of her magnitude, was close to an insult. Out of that came living expenses, agent and manager fees, and all the other necessary expenditures. On the regular road tour, her salary was only $3,000.

"I think Betty was sold down the river," said Kevin Pines. "She didn't even get a percentage. Most stars of her caliber would draw about thirty-five hundred a week plus ten percent of the gross."

But Betty never complained about the salary. There were other things she complained about, and one of them was David Merrick. She felt about as cozy with him as she had felt with Darryl Zanuck. Also, she never quite forgave director Gower Champion for ignoring her. He made no appearance at all until the show played in Omaha, and that was the last anyone saw of him. Despite all this, Betty certainly enjoyed what she was doing and liked the happy turn her career had taken.

If she wanted to feel better, she had only to imagine the alternative. She could be at home alone with nothing to look forward to but creeping old age. Now, she had a hit show with a wonderful cast in her own hometown; she would be home for the birth of her first grandchild and was earning a living. In addition to these pleasant factors, she had happened into a relationship that helped all her troubles seem unimportant. She was well aware that the attraction was rather foolish, but it was working out well. His name was Bob Remick. He was one of the gypsies in the show, a handsome blonde. He definitely went for girls, and she seemed his choice. He was also very, very young.

Remick recalls when Betty first learned what the gap in their age was. He had been hospitalized for a tonsillectomy, and Betty came with a few other cast members to visit him. "For the show I wore a full beard," he said, "so I looked much older. Betty took my hand while I was in bed and glanced down at the hospital ID tag on my wrist. It showed my age. Her eyes widened. 'Twenty two!' she says, not quite believing. She was stunned for a moment, but that was it. She accepted our age difference, and it was never a major problem. Certainly not for me."

As the run of the play extended, Betty saw more and more of Bob, and those around them began to assume their relationship was becoming far more than casual. Yet Betty was extremely careful and discreet. She didn't want her family to know about them; she didn't even want the house maid to know. She was obviously embarrassed about the age difference, whether Bob was aware of it or not.

Betty must have been acutely aware of the difference in their ages when, on February 20, 1966, she became a grandmother. At that time Bob was approaching twenty-three, only a few months older than Betty's eldest daughter. To put it into still another perspective, Bob Remick was born only a couple of months before Betty and Harry James were married.

# Chapter 23

In a newspaper interview done while Betty was playing Las Vegas in *Hello Dolly,* she said, "I'm not much for being away from home on an extended basis, and I would have been reluctant to go with the national company if it hadn't been scheduled for a long run in Las Vegas. But now that I'm into the role, I'd go with it to South Africa. I absolutely love the play and the whole company. When I go out on the stage my tensions and anxieties just fade away. The show brings me great happiness."

Betty's success was almost a rebirth, and she was unashamedly proud of her accomplishment. She wanted all her friends to share her good fortune and invited many good friends to come to Las Vegas to see the show. One of them was dancer Steve Preston.

"I was very pleased when she called," said Preston. "I planned to go over to see the show anyway. She met me at the airport, as always, and on the way back to the house, she said, 'I've got to talk to you before we get to the house. You aren't going to believe this, but I met this really nice kid. Now, we're just friends, understand—but we're running around a lot. Can you imagine me at my age, and I've got a twenty-three-year-old trick.' "

Betty's friends believe her relationship with Bob was platonic for some time, because beneath her bold facade there still dwelled the old-fashioned girl with Victorian morals. When they finally became more intimately involved, Betty required that Bob vacate the house before dawn. He had to scale a wall and traverse a large portion of the Desert Inn golf course to avoid the neighbors' inquisitive eyes. Later, also for appearances, Bob had a separate bedroom in the house Betty ultimately bought.

Betty had a tendency to lash out at Bob when she was drinking, according to Steve Preston. She would call him worthless, boring, or just a kid. "He took it from her," said Preston, "because he knew she didn't really mean it. The apologies would be there in the morning, I'm sure. When Betty drank, she let it all out. Not that she was vicious, but whatever was on her mind came out. She could be especially rough when she was losing at the gaming tables. She was mad at herself, but would tend to take it out on others."

Preston recalls Betty as the one who always reached for the check. When she went out with male guests, she would give them two or three hundred dollars to pick up tabs, so as not to embarrass them. When Betty invited someone to visit her, the invitation always included air fare and *all* expenses. That was the only way she would have it. She was a high-roller and a big-spender, and whatever her faults may have been, she was never accused of being selfish.

"One night she went through a bundle at the tables," said Preston. "And she had markers all over town. She'd say, 'Oh, I can't go to the Desert Inn—I still owe them twenty thousand.' She made a joke of it, but it was true. While she was winning this night, she kept giving me handfuls of chips to play for myself. Eventually her luck changed, but she didn't stop playing. She lost her winnings along with another fifteen thousand.

"The next morning she, of course, hated herself, even

though she didn't say it. But what she didn't realize was that I hadn't played with the chips she had given me. I had cashed them all in and had stashed the money for her. I went to get it then—maybe nine or ten thousand. I handed it to her and said, 'Will this help?' 'Where did you get all that?' she asked me. I told her I had put it away for her, but her reaction wasn't at all what I expected. She said, 'Well, why the hell didn't you give it to me last night—I could have won.'

"She asked what I intended to do with the money, and I said we would take it back to the casino and apply it to what she lost. She didn't care for the idea, but finally agreed. Harry was an even worse gambler than she was. Between them they lost a fortune."

Bob Remick, reared in Brooklyn, was a classical dancer with the Martha Graham Company before he entered musical comedy. From the moment he set eyes on Betty Grable, there was no doubt that she was the lady for him. Betty must have had a similar reaction to him, but the fact that there was a mutual attraction certainly did not assure a smooth sea in their romantic voyage. Much of the trip was stormy.

"Betty may have been jealous," said Kevin Pines. "That was her tendency. Bob never looked at another woman, as far as I could see, but Betty probably didn't believe that. But can you imagine the ribbing that boy took when he came out of the chorus and started dating Betty? He really did adore her."

Pines points out that stars are often like children. They have to be constantly reassured that they are loved. He thinks Betty, very conscious of her age, couldn't believe that this very young, good-looking guy really loved her. Was he out for her money? For reflected glory? What was his true motive? She was probably never convinced of his sincerity. And, partly as a result of these doubts, Betty became very possessive.

"And fans can be inadvertently cruel," Pines added. "When Betty was with Bob, it was hard for her to handle those confrontations. Some character that has aged badly—who looks old enough to be her father—comes up and says, 'Oh, I remember you. I was your biggest fan when I was a kid.' It was that kind of thing that really got to her."

It is also Pines's opinion that Betty and Bob would have eventually married had it not been for Betty's concern over public opinion, more specifically, the opinion of her fans. "Betty stood off from her fans as much as possible," he says, "yet was remarkably loyal to them. She once turned down a very lucrative stage part in a play because she didn't think her fans would like her in that kind of role. She was certainly worried about her fans' reaction to a marriage to a guy half her age.

"And I'll tell you something else about Bob Remick. He had some money saved, maybe four or five thousand dollars, which was a lot for a kid his age to have saved. Betty picked up everybody else's checks, but Bob was spending his own money when they were out together. He went through all his savings while he went with Betty."

Betty seems to have been torn by conflicting emotions about Remick. While she wanted his love, she was never sure she really had it, and she was constantly subjecting him to tests. He had to prove his sincerity every day, and considering the accounts of Betty's treatment of him, he must have been the kindest, most tolerant of all her loves.

Betty's initial alienation from Harry James didn't last long. She couldn't very easily avoid him, since they were in the same small town and had the same friends, so an early truce was called in the divorce war. She, Bob, and Harry often did things together, and it pleased Betty that Harry and Bob got along so well.

"Betty had one of her frequent quarrels with Bob when the three of us were having dinner at a nice French restaurant in Las Vegas," Pines said. "She got up from the table and walked out. At first we made up our minds we would let her go ahead and walk home, but Bob relented. He got the car, and we followed along the streets. As Betty walked, her pants started falling down. We couldn't very well let Betty Grable walk along Las Vegas streets with her ass showing, so we pulled alongside and told her what was happening. Then all of us started laughing. I doubt if she could remember what the fight had been about, but it could be very, very embarrassing when Betty would act up in a restaurant. How Bob put up with it, I'll never know."

Pines says that Betty's capriciousness made her someone to be treated with utmost care, with extreme delicacy. "For example," he said, "she might have someone she wanted you to meet, that she liked very much. She would want you to like that person, too. But you wouldn't dare bring that person's name up a week later, because she could have changed her mind. Then she would be angry that you reminded her of the person. For that reason I really laid back and wasn't very friendly with anyone I met through her. It was impossible to keep up with her allegiances."

*Hello Dolly* closed at the Riviera in mid-September, 1966. From Las Vegas they took to the road with bookings at San Antonio, Fort Worth, and Kansas City, before opening at the Shubert Theatre in Chicago for a two-month run.

When Betty was on the road, it was her practice to notify some of her more ardent fans when the show would be playing in their vicinity. If they showed up at the theater, they were always well-treated. Betty's closest fan of all was Michael Levitt of Chicago, who had corresponded with her for many years.

Levitt's first encounter with Betty occurred in 1949, when he was a young teenager. He and his friends would call columnist Irv Kupcinet's office to find out which stars were due to arrive in Chicago. If sufficiently motivated, they would wait around at the Dearborn Street Station to get autographs. One of Levitt's calls informed him that Betty Grable would be passing through the city en route to New York. He had hit pay dirt; his all-time-favorite star was Betty Grable. He induced a couple of pals to play hooky with him, and they were at the station in plenty of time for the arrival of the Super Chief from Los Angeles.

Travelers from the west disembarked from their Southern Pacific train at the Dearborn Station and take a short cab ride to the LaSalle Street Station, where they boarded a New York Central train to continue eastward.

That was the usual procedure, but in this instance it failed to work that way; Betty was traveling in a private car that was switched intact to the New York Central tracks.

"We ran to the LaSalle Street Station," said Levitt, "and sneaked onto the tracks. We found her car, and I asked the porter if he would take my autograph book inside and get Betty to sign it—to Mikey. He came back and asked which one of us was Mikey. When I told him it was me, and he said to go on up, because Miss Grable wanted to see me. I walked into that compartment, and there she was with that famous smile, wearing jeans, a man's shirt and with no makeup on. We talked for a long time, and she was great. She even brought her small daughters out to meet me. That was how it all began."

Over the years, Levitt sent her letters and greeting cards, and every one was answered. Once, she sent him a cashmere sweater for Christmas.

When *Hello Dolly* came to Chicago, Levitt decided it was time to pay Betty a second visit. It had been seventeen years since their previous encounter. He waited for Betty at the stage door, and, when she finally emerged, he approached her and said, "I don't expect you to remember me, but . . ."

"You're Mikey, aren't you," said Betty.

It was at this moment that the fan-star relationship began its transmutation into pure friendship. Mikey became the next thing to a family member. She called him many times to join her at points along this and subsequent tours. The air tickets were always forwarded ahead of time, and Betty picked up all expenses. It is doubtful that any fan was ever treated more royally by a celebrity. But, despite all her warmth and generosity, Betty's peculiarities still had to be dealt with, and, when she was in a snit, it was every man for himself.

Later Betty implored Levitt to move to Las Vegas. He was her dearest friend, and she wanted him to be around all the time. Mike adored Betty, but by this time he was well aware of her capriciousness. He graciously—and carefully—declined her generous offer. She promised she would set him up in his own hairdressing business and let him stay in her home. What Mike realized was that, when Betty said she wanted him around all the time, it meant just that, *all* the time—and the game would be played precisely according to house rules.

"To be a friend of Betty's," Mike said, "you eat when she eats, sleep when she sleeps, and get up when she gets up. It was a smothering kind of relationship, without much freedom."

Betty especially liked to have someone around in the early hours of the day. It seemed she always found herself aligned with night people. Harry had been, and so was Bob Remick. When she was at home, her early hours would be spent on the golf course, but it wasn't always possible to play golf on the road. Betty was a twelve-handicap golfer, so it was easy to find a game, even though she looked rather absurd, with a golf bag that was like a bouquet of mallets. She used only wood clubs—sixteen of them. But no matter what the game, gin rummy, Scrabble, Monopoly, or going for the big bucks at the casinos, Betty liked to win and was a rotten loser.

She also had a tendency to play cruel little tricks on those close to her. Kevin Pines recalls how reverently she treated him on their first meeting. He was introduced by Dan Dailey, and despite the closeness of her friendship with Dan, he was rudely ignored during the luncheon. "She directed all the conversation to me," said Pines. "I was the star that day. It was a quirk with her. The new person received all the attention. When she liked you, you could do no wrong. When she didn't like a person—forget it."

A similar situation occurred with Levitt. He brought someone to meet her, and Betty treated Mike as a nobody, while she lavished her attentions on the friend. It was almost a warning that one should never take her friendship for granted. Perhaps she wanted the third party to think she wasn't as great a pal as the person making the introductions might have claimed. Maybe this was the result of years of enduring sycophancy, of being surrounded by those seeking favors. She may have been afraid she would be used. She desired friendship desperately, but was compelled to keep her friends under control. The gypsy, the studio grip, the hairdresser, the common herd—they were her kind of people. But were they? She was still Betty Grable, and that made relationships more complicated.

Betty, it would seem, was under a constant bombardment of contradictory impulses. Her problem was gaining a firm grip on her real identity. Was she a "regular" person, or was she special? Who was she? What was she? Betty was an enigma, impossible to assess by even her oldest friends. She could be cruel, and she could be kind. Fortunately her kindness was more prevalent than her cruelty, or many of her dearest friends would not have remained in her company long enough to earn their stature. She was loved for her goodness; her faults were forgiven.

# Chapter 24

After closing in Chicago, the *Hello Dolly* troupe followed a circuitous journey through the South and the East, after bookings in South Bend and Fort Wayne, Indiana. Betty's birthday fell between those two dates, and panic broke out among the cast members when Betty called Max Showalter to say she was remaining in Chicago until Monday's opening in Fort Wayne. A surprise party had been planned for her, but, if Max had not let her in on the plans, there would have been no guest of honor. When informed of the event, Betty promised to be on hand.

According to a Fort Wayne newspaper account, Betty wore a black crepe party dress, accented by red pantaloons. "The elegantly decorated cake," the article said, "was topped with a doll bearing a resemblance to the star of *Hello Dolly.*

Betty was genuinely pleased at the attention showered on her for her fiftieth birthday, and the party was almost as memorable as the surprise given her by Dan Dailey the year before. Dailey had been en route to New York, but detoured to Columbus, Ohio, where he waited three days for Betty and the cast to arrive for their opening there. He watched the show from the audience and surprised her afterwards when he walked into her dressing room. Betty was touched by his visit and grateful for his consideration in waiting until after the show to announce his presence. It was always difficult for her when someone she knew very well was in the audience.

Very few *Hello Dolly* firsts remained for Betty after its long run on Broadway, but her chance to break new earth came with their engagement in Baltimore. Betty's company would inaugurate the sparkling new Morris A. Mechanic Theater.

The trouble was that Carol Channing also wanted recognition for opening the theater. She had left the Broadway company by this time and had formed a second touring group in the show she had played for so long. Betty's contract, however, clearly stated that she would play the date, so little could be done about it. Betty had little doubt David Merrick would have given the date to Channing if he could, because he had never shown much enthusiasm about her. He liked the money she was pulling in, but that seemed to be the extent of his interests. Strangely, it was Max Showalter who frequently received Merrick's praise.

A rivalry had built between Grable and Channing, and one of Betty's agents charged that Channing and her husband were suggesting on radio talk shows that it was a shame a "second rate" company of *Hello Dolly* would be opening the new theater. It had been quite a few years since a major new theater had opened, and it was a feather in the cap for any performer to be the first to play there. Those on Betty's side say Channing wanted very much to wear the feather.

When it was clear which company was to open in Baltimore, it was conveniently arranged that Carol Channing's company would give a command performance the same night at the White House for President Lyndon B. Johnson. This meant that all the Washington critics would attend the White House performance rather than the one only a few miles away in Baltimore.

A few kinks remained at the new theater, not the simplest of which was a leaky roof. It rained heavily on opening night, and umbrellas were needed to shield members of the orchestra. Betty added a parasol to her props, which delighted the audience.

Kevin Pines was responsible for the only gesture David Merrick made on Betty's behalf opening night. He talked him into having a couple of boys run out during curtain calls with two large urns of flowers. "He didn't seem too enthusiastic about the idea," said Pines, "until I suggested she might not show up for the next performance if it wasn't done. Betty deserved that much."

The Baltimore booking was one of the highlights of the *Dolly* tour, but it was the following engagement that held the most significance, because it was the last. After fifteen months and some 600 performances, the first road company of *Hello Dolly* would end after its run in Wilmington, Delaware.

"We were all very sentimental about parting company," said Max Showalter. "We always left the audience crying at the end of the show—even in Vegas. I never used a mike, but Betty did, and it made it especially effective when Betty was on the staircase. Then I could quiet down to sing, 'Hello Dolly it's so nice to have you here where you belong.' She sings, 'Here's my hat, Horace. I'm staying where I'm at, Horace.' And then together, 'Dolly will never ever leave again.' But in this performance, our last, Betty got as far as, 'Here's my . . .' and stopped. She was crying. All she could say was, 'Just hold me.' I held her in my arms, and we stood there with tears running down both our cheeks. We couldn't finish the song."

It was the end of the tour, but, although neither Betty nor Max knew it at the time, it would not be their last performance of *Hello Dolly* after all. Ginger Rogers, who had replaced Carol Channing on Broadway, was ready to take a rest and gave her notice. Betty was asked if she would replace Ginger. She refused. There was an inexplicable enmity between Betty and Ginger, and the thought of replacing her was something Betty could not accept. Throughout Betty's career, Ginger Rogers played the superstar and, according to Betty, treated her superciliously. She had as little to do with Ginger as possible.

When Betty's tour closed, several of the dancers were signed on for the New York company. Since they were friends, Betty and Bob were anxious to see them perform, yet Betty did not want to attract attention in the process. They bought their tickets under an assumed name, and Betty wore a brunette wig to disguise herself. She and Bob sneaked inside and watched the show in what they believed was total anonymity. But then Ginger came out for her curtain speech. "Ladies and gentlemen," she said, "I'd like you to meet my replacement. I'm sure all of you would like to give a round of applause to Miss Betty Grable."

Betty was mortified. To her, it was a replay of *Gay Divorcee,* where Ginger ruled as the star and Betty was the dumb little chorus girl. Betty thought Ginger was saying, "I'm getting fed up doing this show, so they went out and found this actress to take my place." Betty had never been angrier. When they reached the street, Betty bolted for the stage door with every intention of staging combat with Ginger Rogers. "How dare she say I'm her replacement!" Betty raged. Remick finally managed to alter her course and, with much cajoling and reasoning, removed her from the battle arena.

It was Martha Raye who replaced Ginger and Max Showalter who replaced David Burns. A few months later Ginger would take the show on tour, and thus, it was, in a sense, Ginger Rogers who replaced Betty Grable. At least, Betty enjoyed thinking of it that way.

Martha Raye went into *Dolly* February 20, 1969, and Showalter came in about a month later. Business dropped dramatically after Ginger Rogers left the show, and David Merrick was frantic for a solution to keep the show alive. He once more turned to Betty, who, by this time, would just as soon have scrubbed floors as work again for him. But Kevin Pines went into negotiation with Merrick and came out with a contract that could not easily be dismissed, not even by Betty Grable. She would get $5,000 a week plus ten percent of the house. She would be earning more than Channing and, more importantly, more than Ginger Rogers. Betty said yes.

When Martha Raye was the star, box-office receipts dipped to about $43,000 a week, according to Pines, and the theater would have been lost if they had gone down one more thousand.

"Betty came in," said Pines, "and the grosses went right

back up into the eighties. Betty saved the show in a really big way, and—would you believe it—neither Merrick nor Gower Champion stopped into Betty's dressing room to offer congratulations or to say so much as hello."

Most of the reviewers liked Betty on Broadway, though once more they criticized the weakness of her voice. Dan Sullivan of the *Los Angeles Times* was an exception. He suggested Betty arrived at the St. James Theatre with her own claque. Pines says this was a cheap shot, that Betty had at most a half dozen friends in the audience opening night. The audience loved her and gave her standing ovations throughout the evening.

"After curtain," says Pines, "the police came back and told Betty she would have to wait a while before leaving the theater, that, with so many fans outside, the police couldn't be responsible for her safety. She couldn't leave by the front of house either, because the fans were there as well. The whole street was roped off. We waited a while and started out, but recoiled when we saw the seething mob outside. We went back to the dressing room, and had a few drinks while the crowd dispersed.

"Later on, with the help of a wedge of mounted police, we made it to the limo. Nothing like this had ever happened to Betty before. Not in her entire career. She had made personal appearances before, but I think this was her first Broadway appearance since *Du Barry Was a Lady.*"

Betty's Broadway engagement in *Hello Dolly* was a personal conquest as well as a financial windfall—especially for David Merrick—but even though it was her habit to extend her contract whenever possible, to keep everyone working, she had no such inclinations this time. When the six months were up, she quit.

Her departure from the show opened the way for the first brunette *Dolly* to take over. It was Pearl Bailey, who did excellent business during her run. Later, Dorothy Lamour became the second brunette to play Dolly Levi, not on Broadway, but with the show's touring company. At first she experimented with a blonde wig, but no one could quite believe Lamour as a blonde, so once again an exception was made.

During the interim between the national company of *Hello Dolly* and the Broadway run, Betty had made some important changes. During the span of about a year she bought a pleasant home on the Tropicana Golf Course in Las Vegas and moved into it. She left the larger home at the Desert Inn to Harry, who later sold it.

In line with Betty's pledge to take things easy, she stepped beyond the continental boundaries of the United States for only the second time in her life. Several years earlier she played a nightclub engagement in Puerto Rico, which carried her across a minimal expanse of ocean, and this time she and Bob flew a bit deeper into the Atlantic to visit the Virgin Islands. A month was spent in total relaxation, something Betty hadn't done in a long time.

When the Broadway stint in *Dolly* was behind her, Betty was ready for another vacation. Kevin Pines had a booking for her with the Kenley theaters to do *Born Yesterday,* but she turned it down, even though her salary would have been tremendous. At the time she believed her fans wouldn't accept her in a straight comedy role. She and Bob went ahead with their second vacation within two years and chose the other direction. They languished on the sands of Waikiki for a month.

Betty was once more ready for work upon her return and ironically accepted an offer to do *Born Yesterday,* which she so recently had turned down. The pay was a fraction of the deal Pines had set up for her earlier, but she played the date at a dinner theater near Chicago and was happy with the results. She loved the role of Billie Dawn, and the audiences loved her.

With this encouragement, Betty agreed to a tour with the show, which would start in a theater near the one where she had debuted the show. She had been out of touch with her friend Betty Ritz, who had since become Mrs. Raphael Baez, and wrote her at her home in Acapulco to let her know what had been going on:

*My Dear Betty,*
*I'm back in Vegas and leave Sunday August 25 to go to Chicago to play* Born Yesterday *for three weeks. Then I come back home for a week, and then go to Houston to do it for two weeks. After that I'm going to cool it for a while, and maybe if all is well can come visit*

*you sometime before the first of the year. I don't guess there will ever be a chance for you to come visit me. After Harry and I got the divorce I bought a real cute house on the Tropicana Golf Course. It would be so groovy to have you stay with me.*

*About Bob—For a kid he's got poise and the sense of a much older person, and for some reason, although I try to dissuade him, he adores me. He's kind and thoughtful, and though I know it's not right, we've developed a wonderful companionship, which has lasted almost three years. He should be with someone his own age, but what the hell—if we're happy together so why not let it last as long as we can.*

*Harry has a new baby boy. I can't figure out what our grandchildren are to it in relationship. That's wild, isn't it? Jessie, I guess I told you, has a girl and a boy now. They're both very happy and thank God. So I go on my own little way, and I guess everything is about as good as could be expected.*

*You sound happy, which you know means a lot to me. Do you think we'll ever make that trip we talked about—in our old age? I'm old now, so we had better not wait too long. I think so often of the things we used to do, and of the funny, funny scenes we used to get into. I went to Del Mar for a couple of days last week, and that really brought back memories. It's not the same anymore, but for God sakes, it's been twenty-one years. Well, honey, I'll say bye-bye for now and remember I'll always love you and you'll always be my very, very best friend.*

*Betty*

The trip to which Betty referred was a pledge made by her and Betty Ritz years earlier, to take a luxury liner cruise to Europe. It was a standing joke that found them seated in deck chairs with other passengers walking past them, wondering, "Who are those little old ladies?" Then, someone would say, "Oh, that's Betty Grable, isn't it?"

# Chapter 25

Betty's management team had a grand fantasy. It seemed like a natural—a sure thing. They visualized Betty Grable returning to her old studio, the place where she had achieved her incredible heights of movie stardom. Now, as a mature but still beautiful woman, she would play the lead in *Hello Dolly* on the screen. And who would play Horace Vandergelder? Why, Dan Dailey, of course. One of the great teams of modern time would reunite to regale their fans with their charm and talent again.

But the ruling powers at Twentieth Century-Fox had a much younger person in mind to play Dolly Levi. Although they didn't say so at the time, Barbra Streisand had already been chosen for the role, and Gene Kelly would play Vandergelder.

It's doubtful that Betty harbored any hopes for the miracle that was fantasized by her agents, because she knew better than anyone the burned-bridge status she had at Twentieth. However, she probably didn't realize that this would be her very last shot at movies—that, indeed, her film career had ended fifteen years earlier. She would have loved a comeback, just to be able to say, "Look at the old girl now," but it was never to be.

A play proposal came Betty's way in late 1968, and, despite just about everyone's advice, she jumped blindly into it. The play was a musical called *Belle Starr,* with the score written by Steve Allen. It was to be produced by a man named Jerry Shafer, along with a former leading man of Betty's, Rory Calhoun. What attracted Betty, and caused her to ignore all warnings, was the where rather than the what. The musical was to open in Scotland and settle in for a run in London. If there was ever a place she wanted to go it was London, so she accepted the offer.

Kevin Pines parted company with Betty at this juncture, because his advice went unheeded. He said she signed her name on a grocery bag, and off she went. Betty and Bob went to Glasgow by air, and after the passage of about a week she was calling Pines to come over and help her out. The play was a shambles, and she didn't even have a decent costume to wear.

"I went over and saw the show," said Pines, "and it was awful. She had two shabby costumes, and her biggest number was a thing where she drew a pair of guns out of their holsters and sang, 'I've Got the Biggest Pair of 38s in Town.'

"It was very funny about Betty—she was so incredibly inconsistent. Waiting for her to sign the contract for *Hello Dolly* was like sweating bullets, yet she went racing into this bomb full steam ahead. I was never able to figure her out."

Pines scurried about trying to come up with decent costumes for Betty, and she was trying to hire a script doctor to suture some of the gaping wounds in the script. She would have paid for it out of her own pocket, but it was too late. Steve Allen's songs were good, but by this time even he had washed his hands of the fiasco.

While everyone was wringing their hands in despair and bustling vainly to keep Betty from the brink of disaster, she, unknown to practically everyone, was having the time of her life. She heard from old and loyal fans, was absorbing London's charm, and was taking every sightseeing tour her free time would allow.

"They at least provided us with a lovely flat," said Bob Remick. "It was on Grosvenor, across from the U.S. Embassy. The people loved Betty and were incredibly gracious. The rehearsals were in a kind of industrial area with open markets all around. We'd walk along the streets, and Betty would get greetings like, 'Hello, Betts.' Shouts would come from passing autos, or from across the street, but no one ever approached her directly. They honored her privacy to that extent. When we would walk into a pub for our lunch break, the entire patronage would rise as though she were visiting royalty. As far as the show was concerned, it was hopeless. It ran three weeks in Scotland and three weeks in London."

The *Daily Express* described Betty's talents as "modest at best," and the *Evening Standard* said, "She had a voice so weak that not even a microphone could aggrandize. She had a timid wiggle, masquerading as voluptuousness, and the wholesome appeal of Miss Vanilla Ice Cream of 1936." The *Daily Telegraph*'s observation: "She is just left standing there while the company rampages around her."

No matter how cold and cruel the reviews, the fans still adored Betty Grable and gathered together to carry placards in front of the theater. "We Love You Betty," said one. "Come Back To London," said another.

The trip not only allowed Betty an opportunity to make contact with many of her English fans, but also brought her together again with Paula Stone Sloan, who was living in London at the time. Betty lost no time in asking Paula's help with the show. But, because it was highly unethical for one producer to meddle in another's production, this was something Paula could not do. "I saw the show opening night," said Paula, "and didn't like it at all. And it was a shame, because Betty was so dearly loved in London. When I went backstage, Betty just looked at me. I said, 'You're absolutely beautiful.' There was nothing left to say."

This was Paula's first meeting with Bob Remick, and she was very favorably impressed. She recalled, however, that Betty called her aside before the meeting to ask that she not mention

George Raft or any of her other boyfriends. Paula thought this strange, but, of course, complied with Betty's request.

There had been some travel money up front, a round-trip air ticket, and, of course, the beautiful flat near the American Embassy, and that was it. There was little hope any additional money would be forthcoming, but Betty adopted a philosophical attitude toward the fiasco. It had been her own decision, and she had to accept the way it turned out. When the play was behind her, Betty was determined there would be at least one other dream she could fulfill—that voyage on an ocean liner. Betty Ritz wouldn't be there to share it with her, but Bob was on hand. It would serve as a very happy ending to a questionable venture.

The trip was pure pleasure. Betty could hardly believe any of it was happening. She vowed again to devote as much time as possible in travel. There were a hundred places she wanted to see, and now, by God, she would see them.

Betty's euphoria remained throughout the voyage, but came to a sudden halt when the ship reached New York Harbor. Betty was mystified by the battery of reporters on hand to greet her—she knew she was no conquering heroine returning to the homeland. When the gangplank was lowered, she soon learned what it was all about. While on the voyage, Rory Calhoun's wife, Lita Baron, had filed for divorce. Betty Grable was listed as one of seventy-eight women Mrs. Calhoun named as adultresses with Rory. Betty's first reaction: "Rory Calhoun?"

"It didn't even upset her," said Remick, "because the charges were too bizarre. She had done a couple of movies with him in the fifties, but she never really got along too well with him. And she certainly didn't go to bed with him while we were in London. That, I know for sure."

The headlines soon faded, and it is doubtful anyone—with the possible exception of Lita Baron—believed Betty Grable had had an affair with Calhoun. After the pummeling the gods dealt Betty in London, the closing insult by Calhoun's wife was probably accepted as a logical ending to a very bizarre chain of events.

# Chapter 26

After her return from London, Betty loafed as long as her finances would allow and finally accepted the proposal to tour with *Born Yesterday.* Before long, Betty would become as closely associated with this show as she had been with *Dolly.* Over the next few years she would crisscross the nation playing Billie Dawn to the cheers of her loving fans. Often she would invite Mike Levitt—her number one loving fan—to join her at stops along the way. He was on hand when the show played in Sullivan, Illinois, in late 1969.

It was during this visit that Levitt introduced Betty to Hostess Twinkies. "Betty took one look at it when I handed one to her," said Levitt, "and said, 'I don't know whether to eat it, or play with it.' From that time on, she never failed to have them in stock whenever I would visit her. She remembered little things like that."

Mike really suspected that he had hooked her on them, but she refused to admit it. She always insisted that she bought them for him, and that he would have to finish them off before he left, but periodically she would say, "Get me one of those Blinkies, or whatever you call them."

The tour started from Sullivan, and it may have been there that Betty earned the highest weekly salary of her life. The show played in a converted movie house that seated 800, and Betty's contract gave her one-third of the gross. Every performance was sold out, and there was standing room only for the four-week run. If she could have matched this contract on subsequent dates, she would have come out of *Born Yesterday* with a tidy nest egg, but most managements were less generous.

For the following year and a half Betty toured the country from Illinois to Kansas to Maine. There were disasters and delights, horrible playhouses and majestic palaces. Often there were breaks between bookings when Betty could hop home to Las Vegas for a brief respite. Mike Levitt joined Betty and Bob on one of those stops. During his stay, Levitt went gambling with Betty for the first time.

"We were playing blackjack," said Mike, "and she gave me a stack of chips. It would be my tendency to play a couple of dollars at a time, but she didn't want it that way. She said, 'You either play my way, or not at all.' I played her way, and we both lost.

"Bob went off somewhere, and, when Betty was ready to quit, she had him paged. When he failed to answer the page, Betty decided to leave without him. She was bombed, and, when the doorman was asked to bring the car around, he turned to me and said, 'She isn't going to drive, is she?' I said, 'She'd better–I don't know how.' "

Betty had become a bit sour, and Levitt believes it was caused by more than her losses at the blackjack table. "When people say things," he said, "they always seem to do it so you can hear it. It's almost like they're in a dark theater whispering to the person next to them, without the characters up on the screen being able to hear what they say. That's how it sometimes was with Betty. A woman said something like, 'She sure doesn't look the way she used to, does she?' This upset Betty, and who can blame her? She told me she hoped someday to have the nerve to turn around at times like that and say, 'Who the fuck does look the way they used to?' She said, 'Am I supposed to walk around the rest of my life with my hand on my hip, looking over my shoulder?' "

Betty got behind the wheel of the car and burned rubber. She was aware that Mikey, being a city boy, was a rather timid auto passenger, so she planned to give him a ride he would remember. She careened around corners, through narrow streets and back alleys, on a shortcut that only she knew. When she glanced over and saw the terror on Mikey's face, she began laughing. Any anger she had felt at the beginning of the trip was gone now. Her sense of humor returned, and everything was hilariously funny. By the time they reached home, the inevitable had happened—she had wet her pants.

"She had a big lounge chair in her den," said Mikey, "where she liked to plop after dinner. That was where she headed when we got home, and I tried to help her get out of her clothes—so she could be more comfortable. 'Don't touch me,' she said. 'You're trying to steal my jewelry—just stay away.' So, I let her sleep."

Once, in a mellow mood, Betty told Mikey that he was the best friend she had in the whole world. "It bothered me," he said, "because to say that to me showed how insecure she was. With all the important people in her life, she singled me out as her best friend. That was when she asked me to move to Las Vegas, but I was afraid to do that. In short visits our friendship was perfect. That was how I hoped to keep it."

Their friendship was not perfect, even in brief encounters, but on a short term basis it was probably easier to forgive and forget. One of Betty's stormy sieges took place when she went to New York to do a Geritol television commercial. She invited Mikey to come along and join her and Bob at the Plaza Hotel at the time of the shoot.

It was red-carpet treatment all the way: limousine, theater tickets, champagne in the room. There was also carte blanche on room service in the most esteemed of New York hotels. On the first evening, Betty planned a conservative regime. They would have a few cocktails, order a snack from room service, and turn in early to be fresh for the 5:00 A.M. wake-up. The austere schedule was followed religiously to the point of ordering the food. They may have had one or two extra cocktails, but it was still early when Betty started her examination of the room service menu.

"She looked at the room service menu," said Mike Levitt and gave kind of a helpless shrug. 'You know,' she said to us, 'No matter whose paying for it, I just can't do it.' She was reacting to the prices on the menu. She gave me a handful of money and asked me to go to Rubin's and bring some things back to the room. I came back with two shopping bags full of great food, including cheesecake, and it cost a fraction of what three room service meals would have cost.

"She gave that familiar wrinkle of her nose, and said, 'Let's sit on the floor, okay? Like a picnic.' That's what we did, and had a great time eating cold cuts, potato salad and malts."

Betty had been drinking throughout the wait for the food, and by the time they finished eating the early-to-bed vow went down the elevator shaft. She suggested that maybe they could go to one place for quick drink. They went to a nearby bar with all good intentions, but the piano player spotted Betty and started playing all her movie hits. Soon she was standing at the piano providing her own words to the music. The patronage was enthralled. It happened to be a gay bar, and gays were always among Betty's most ardent fans. With that kind of audience, and with the drinks coming her way, Betty stayed on and on and on.

Remick had passed on the bar stop, so Mikey was burdened with the responsibility of attempting to pry Betty away from the piano bar. By this time Mikey knew Betty well enough to be wary of the task that lay ahead, but he did try. He asked rather timidly if she knew how late it was. It was nearly two o'clock and she had to be up at five.

Betty sent him a searing glance. "It really bothers you that I'm having a good time, doesn't it?"

Mikey retreated.

A few minutes later, Betty smiled over at Mikey and beckoned him closer. When he came to her, she leaned forward as if to invite a kiss. Mikey pressed his lips to Betty's, but her kiss was a bit more than he expected. "When she kissed me," said Mikey, "she got my upper lip between her teeth and bit hard. She bit all the way through my lip, and I still have a scar to remember it by."

With this gesture completed, Betty stormed out of the bar and returned to the hotel. By the time Mikey followed her into the suite, she was complaining to Remick about her hair. It wasn't quite right—the color was off. She would look awful tomorrow for the commercial. She dispatched Bob to Times Square to an all night drug store, where he could buy an assortment of hair preparations. When Remick returned with the order, Betty set out to color her hair. It took all but an hour-and-a-half of her remaining sleep time. Despite the minimal sleep, Betty was awake at the appointed hour.

Considering what had transpired the night before, Betty looked surprisingly fit and beautiful for the shoot. When the director ordered "Action," Betty delivered her lines perfectly. It was a take on the first try—almost. She was fine, but a technical problem required shooting the commercial again.

Betty went into the retake with confidence, but her spontaneity was missing. She tried again and again, but after that first perfect take, there were no others. They worked hour after hour attempting to get it right, but it was hopeless. In the end the client rejected the entire concept. The shoot was written off and rescheduled with a new script. The next setting would be in California.

It was almost as if the gods had been watching over Betty, because the second stab at the Geritol commercial was superior in every way to the first. This time Betty was joined by her daughters and her four grandchildren. The gathering was staged to give living proof that the tonic could produce the world's most glamorous grandmother.

During the shooting of the second commercial, Betty was registered in one of the plush bungalows at the Beverly Hills Hotel, and she loved it. She had been around Hollywood many years, but had never seen the interiors of the pink cottages, and at this juncture in her career Betty felt very well treated indeed. The commercial was a huge success, and the previous disaster in New York was forgotten—except, perhaps, by Mike Levitt.

Less than one year later, she again was booked into the Beverly Hills Hotel. This occasion was another first for Betty Grable; along with Dick Haymes, she would present the 1971 Academy Award for Best Musical Score.

Betty had always avoided participation in events of this kind. She had never even attended a premiere as a spectator; she refused studio publicity appearances, or any other event that would cast her into throngs of movie fans. She was not timid if she were performing—but the impromptu ad-lib situations terrified her. It was never easy for her to explain, because she didn't really understand it herself. There had been times when she was tempted to turn out for some of the more glittery functions, if only out of curiosity, but at the last minute she always backed down.

In the 1957 Academy Awards she appeared on the telecast, but that time she and Harry James acted as performers and introduced that year's nominated songs. Actually, she and Harry were in that show's opening number, a medley of former Oscar-winning songs, and they worked with about ten other stars in the extravagant production number. It was well-planned, carefully choreographed and directed, and no problem for Betty at all. It was different in 1972. She was to make her entrance with Haymes, read their lines off a teleprompter, go through the envelope opening business, then name the winners and hand them the Oscars. She very nearly turned down Howard Koch's invitation, but then thought better of it. Not for herself. The glitter no longer made much difference to her. But what about Bob Remick? He would enjoy it—and Mikey. Mikey would love it. She accepted.

Betty gave Bob and Mikey as her reasons for doing the show, but there may also have been an inner voice of gentle persuasion. Some cryptic message from her subconscious may have been telling her that this would be her last chance to communicate with her millions of fans, the last hurrah of all.

Betty had scarcely hung up the telephone after her affirmative reply to Koch, when she picked it up again. She couldn't wait to tell Mikey. She asked him to join her and Bob, and he accepted eagerly.

Early 1972 was a time of great excitement for Betty. Besides the Academy Awards, she had signed a contract to go to Australia to play in *No, No Nanette.* She had forgotten her fear of flying and would traverse more than ten thousand miles of ocean to visit down under. She was rather proud of her bravery. Since she and Bob Remick teamed up, she was young again, willing to take risks, ready to expand her horizons.

After assembling her coterie for the Awards ceremonies, Betty called the Beverly Hills Hotel to book one of the bungalows she had enjoyed so much those months earlier. So far, everything had been working in her favor, but at this point her good luck faltered. All the bungalows were booked; the last three had just been taken by Charlie Chaplin for his party.

This didn't make Betty very happy, but she would have to accept it. It was true that Charlie was being honored in the Awards ceremonies, but did he have to grab all the remaining bungalows? She was given a very comfortable suite on the big day and had little cause for complaint. Her heart was still set on her first choice, however, and she paused in unpacking when she heard the sound of a nearby siren. "See what that is," she said to Mikey.

Mikey went to the window that presented a broad view of Sunset Boulevard. "It's an ambulance," he reported.

There was a mischievous glint in her eye. "Mikey," she said, "call downstairs. Maybe Charlie didn't make it—and we can get a bungalow after all."

It was a grand homecoming for Betty. She had made very few visits to these environs since she moved to Las Vegas, and she couldn't resist taking a tour of all her previous homes. Bob and Mikey went along, of course, and there were a couple of other friends from Betty's movie days. The first stop was Betty's first home on the West Coast, the charming house at 250 Chadbourne in Brentwood. This was where she had spent the later thirties with her mother, and at times her sister, brother-in-law and nephew as well. Then they saw the familiar Stone Canyon address where she lived when Harry James entered her life. There was the honeymoon home at Heather and Coldwater Canyon, and finally the majestic Beverly Hills Estate at 600 Doheny Road, where the girls spent their developing years. This was the home that was later purchased by Carol Burnett. The last stop on this leg of the tour was the last residence of the James family prior to the Nevada exodus, the house off Beverly Drive, near Coldwater Canyon.

At each stop, Betty had reminiscences to share with everyone. "There was no house on this corner when we lived here," she said of the Doheny home. "We had all this land. And I can almost see little Jessie waving to me from that window—right up there." It went that way from place to place, and Betty was especially quiet when they paused at the tiny home at 257 Rodeo Drive. This was the home Betty bought for her mother in 1945. Lillian lived there snugly, among Betty's antiques, until her death in late 1964. The years were rolling past, gaining momentum as they went. It didn't seem as though eight years had passed since Lillian's death.

Betty must have seen a clear vision of her small mother with her misshapen hip, clip-clopping along lonely corridors with masked pain and iron determination, set on a mission of good for her young daughter. If there had ever been hate mixed with the love for her mother, it was not evident now. Tears came to Betty's eyes.

The tears were swept away quickly by a brush of the hand and a typical Grable-ese quip, but her friends were aware of her deeper feelings. They were also tuned into the significance of their experience. They were seeing, in an hour or two, the career of one of Hollywood's most coveted stars. It was a fleeting recapitulation of the whole story: the struggle from anonymity to recognition, from aspirant to star. They could sense the joys, the pain, the sorrow and the ecstasies. It was a moving journey through time, and more moving later when each of Betty's friends would realize that they were included in the final excursion into her past. Time for sentimental journeys was running out for Betty.

The Forty-Fourth Annual Academy Awards ceremonies were held at the Dorothy Chandler Pavilion of the Los Angeles Music Center April 10, 1972. Jack Lemmon was master of ceremonies, and the evening's highlight came with Charlie Chaplin's Honorary Oscar for his outstanding achievements in filmmaking. This came at the end of the program which awarded *The French Connection* for the Best Picture, to Gene Hackman for Best Actor, and to Jane Fonda for Best Actress.

Somewhere midpoint in the proceedings, Betty Grable and Dick Haymes were introduced to present the award for the Best Musical Score. It was Haymes who said, "And the winner is . . ." Betty fumbled with the envelope and, clearing the card, read, *Fiddler On the Roof.*

It was all over in minutes, but it was a long evening backstage in the mayhem of a progressing live television presentation in progress. Betty was clearly nervous as she paced in the back stage cavern—and beautiful, in her low cleavage, lamé gown, with its split up the front to reveal the "million dollar gams."

"I'm having a nicotine fit," she said to those near her and stepped out of the restricted area for a cigarette. Upon her return she seemed to be hyperventilating and mentioned a ponderous feeling in her chest. She passed it off as stage fright, panic, plain nervousness—whatever. She considered her personal diagnosis valid because, when her cue came to go on stage, she felt fine. No hint of nervousness was evident during her brief appearance, and the crowd was generous, as always, in applause.

The nervous energy kept Betty afloat following the program, and it wasn't until the long drive to Los Angeles International Airport that her earlier malaise erupted into a near seizure. She had difficulty breathing, and the heaviness returned to her solar plexus. Remick was alarmed and asked if they should find a doctor. The spasms abated by the time they reached the airport, and Betty was sure everything was fine. If she felt poorly in the morning, she would see a doctor, but she was sure that whatever it was had passed for the time being. She was tired, was all. All the excitement was taking its toll, and everything would be fine after a good night's rest.

Betty was certain everything was all right in the morning and could see no reason to visit a doctor, but Bob was insistent. There had to have been a reason for such incapacity the night before, and a doctor's examination would explain it. Betty finally agreed just to satisfy Bob, but was certain it would turn out to be a waste of time.

The appointment with the family physician was set for the following morning. In his office Betty explained the symptoms—severe dips in energy, heaviness in the chest, occasional sharp stabs of pain. There was a general examination and then x-rays. The doctor seemed to be spending an inordinate amount of time examining the x-rays, and Betty asked him about it. He smiled assuringly and told her there might be something there—what it was he couldn't be sure. He did, however, insist that Betty make an appointment with a specialist. It was only a precautionary measure, of course, but they had to be sure.

Betty was apprehensive now. She knew the doctor well and also knew when he was concerned. Despite the inconvenience, she agreed to return to the Los Angeles area to see Dr. Robert Kositchek. Chief of Staff at St. John's Hospital, Kositchek was a revered friend of the family. It was he who had treated Betty's mother, and he was the attending physician at the time of her death.

An appointment was made at St. John's, and Betty was admitted for tests. She was assigned a private room, and a nurse's aide helped her settle in. "May I help you hang up your lingerie, Mrs. James?" said the girl. Betty smiled, but assured the girl that a hospital gown would be fine for her. Later, in recounting the incident to Remick, she said, "Who the hell did she think I was, Joan Crawford?"

After the tests were underway, she called her sister Marjorie. "Guess where I am?" she said.

"Where?" said Marjorie.

"I'm at St. John's Hospital."

"You're where?"

Betty laughed. "Don't worry. I'm just here for some tests. I haven't been feeling too great lately and thought I'd better get it checked out. I'll be out of here in three or four days."

Marjorie said it was the next day that the doctor "dropped the bomb." He told Betty she was suffering from lung cancer.

# Chapter 27

Only Betty's closest friends were apprised of her illness, and as far as she was concerned the event wasn't of sufficient import to broadcast it more generally. She could accept that she had cancer, but there was no doubt in her mind that she would survive.

One of the friends was Steve Preston, who had danced with her in her nightclub act in better days. "I went to see her," he said, "and she was sitting up in bed looking beautiful. She was smoking, of course, and was still chewing on the ever-present Dunhill cigarette holder. I didn't ask what was wrong with her, but she eventually brought it up. 'It's interesting,' she said, 'how we always joked about smoking and lung cancer. Well, I've got it—I've got the big C.' "

Betty's prediction to her sister that she would be out of the hospital in a few days wasn't far off on this occasion. After the tests she was scheduled for chemotherapy and cobalt treatments, much of which could be administered on an out-patient basis. Her cancer was inoperable because it was in the center of her lungs. Had it been elsewhere, surgery might have checked it permanently. Now it was a matter of chance. The treatment could be successful, but the prognosis was negative. Betty was never told.

Bob and Betty were seeking a furnished apartment in the proximity of the hospital when friends invited her to stay in their guest house in Bel Air. It was charming and very private, and, although Betty was reluctant to accept the offer for fear she would be an imposition, she finally took them up on it. It worked out well. The weeks of treatment were grueling, but it helped to have a comfortable place to come home to. The cobalt caused constant aching in her chest, and nausea was a steady companion. Betty never complained.

When the treatments were completed, Betty and Bob returned to Las Vegas for a long convalescence. With the passage of time, Betty was more and more confident that her battle was being won. Remick recalls only one dip in her spirit during those months. They were watching a television drama on "Medical Center." "It was about a cancer victim who was taking morphine," said Bob. "It was losing its effects, and the patient was in agony. I glanced at Betty to see her reaction and caught her just as she was brushing a tear from her cheek. I think she knew even that early that the person on that screen could easily be her. Her spirits were always high otherwise. She knew she would beat it."

As her strength increased, Betty felt more like getting out of the house. She got in some putting practice at the golf club, and on one special occasion she and Bob attended the Desert Inn opening of the Debbie Reynolds Show.

"Betty could never say no to her fans," said Remick. "That was one of the reasons we seldom went out. After the show, Debbie stepped out and introduced Betty. The crowd immediately began to close in. There were twelve hundred people in the room, and most of them wanted a Betty Grable autograph. She was still signing her name forty-five minutes later, when somebody finally came out to escort her backstage to see Debbie. Betty always knew where her bread was buttered and was eternally grateful to her fans. I think she enjoyed giving out the autographs on this occasion. To know that she was still popular, with everything that was happening to her."

Betty was extremely disappointed and disturbed at having to cancel the tour to Australia. She had hundreds of fans there and in New Zealand. A large contingent of them had planned to travel to London to see her in *Belle Starr,* but the show had closed before they could get the trip organized. When that failed, and when Betty knew she would be going to Australia, she wrote to key members of the group to let them know about it. She felt terrible having to disappoint them again.

With autumn Betty was feeling so well she wondered if she had been hasty in canceling the Australian tour and actually made inquiries about the possibilities of reinstatement. Bob convinced her to wait a while, just to be sure. One thing was certain: Betty had had all the loafing she could handle. She was determined to go back to work. She contacted an agent who quickly found her a lucrative booking for *Born Yesterday.* It was a short-term run at the Alhambra Theatre in Jacksonville. She had never been more ready to go to work.

Although Bob Remick insists Betty was never suspicious that her condition was terminal, Betty Ritz Baez believes otherwise. Her belief is based on Betty's own comments. Betty Baez surprised Betty Grable by accepting her invitation to join her and Bob for Thanksgiving and flew to Las Vegas from Acapulco. Mike Levitt joined them also.

What motivated Betty Baez to make the trip was a letter written by Grable the previous August. It said in part:

> I was supposed to go and do *No, No, Nanette* in Australia for six months, however, I finally decided after all these years it might be a good idea to get a physical before I went, because I haven't been feeling well for a long time. Well, it's a good thing I did, cause my chest x-ray came back abnormal. Lucky me, just in time. Here I was with a big malignancy. Went to Dr. Kositchek, and he put me in St. John's Hospital in Santa Monica. Constant nausea for seven weeks, because of the cobalt treatment every day. I've been home for six weeks now, limp as a rag, and still taking medication, chemotherapy. It's been scary, but I think it might be

licked . . . I'm up to 137 pounds. Isn't that murder? I'm still with the damn pills, too. How about that, you and me sick at the same time, and with cortisone. God, wow, could we cut up touches about each other if we were ever together to discuss our illnesses . . . . God love Vicki, she wanted a girl so badly. Maybe next time. Jessie is fine, and came to see me a lot in the hospital. Sweetheart, I'm so glad you're over that really terrible time you went through, and if it's any comfort to you, I can't make the martini bit anymore either. How about us? I love you, and take care. . . . Always, Betty. P.S. Bob sends love and kisses.

When Betty Baez saw Betty, she found her looking fit enough, even though she was a bit plump from the cortisone. "She came running to open the door," she said. "She hugged me, and said, 'Oh, honey, wait 'til you see what they've done to me.' We were both in tears, and she showed me the biopsy scar along her shoulder. We had a wonderful two days and talked for hours. Thanksgiving night, after dinner, Bob and Mikey were in watching television, and we sat in front of the roaring fire. She said, 'You know, this is really it. I'm not going to be here much longer.' She said I shouldn't feel bad about it, because she didn't. She even made a joke about it. She said her greatest regret was that the doctor had restricted her to a single martini before dinner, and she really loved her martinis.

"It reminded me of the time she had a cyst removed from her cheek when she was making *Beautiful Blonde From Bashful Bend.* She said, 'Now, don't make me laugh—I had surgery today.' She would exaggerate just to make people laugh. Betty hadn't lost her sense of humor that last Thanksgiving of her life. She was facing death, but acted as though it was no more serious than the time the cyst was removed. I'll always admire her for that.

"On the day I left, when Bob drove me to the airport, I knew it would be the last time I was going to see Betty alive. I made her promise to call if anything happened, or if she needed anything. But I knew she would never call, especially if things weren't going well. She would want me to remember her the way she was then.

"I heard from Betty the following February. She sent a card from Jacksonville. It said, simply, 'It's sure good to be busy again, and I feel much better too since I'm finally doing something.' A few months later I would hear her voice for the last time."

*Born Yesterday* opened at the Alhambra Dinner Theatre on January 24, 1973, and closed in mid-March after the four week extension. During the run of the play, Betty felt good enough to agree to a later booking in Tampa, but that was before her energy began to fade and prior to the increasing pains in her stomach.

She called her sister, Marjorie, after the pain had become severe. "She told me she was in absolute agony," said Marjorie. "I was alarmed and asked if I should call Dr. Kositchek. Betty said she could call a doctor herself, because she was seeing a doctor each week in Jacksonville, but they weren't of any help. She said that the minute she set foot on stage she was fine. But then when she got back to the apartment, she would be walking the floors all night."

Betty felt certain a rest would put her back in good order, but shortly after her return to Las Vegas she knew she was in for another visit to St. John's. The pains continued and were becoming unbearable.

Her second admittance to the hospital resulted in major abdominal surgery. The cancer in her lungs had cleared up entirely by this time, so, in a sense, the chemotherapy had been successful, but the cancer had changed location. Now it had spread throughout her entire body. A very large tumor was removed from her stomach, and it was discovered that cancer cells had even reached into her brain. There would be no brain damage, but there was no way to deal with it either. It was simply a matter of time.

# Chapter 28

If Betty was the darling of the common worker during her contract days at Twentieth Century-Fox, she was now the model patient at St. John's Hospital. She asked for no special privileges, and was timid when it came to the simplest requests. She was the same rather diffident young woman who was willing to stand in the snow at Basin Street East to get in to see Harry James.

After surgery Betty was trussed up with sutures and clamps, and it was a major undertaking to lift herself out of bed. Once, when she felt the need to go to the nearby bathroom, she didn't want to ring for assistance for this trivial task. She tried to make it on her own, failed, and had to seek help. In her struggle to manage the matter alone, she had a typical Betty Grable accident: she wet herself—and all the sheets.

Betty was in tears when the aide answered the call and was abject in her embarrassment. After she had been helped to the lavatory and the sheets had been changed, Betty said to the girl, "Just you remember, now. If you ever wet the bed, call me and

I'll come to your house and change the sheets." This was Betty's way: the imperative to turn adversity into humor.

There were few moments, however, when Betty was alone. Her days were almost entirely filled by Marjorie's and Bob's company. They had admittance passes for any hour, day or night. Betty's second hospital confinement lasted seven weeks, and during that time Marjorie missed only five days. Marjorie was not entirely healthy herself. With osteoporosis and arthritis, she required a walker for ambulation—yet she was always on hand to care for her loving younger sister.

Marjorie was with Betty a great deal, but Bob Remick was there almost twenty hours a day. He frequently shuttled back and forth to Las Vegas upon Betty's command, mostly to make sure the dogs were well cared for. What demands Betty shielded from hospital personnel, were thrust less timidly upon Remick.

"She didn't give that poor boy a minute's rest," said Marjorie. "She wanted to know if he had done this or attended to that. It was always something. Maybe she needed a whipping boy, and darling Bob was it. She was on him all the time, and you would never find a more totally devoted person anywhere. The James family owes him a great deal. I hope they realize it—I know I do. If Betty wanted him to sit up all night and hold her hand, hold her hand he did. She had only to say it, and he would do it."

There were a couple of sources of extreme aggravation to Betty during her hospitalization. The least serious involved the producers for the Australian tour of *No, No Nanette.* They didn't believe Betty was too ill to honor her contract and suspected she merely wanted to renege on the deal as so many Hollywood stars were wont to do. Just the fact that they suspected such a motive disturbed Betty greatly. She could hardly blame the men, because the tour had been sold out for months, and they stood to lose a small fortune.

They made a special trip to Los Angeles to check out Betty's story and were satisfied it was true. But this didn't satisfy Betty. It was on her mind when Cyd Charisse came to the hospital to visit, and Betty mentioned it to her. She had only to bring it up to be offered a solution. Cyd would gladly substitute for Betty and would see that her husband, Tony Martin, was included in the bargain. The proposal was offered to the Australians and accepted. That ended one source of Betty's consternation, but the other matter was not so easily remedied.

In her syndicated column, Joyce Haber announced to the world that Betty Grable was dying of cancer. Betty's loved ones tried everything possible to keep it from her, but it was impossible. Phone calls started coming in, and then came letters—hundreds of them. But it was a call from her friend Betty Ritz Baez that first brought the matter to Betty's attention. Baez read the column in a Mexican newspaper and called at once. It was Betty who had to reassure her concerned pal that the news was entirely without foundation. She said she would have called had her condition changed.

Betty was deeply depressed for a few days. Perhaps the fact that it was stated so emphatically added impact to something she already knew, or maybe she didn't really believe she was going to die, but the published information was a source of severe upset to Betty, and she put it into words when she spoke with her friend Jim Bacon, movie columnist for the *Los Angeles Herald Examiner.*

"You know," she told him, "until I read that, I thought I was doing fine."

Whatever Betty's deeper feelings may have been during this trying time, she expressed them to no one. It could have been that she really did believe she would win her battle—at least until she had the surgery—and perhaps the newspaper item helped establish her doubts. But her spirits would rise once more.

What Joyce Haber said in print, everyone close to Betty had known for some time. The only affirmative goals now were to keep her as comfortable as possible, and Dr. Kositchek promised that Betty would not suffer needless pain. Each time the pain became intolerable, Betty would press the buzzer. Then, with the appearance of the nurse, Betty would ask with a guilty smile: "Could I have a fix, please?" She would get it at once.

There were good days and poor ones. Some days Betty

would want no company other than Marjorie and Bob. "I could tell when Betty was feeling good," Marjorie said. "If she put on the eyelashes, that meant she felt up to having visitors." Among Betty's frequent visitors was her daughter Jessica, who then lived in the Los Angeles area with her daughters.

"My mother and I got very close while she was in the hospital," Jessie said. "We started to come together when I was about twenty-three. We weren't really alienated before, but I hadn't yet learned to like her. I didn't understand what she had been going through before then, and I had plenty of my own problems when I was young.

"Bob Remick practically saved my mother's life, because when she went through the divorce, her mother's dying, and my leaving home, he came into her life. At first, I was afraid he might have been using her, but I soon realized he wasn't, and I thought it was great."

During these long, warm visits, Betty finally was able to tell her daughter that she envied her independent spirit, that she was strong enough to strike out on her own. She confessed that she had never been able to do what she wanted. Jessie said she finally realized that her mother never really knew who she, Betty, was. Betty was always there for somebody else.

Jessie had had very few birthday celebrations as a child. She had felt neglected and unloved as she was growing up. Now as an adult her affinity for her mother, which had always been there just beneath the surface, finally sprang to life. Betty became loving and warm. She was finally able to express her love in simple terms. She asked her daughter for understanding for past failures. And on Jessica's twenty-sixth birthday—May 20, 1973—she gave her a surprise party in the hospital room. Marjorie brought in a cake, and Jessica's children, Kelly, nine, and Scott, eight, were given hospital permission to come to the room to see their grandmother.

"Mom gave me a hundred dollars," Jessie said, "and I didn't want to take it. Mom said, 'Look, I haven't much time left, and I should be able to give you whatever I want to.' "

But it wasn't the money that made Jessica happiest. It was

the feeling of love and the closeness she finally realized with her mother. Despite the reality of approaching death, this birthday would be one of the most memorable and happiest of Jessica's life. It was late—but not too late to become acquainted with, and to learn to love, her mother.

Dozens of Betty's friends called, and, depending on her mood and physical well-being, she either received them or put them off. She was extremely conscious of her appearance. First there was the plumpness from the cortisone, which upset her, but later, when her weight began to plummet sharply, it was much worse. Max Showalter called, and she denied his visit with assurances that she would only be hospitalized a few days, that everything was fine. Dan Dailey visited her early on and called many times afterward, but Betty did not want to see him. Rather, she didn't want him to see her. There was no one she enjoyed visiting with more than Dan, but her vanity simply would not permit it. She always wanted to look her best for him.

Mike Levitt was the third person, after Marjorie and Bob, to have carte blanche visiting rights, and his visits from Chicago were the source of great comfort to Betty. He had indeed become one of her dearest friends, and surely one of the most loyal.

By the time Mike started paying frequent visits, Betty's mail was arriving by the truckload. She received hundreds of letters each day, and much of her time was spent reading them. She became almost possessive about her daily mail, and it was with some reluctance that she shared the fun of reading. Soon, however, the task became so great she was forced to pass the mail around. It was Mike Levitt who was usually delegated to come up with the daily count. "How many today?" Betty would ask.

"Almost eight hundred," he replied on a record day.

Betty was excited the next day when the count was being made. "How many today?" she asked when the task was completed.

"Seven hundred and thirty," Mikey replied.

"How quickly they forget," Betty sighed, in her inimitable way.

Levitt, himself a hairdresser, was always aware of Betty's

deficiencies in that regard. "She always had kinky, unattractive hair," he said, "and would cover it up with any number of turban-type hats. The chemotherapy was the coup de grace. When she ran a comb through her hair, it would come out by the handfuls. She didn't make a big thing of it, though. She was able to kid about it."

Betty, fortunately, possessed the faculty for turning almost anything into a joke, which helped her immensely during her hospital confinement and made it infinitely easier for those attending her.

Mikey was in the room one day when a nurse was helping Betty into the lavatory. Betty became concerned about the backless hospital gown and, while attempting to pull it together, said to Mikey, "Bet you never thought you'd be seeing this much of me, did you?"

"Come on, don't worry about that," said Mikey.

The nurse interjected. "Don't worry, Mrs. James, nobody's looking."

"They would have once," Betty retorted.

Marjorie remembered a morning when she had been up late the night before to watch *My Blue Heaven* on television. "When the movie started," Marjorie said to Betty, "and you were singing "My Blue Heaven," I just couldn't help crying."

"That bad, eh?" said Betty.

# Chapter 29

Betty entered a plateau of apparent well-being and rallied to the point of ambulation. The operation incisions had healed, and she wanted to get out of the hospital, to go home. She had been constantly worried about Elva and Kato, the dogs, and longed for familiar surroundings. The doctor agreed. If she wanted to go home, and as long as she was comfortable, why not? Bob arranged for a private plane to transport her to Las Vegas.

As Betty was helped from the wheelchair to the taxi, she tried to stand on her own, but failed. Secure inside the cab, she joked about it. "These million dollar legs won't even hold me up," she laughed.

The driver was silent throughout the trip to the airport, but, when they reached their destination, he leaned over the back seat. "Miss Grable," he said, obviously choked up, "I have to say this to you. You've given me some of the greatest joys of my life—God bless you."

The message, short and sweet, made Betty's day.

Remick hired a nurse to minister to Betty, but it didn't work out. "Just my luck," said Betty, when the girl's mistakes became too obvious to be ignored, "I'm the girl's first job."

Bob took on the nursing chores, but the young nurse's residue remained. She had fluffed up cushions for Betty to rest on, but they happened to be the dogs' cushions. Periodically Betty would complain good-naturedly, "I'm still sucking up dog hair."

For a brief term Betty's homecoming was second only to pure ecstasy. It was so fulfilling to see her beloved animals, to be able to have breakfast on a sun-drenched patio, to see the irrigated expanses of rolling fairways, to be able to visit with her pals in the old neighborhood. It seemed as though she had been away for eons.

It was subtle at first, but there was no question that Betty was slowly beginning to fail. She was becoming more and more dependent on morphine as the pain returned, and her weight began to diminish rapidly. She would try to eat, but the food refused to stay down. It reached a point where she was practically existing on medication and the water used to wash it down. But she kept looking ahead; it was essential to set goals. She talked of what they would do when she was well, the trips they would take, the adventures she had thought about—dreamed about—but never embarked upon. The date of July 4 bloomed in brightness on her now limited horizon. It towered in front of her as a kind of milestone.

"Call Mikey," she asked Bob excitedly. "Ask him to join us on the Fourth of July. Now, don't take no for an answer—he absolutely has to come. It'll be just like old times."

The call was made, and Mikey promised he would be there without fail. He spoke briefly with Betty and was pleased at how well she sounded. It would be like old times for him, too, to be with his dear friends over a holiday. He was looking forward to it.

The weeks passed, and toward the end of June Levitt made his reservations for Las Vegas. He called Betty's number on Thursday June 28 to advise Bob the time of his arrival the following Tuesday, July 3. It was Remick who answered the phone, and, before Mikey could explain his call, Bob said he was just getting ready to call *him.* The Fourth of July get-together had to be canceled.

At that moment Remick was rigging a friend's camper to transport Betty back to St. John's Hospital. If there was to be a reunion, it would have to take place in Betty's hospital room. Mike asked no questions, in case Betty was listening in on the extension. Instead he accepted the change in plans cheerfully and said he would change his reservation for Los Angeles, and would see both of them there.

Betty's mode of transportation to Santa Monica became a major dilemma. Her pain was so great the chartered aircraft was out of the question. She would have to sit up, and Betty simply wasn't capable of doing so. It would have been possible to arrange for comfortable accommodation in the first class section of a passenger jet, but not total privacy. Betty could not have sympathetic fans gazing at her; Bob refused to allow that. He knew that Betty would just as soon die as have her fans see her the way she looked now. He finally devised a plan of outfitting a camper with a hospital bed, and their mutual friend Bob Blattin had such a vehicle. Blattin, who had been Betty's hairdresser throughout the run in *Hello Dolly* was more than happy to volunteer the vehicle and his own services. The two Bobs boarded Betty into the bed of the van and alternated as drivers in the long midnight journey westward over the Mojave. Betty was checked into the hospital just past dawn on Friday June 29.

Mike Levitt's initial intention was to join them in Santa Monica on July 3, but a curious compulsion drew him to the telephone on July 2 to inquire about flights to Los Angeles. He was told a flight was leaving within the hour, and Mike booked passage. He packed a pair of jeans and, for no logical reason, his navy blue suit.

Both daughters and sister Marjorie had been summoned that day by Remick, and he attempted to call Levitt, who, unknown to Bob at the time, was en route to Los Angeles. Betty had little time left.

Betty was fading in and out of consciousness throughout the

day, and while she was conscious she could seem quite robust, at least in spirit, and was surprisingly sentient. She greeted everyone warmly and didn't seem alarmed by their collective presence. The brief conversational subjects were trivial, small talk topics, no talk of death or pain.

As Marjorie watched her sister's emaciated form, something registered: though the upper part of Betty's body had wasted away literally to skin and bone, below the waist there remained almost intact the million-dollar legs. Daughter Jessica looked at her mother's hands to find something of the former identity. "Her hands hadn't changed," said Jessica. "They were still mother's hands."

And it was Remick who clutched Betty's hands and had done so for endless hours, both as she slept and during her brief moments of wakefulness. He left her side for only a moment at 3:30 P.M. when he saw Mike Levitt outside the door. He wanted to intercept him before he entered the room.

"You haven't seen Betty in a little while," Bob told Mikey, "and I had to prepare you. Betty's changed—changed a lot."

Mike entered the room and studied the figure in the bed. He would never have recognized her. Her tiny nose seemed huge now, because there was no flesh remaining on her cheeks. She looked almost skeletal.

Daughter Victoria saw Betty's eyes flutter. "Mother," she said. "Look who's here."

Betty's eyes swept the faces and managed a smile. "Oh, Mikey," she whispered. "Mikey, you're here."

Betty tried her best to give Mikey's hand a squeeze, but little strength remained. Bob gathered her hands again into his own, and the vigil continued. There would be a few words, sleep, and once Betty became quite alert. "Where is everybody?" she questioned.

"We're still here," Bob replied.

"Marjorie isn't here," she said.

"Yes I am. I'm right here," Marjorie assured her.

With a smile fluttering, she drifted off again. The nurse appeared to take Betty's pulse and straightened. All she managed to say was, "Excuse me," and she walked rapidly out of the room.

Bob knew then. He saw tears in the nurse's eyes, and, although she didn't announce it, Bob knew that Betty had died. He gathered everyone together and ushered them through the door and into the corridor. The end had come.

# Chapter 30

The nurse who so abruptly excused herself from Betty's hospital room at the moment of her death did it because she had no other choice. Had she stayed a second longer, she would have given in to uncontrolled sobs. In a letter written to Marjorie several days later, she apologized profusely. "I know it wasn't professional of me to break down like that," she said, "but I had been a Betty Grable fan for so many years, and then finally getting to meet her, and then having to watch her die. It was just too much for me."

How fitting it was that one of those most anguished at the time of Betty's final curtain would be a fan, a total stranger. Only a few knew Betty Grable closely, but there were legions who knew and loved her from afar. Betty Grable belonged as much to this practical nurse as she did to her own family and friends. When Betty's spirit drifted out of that antiseptic hospital room, she was probably smiling.

The time of death was 5:15 P.M. July 2, 1973. The Fourth of July passed without the celebration for which Betty had hoped.

The funeral was held the following day at All Saints Episcopal Church in Beverly Hills. There were about 600 mourners in all, including family, friends, and fans. Both ex-husbands were there, Jackie Coogan and Harry James; George Raft was too ill at the time to make it. All family members were present as well as the man who loved Betty more than almost anyone, Bob Remick. As Mikey Levitt dressed for the one o'clock services, he knew why he had packed the navy suit.

Among the stars paying respect were Alice Faye, Dorothy Lamour, Mitzie Gaynor, June Haver, and Dan Dailey. Red carnations, Betty's favorite flower, were everywhere. Most noticed among the selections played on the chapel organ was "I Had the Craziest Dream."

The song must have struck a particularly poignant chord for Harry James. It was originally sung in 1942 in *Springtime in the Rockies,* when Betty and Harry worked together for the first time. She introduced the song, and he and his band had kept it alive through the years. Harry sat with his daughters during the services. Afterward, on his way out of the chapel, he turned to his former sister-in-law Marjorie Arnold. "You know," he said, "today is our thirtieth wedding anniversary."

During Betty's final days Harry was appearing with his orchestra in nearby Anaheim. Had she been aware of it, Betty would have surely attended had it been possible, because until the end she remained Harry's greatest fan. Betty had always been proud of Harry, and her love for him never died.

There were detractors on hand, those who insisted the funeral was tasteless and unworthy of Betty's memory, but what can be said properly in final tribute to a person as revered as Betty Grable? She was gone, and the final services were an anticlimax.

Harry James was quoted as saying to reporters, "If she were here I could tell you a hundred memories. We had a wonderful life. But right now, I don't feel free to discuss the little gal."

Hugh O'Brien, who worked with her in a road company of *Guys and Dolls* said: "She could have done more good in New York Harbor than the Statue of Liberty."

Dan Dailey recalled that "She was always fun—a great professional, vital and alive with the best sense of humor I've ever heard from anyone, anywhere. I always felt I owed her my career. I miss her already."

Betty once did a guest appearance on a Perry Como television show. When they showed her a script and described what she was expected to do, Betty was quoted as saying, "It's loud, it's cheap, it's gaudy. It's like everything I've ever done—I LOVE IT!"

The *Daily Variety* obituary recalled Betty's response to being named the year's worst actress by the *Harvard Lampoon.* Her responding wire read: "You're so right."

That was Betty Grable. She was a simple girl from St. Louis with obedience toward her mother and high morals. She was rowdy and ribald and fast with a quip, but that was with the gang or on the set. At home, her children never heard a four-letter word stronger than "damn." She was a person of many facets, with something for everybody. Even her life was a succession of acting roles. In the process of living out her various roles, the real Betty Grable sometimes became clouded, hard to find. But no one had more trouble finding who she was, than Betty herself. She was funny, she was kind; she was strict and sometimes cruel. She was the life of the party, who could storm out only moments after wearing the lamp shade. She would shower her friends with gifts, to accuse them later of using her. But, despite her paradoxical qualities, her goodness prevailed. And she was loved.

She always deferred to other female stars, insisting they were the *real* stars, and that she was something of an imposter. It wasn't true at all, but perhaps she believed it because personal ambition was missing. She was pushed and somehow caught on, but she always considered it something of an accident. Her mother told her she was special, but the only way Betty considered herself special was that other kids went on family vacations and had birthday parties, and she didn't.

Betty needed to be loved and always had doubts that others did indeed love her. She seemed most insecure with those who mattered most, and in her self-doubt she often treated them worse than anyone else. There were great loves in her life, and the last was certainly not the least. No one ever could have loved Betty more than Bob Remick, and he proved it through the very end.

If Betty had demanded less of his attention, Remick might have developed more of his ready talents. He was a fine dancer and a competent photographer. But Betty wanted Bob at her side—always. She would have him signed on as road manager or whatever nondescript title was available on her tours, but it amounted to a device to keep him close at hand. He went through his life savings during the seven and a half years he lived with Betty and ended up with what he wore on his back and carried in his pockets. Some states demand community property for a common law union of this length, but Nevada is not one of them.

While Betty was hospitalized, her manager spoke to her about drawing up a will, but nothing further came of it. When she and Bob traveled to London, she scribbled out a directive that would leave all her possessions to her daughters in the event of her death. This crude document was what turned up after Betty's death.

After the funeral, when Bob returned to the home he had shared with Betty in Las Vegas, he found all the furniture, paintings, and other possessions and valuables stacked up in the middle of the living room floor—a result of Victoria's inventory. She had been advised that, when property goes into probate, items tend to disappear. Bob didn't object to the inventory, recognizing it as common procedure, but they—Victoria and her husband—had disrupted *his* home. He lived there too. He asked that the items be returned to their proper places and that they remain there until he was able to find another home. He remained a few months longer, until the house was sold back to the Tropicana Hotel, and then found an apartment of his own. The house was sold for $125,000.

Marjorie Arnold said the daughters had intended to give Bob the Mercedes SL with license plate ERG. But, as it turned out, the car represented the only available cash, of which plenty was needed. "That took care of that," Marjorie said. "I was disappointed, because it would have been a nice thing to do."

Betty's hospital expenses were huge, and there was the ever-present IRS to deal with. "Everything had to be sold," said Jessica. "We were lucky with the personal debts, because one woman she owed money to only claimed half of it, but even then it amounted to about sixteen thousand dollars. The markers in the gambling casinos must have all been written off."

There are friends of Betty's who insist she would have been extremely well-off at the time of her death, had it not been for paying off Harry's back taxes and gambling debts, totaling nearly half a million dollars. As it turned out, the estate was almost nonexistent. Daughter Jessica says her inheritance came to $11,000, a miniscule amount in light of the millions Betty earned. She is said to have made more than five million dollars during the forties and early fifties.

The horses cost them heavily—no matter how Betty defended their ownership—and Betty wasn't far behind Harry when it came to gambling losses; both were naive in business acumen. What may have mattered more than any of this was their misplaced trust in the self-acclaimed business geniuses who handled their tax matters. Betty had competent advisers during the latter years, but it was too late then. Their fortunes had dwindled.

Gambling was one of Betty's major failings, unless it was the ultimate gamble on which she was judged: the gamble of life itself. If it were there that judgments were made, then Betty was a winner all the way. When it came to living, Betty Grable hit the million dollar jackpot.

Following are the lyrics to a song recorded in 1974 by Neil Sedaka. It was written by Sedaka and Howard Greenfield.

*BETTY GRABLE*

When I Used To Be a Little Kid I Used To Go
Every Saturday Afternoon To the Picture Show.

Close Up To the Screen My Life Was So Serene.
I Lived Thru Ev'ry Scene With My Movie Queen
. . . Betty Grable.

Three Hundred Howling Kids Would Always Pack the House
But They Just Came For Donald Duck and Mickey Mouse.
But There Would Be a World Of Fantasy Wrapped In the Melody
She Sang and Danced For Me
. . . Betty Grable.

Lots and Lots of Pin-Up Shots, I Had 'Em All
And There They Were Pasted up Upon the Wall.
When Mama Said That It Was Time For Bed
I'd Eat Some Jam and Bread And Watch Her Overhead
. . . Betty Grable.

Just the Other Night I Saw Her On Some Late Late Show
And It Occurred To Me I'm Someone That She'll Never Know.
So I Wrote This Little Song For the Lady I've Loved So Long
. . . Betty Grable!

# epilogue

Not long after Betty's death, her sister Marjorie and husband Dave sold their Bel Air home, and packed as many belongings as possible into a pleasant retirement condominium in Laguna Hills, about sixty miles south of Los Angeles. With assistance from a part-time maid, Marjorie cared for the household with courage and good spirits, often relying heavily on the Grable sense of humor to carry the day. Although in failing health, she managed to look after Dave, who for the most part was bedridden. A few days prior to Thanksgiving 1980, Marjorie died of a stroke. She was seventy-two.

In recent years, Jackie Coogan also suffered a stroke, but he is fully recovered. He works occasionally in movie and television character roles but is essentially retired. He did finally come into his inheritance at the death of his mother a few years ago. Upon her death, the corporate holding company went into a trust that amounts to about $500,000. Jackie will receive its annual interest as long as he lives.

During his latter years, George Raft held down a steady job—or perhaps a sinecure—for Riviera Hotel Reservations in Beverly Hills. He served in a public relations capacity for the Las Vegas organization. Toward the end he was in and out of hospitals and away from his desk much of the time. His wife, the former Grayce Mulrooney, died several years ago still carrying the name Mrs. George Raft; George himself died on November 24, 1980, of leukemia at age eighty-five. He had been chronically ill with emphysema for several years. Shortly before his death he asserted once more that Betty Grable was the only girl he ever really loved.

Harry James's ex-wife, Joan, has custody of the teenage son who resulted from their rather brief marriage. Harry owns homes in Las Vegas and Carlsbad, California, where he enjoys playing golf. He still plans his road tours and concerts to permit attendance of the racing meets at the Del Mar Race Track. Although past Social Security retirement age, Harry's lip remains intact, and he tours the country on frequent big band concert engagements.

Dan Dailey, who survived Betty by five years, had attained substantial wealth before his death October 16, 1978, but he was not a happy man. While attending high school in Long Island, Dan's shin bone had been crushed and his leg muscles severely damaged in a football scrimmage. There was some doubt at the time about his full recovery, but he was dancing in burlesque only a few years later. Dan was injured again in 1977, when he fell from the stage in Raleigh, North Carolina, where he was playing in *The Odd Couple.* A broken hip and later complications, reduced Dailey to invalidism. His right leg was an inch shorter than the left, and this infirmity made him a recluse. He was too proud to be seen in public in this condition, and was drinking heavily. His cause of death was listed as anemia.

Max Showalter was in Rome when he learned of Betty's death. He was approaching a TWA ticket counter to buy a ticket home when a newspaper front page caught his attention. It carried Betty's picture. The headline read: MORT. "It hit me like a hammer in the pit of my stomach," he said. "My legs gave way from under me, and I sank down to my knees. I didn't really know she was that ill."

Betty's daughter Jessica now lives in Oregon, where she recently began a hospital career as a respiratory therapist. Though she hasn't seen Harry since her mother's funeral, her father provided financial assistance during her three years of training for the position. Jessie takes special care of her teenage son and daughter, and is content without current romantic involvement and has no interest in moving closer to the bright lights of Hollywood or Las Vegas.

Victoria Elizabeth resides in a comfortable suburb of Detroit, Michigan, with her husband and one remaining child. The younger son suffered a congenital illness and succumbed to it a few years ago. Harry, despite his aversion to hospitals, did visit his grandson during his confinement with the illness. Vicki and her father keep in rather close touch, and he manages to pay occasional visits to her and her family when his travels bring him into her vicinity.

Bob Remick remained in Las Vegas. Through friends he made during his relationship with Betty, he was able to enroll in croupier school and is now employed as a dealer at one of the casinos on the Las Vegas Strip. He is married and recently became the father of a baby boy. Betty's surviving dogs, Elsa and Kato, have been integrated into the new Remick household, and are finding life almost as enjoyable as when Betty was alive—*almost.*

# BETTY GRABLE MOVIES

**LET'S GO PLACES.** (1930 Fox) Betty is a chorus girl. Director: Frank Strayer. Cast: Lola Lane, Sharon Lynn, Frank Richardson, Walter Catlett, Dixie Lee (who would marry Bing Crosby in 1935), Charles Judeis, Ilka Chase, Larry Steers, Betty Grable.

**NEW MOVIETONE FOLLIES OF 1930.** (1930 Fox) Betty is again in the chorus. Director: Benjamin Stoloff. Cast: El Brendel, Marjorie White, Frank Richardson, Noel Francis, William Collier, Jr., Miriam Seegar, Huntley Gordon, Paul Nicholson, Yola D'Avril, Betty Grable.

**WHOOPEE.** (1930 Goldwyn-United Artists) Betty is a chorus girl, elevated by title to "Goldwyn Girl." Director: Thornton Freeland. Cast: Eddie Cantor, Sally Morgan, Paul Gregory, Jack Rutherford, Ethel Shutta, Spencer Charters, Chief Caupolican, Albert Hackett, Will Philbrick, Walter Law, Marian Marsh, Barbara Weeks, The George Olsen Band, Betty Grable. Hit songs: "Whoopee," "My Baby Just Cares For Me."

**KIKI.** (1931 United Artists) Grable is just another face in the crowd. Director: Sam Taylor. Cast: Mary Pickford, Reginald Denny, Joseph

Cawthorn, Margaret Livingston, Phil Tead, Fred Walton, Betty Grable.

**PALMY DAYS.** (1931 United Artists) Betty resumes her work as a Goldwyn Girl. Director: A. Edward Sutherland. Cast: Eddie Cantor, Charlotte Greenwood, Spencer Charters, Barbara Weeks, George Raft (his fourth small film role after three years in Hollywood), Paul Page, Harry Woods, Charles B. Middleton, Betty Grable. Songs: "Bend Down, Sister," "My Baby Said Yes, Yes," "There's Nothing Too Good For My Baby."

**THE GREEKS HAD A WORD FOR THEM.** (1932 United Artists) Betty shows off a sexy evening gown by Chanel. Director: Lowell Sherman. Cast: Madge Evans, Joan Blondell, Ina Claire, David Manners, Phillips Smalley, Sidney Bracey, Betty Grable.

**THE KID FROM SPAIN.** (1932 United Artists) Betty is a Goldwyn Girl for the last time. Director: Leo McCarey. Cast: Eddie Cantor, Lyda Roberti, Robert Young, Ruth Hall, John Miljan, Noah Beery, J. Carroll Naish, Robert Emmett O'Connor, Stanley Fields, Paul Porcasi, Walter Walker, Julian Rivero, Theresa Maxwell Conover, Ben Hendricks, Jr. Paulette Goddard and Toby Wing (Jackie Coogan's first love) are also Goldwyn Girls along with Grable. Songs: "In the Moonlight," "Look What You've Done," "What a Perfect Combination."

**CHILD OF MANHATTAN.** (1932 Columbia) Betty gets seventh billing in role of Lucy. Director: Eddie Buzzell. Cast: Nancy Carroll, John Boles, Warburton Gamble, Clara Blandick, Jane Darwell, Gary Owen, Betty Grable, Luis Alberni, Jessie Ralph, Charles Jones, Tyler Brooke, Betty Kendell.

**HOLD 'EM JAIL.** (1932 RKO) Betty plays a principal part as the daughter of the warden in this screenplay written by S.J. Perelman. Director: Norman Taurog. Cast: Bert Wheeler and Robert Woolsey, Edgar Kennedy, Betty Grable, Edna May Oliver, Roscoe Ates, Paul Hurst, Warren Hymer, Robert Armstrong, John Sheehan, Jed Prouty, Spencer Charters, Monty Banks, Lee Phelps, Ernie Adams, Monte Collins, Ben Taggart.

**PROBATION.** (1932 Chesterfield) Betty moves up in billing to fifth place in this straight role. Director: Richard Thorpe. Cast: Sally Blane,

J. Farrell MacDonald, Eddie Phillips, Clara Kimball Young, Betty Grable, David Rollins, Mary Jane Irving, Matty Kemp, David Durand.

**CAVALCADE.** (1933 Fox) Betty drops in stature to "Girl On Couch" in this Noel Coward, Academy-Award-winning screenplay. Director: Frank Lloyd. Huge cast is headed by Clive Brook and Diana Wynyard. Ten-year-old Bonita Granville makes her film debut.

**SWEETHEART OF SIGMA CHI.** (1933 Monogram) Betty sneaks into this one as a member of the Ted Fio Rito orchestra. The male singer in the band is Leif Erickson, who goes on to bigger roles in movies. Director: Edwin I. Marin. Cast: Mary Carlisle, Buster Crabbe, Charles Starret, Florence Lake, Eddie Tamblyn, Sally Starr, Mary Blackford, Tom Dugan, Burr McIntosh, Major Goodsell, Grady Sutton, The Ted Fio Rito Orchestra. Songs: "Fraternity Walk," "It's Spring Again."

**MELODY CRUISE.** (1933 RKO) Betty lands the role of a stewardess in this mild musical. Director: Mark Sandrich. Cast: Charlie Ruggles, Phil Harris, Greta Nissen, Helen Mack, Chick Chandler, Jane Brewster, Florence Roberts, Marjorie Gateson, Betty Grable. Songs: "I Met Her At a Party," "He's Not the Marrying Kind," "This Is the Hour," "Isn't This a Night For Love."

**WHAT PRICE INNOCENCE.** (1933 Columbia) Betty is Jean Parker's pal in this juvenile message drama. Director: Willard Mack. Cast: Willard Mack, Jean Parker, Betty Grable, Bryant Washburn, Ben Alexander, Beatrice Banyard, Louise Beavers.

**BY YOUR LEAVE.** (1934 RKO) It's eighth billing for Grable in a straight role. Director: Lloyd Corrigan. Cast: Frank Morgan, Genevieve Tobin, Neil Hamilton, Marian Nixon, Glenn Anders, Gene Lockhart, Margaret Hamilton, Betty Grable, Lona Andre, Charles Ray.

**STUDENT TOUR.** (1934 MGM) Betty is billed eighth in her first "Betty Coed" role. Director: Charles Reisner. Cast: Jimmy Durante, Charles Butterworth, Maxine Doyle, Phil Regan, Florence McKinney, Douglas Fowley, Monte Blue, Betty Grable, Fay McKenzie, Bobby Gordon, Mary Loos, Pauline Brooks, Bruce Bennett, Nelson Eddie, Mischa Auer, Arthur Hoyt, Dave O'Brien. Songs: "A New Moon Is

Over My Shoulder," "The Carlo," "Snake Dance," "The Taj Mahal," "From Now On," "Fight 'Em," "I Say It With Music."

**THE GAY DIVORCEE.** (1934 RKO) Betty is billed sixth and is given a featured dance number, "Let's K-knock K-nees," with Edward Everett Horton. Director: Mark Sandrich. Cast: Fred Astaire, Ginger Rogers, Alice Brady, Edward Everett Horton, Erik Rhodes, Betty Grable, Charles Coleman, William Austin, Lillian Miles, George Davis, Alphonse Martell, E.E. Clive, Paul Porcasi, Charles Hall. Songs: "Looking For a Needle In a Haystack," "The Continental," "Don't Let It Bother You," "Let's K-nock K-nees," "Night and Day."

**THE NITWITS.** (1935 RKO) Betty is a comedy murder suspect and receives third billing. Director: George Stevens. Cast: Bert Wheeler and Robert Woolsey, Fred Keating, Betty Grable, Evelyn Brent, Erik Rhodes, Hale Hamilton, Charles Wilson, Arthur Aylesworth, Willie Best, Lew Kelley, Dorothy Granger.

**OLD MAN RHYTHM.** (1935 RKO) Betty does her coed routine, but gets to know Hermes Pan with whom she will work many times in the future. Director: Edward Ludwig. Cast: Charles "Buddy" Rogers, George Barbier, Barbara Kent, Grace Bradley, Betty Grable, Eric Blore, Erik Rhodes, John Arledge, Johnny Mercer, Donald Meek, Dave Chasen, Joy Hodges, Douglas Fowley, Evelyn Poe, Margaret Nearing, Ronald Graham, Sonny Lamont, William Carey, Lucille Ball, Marian Darling, Jane Hamilton, Maxine Jennings, Kay Sutton, Jack Thomas, Erich Von Stroheim, Jr., Carlyle Blackwell, Bryant Washburn, Jr., Claude Gillingwater. Songs: "I Never Saw a Better Night," "There's Nothing Like a College Education," "Boys Will Be Boys," "When You Are In My Arms," "Comes the Revolution, Baby."

**COLLEGIATE.** (1936 Paramount) Betty Coed strikes again. Director: Ralph Murphy. Cast: Joe Penner, Jack Oakie, Ned Sparks, Frances Langford, Betty Grable, Lynn Overman, Betty Jane Cooper, Henry Kolker, Donald Gallagher, Albert Conti, Helen Brown, Edgar Dearing, Guy Usher, Marjorie Reynolds. Songs: "I Feel Like a Feather In the Breeze," "You Hit the Spot," "Rhythmatic," "My Grandfather's Clock," "In the Hallway," "Who Am I," "Will I Ever Know," "Guess Again," "Learn To Be Lovely."

**FOLLOW THE FLEET.** (1936 RKO) Betty comes on the screen as one of three showgirls. Director: Mark Sandrich. Cast: Fred Astaire, Ginger Rogers, Randolph Scott, Harriet Hilliard, Astrid Allwyn, Ray Mayer, Harry Beresford, Russell Hicks, Brooks Benedict, Lucille Ball, Betty Grable, Joy Hodges, Jenny Gray, Tony Martin, Maxine Jennings, Frank Jenks, Jane Hamilton. Songs: "I'm Putting All My Eggs In One Basket," "We Saw the Sea," "Let's Face the Music and Dance," "Let Yourself Go," "But Where Are You," "I'd Rather Lead a Band," "Get Thee Behind Me Satan."

**DON'T TURN 'EM LOOSE.** (1936 RKO) Betty emotes in film depicting dangers of parole laxity. Director: Ben Stoloff. Cast: Lewis Stone, James Gleason, Bruce Cabot, Betty Grable, Nella Walker, Louise Latimer, Grace Bradley, Frank M. Thomas, Maxine Jennings, Frank Jenks, Harry Jans.

**PIGSKIN PARADE.** (1936 20th) Betty returns to the campus, with little to do. Director: David Butler. Cast: Stuart Erwin, Patsy Kelly, Jack Haley, Johnny Downs, Betty Grable, Arline Judge, Dixie Dunbar, Judy Garland, Tony Martin, Fred Kohler, Jr., Elisha Cook, Jr., Pat Flaherty, Jack Nurphy, Dave Sharpe, Si Jenks, Jack Stoney, John Dilson, Ben Hall, Lynn Bari, Charles Wilson, Alan Ladd. Songs: "It's Love I'm After," "Balboa," "You're Slightly Terrific," "You Do the Darndest Things Baby," "Hold That Bulldog."

**THIS WAY PLEASE.** (1937 Paramount) Betty plays her first bride in slapstick. Director: Robert Florey. Cast: Charles "Buddy" Rogers, Mary Livingstone, Betty Grable, Ned Sparks, Jim and Marian Jordan, Porter Hall, Lee Bowman, Cecil Cunningham, Wally Vernon, Romo Vincent, Jerry Bergen, Rufe Davis. Songs: "Is It Love Or Is It Fascination," "This Way Please," "Delighted To Meet You," "What This Country Needs Is Voom Voom," "I'm the Sound Effects Man."

**THRILL OF A LIFETIME.** (1937 Paramount) Betty plays Leif Erickson's flame. Director: George Archainbaud. Cast: Judy Canova, Betty Grable, Buster Crabbe, Dorothy Lamour, Johnny Downs, Ben Blue, Eleanor Whitney, Leif Erickson, Howard M. Mitchell, Franklin Pangborn, Tommy Wonder. Songs: "Keeno, Screeno and You," "I'll Follow My Baby," "Thrill Of a Lifetime," "Paris In Swing," "Sweetheart

Time," "It's Been a Whole Year," "If We Could Run the Country For a Day."

**COLLEGE SWING.** (1938 Paramount) Betty lands a role for Jackie Coogan in this one, but there are a few other stars. Director: Raoul Walsh. Cast: George Burns and Gracie Allen, Martha Raye, Bob Hope, Edward Everett Horton, Florence George, Ben Blue, Betty Grable, Jackie Coogan, John Payne, Cecil Cunningham, Robert Cummings, Skinnay Ennis, The Slate Brothers. Songs: "I Fall In Love With You Every Day," "What a Rhumba Does To Romance," "The Old School Bell," "Moments Like This," "What Did Romeo Say To Juliet," "College Swing."

**GIVE ME A SAILOR.** (1938 Paramount) Betty adds love interest to a Bob Hope comedy. Director: Elliott Nugent. Cast: Martha Raye, Bob Hope, Betty Grable, J.C. Nugent, Jack Whiting, Clarence Kolb, Nana Bryant, Emerson Treacy, Bonnie Jean Churchill, Kathleen Lockhart, Ralph Sanford. Songs: "What Goes On Here In My Heart," "The USA And You," "A Little Kiss At Twilight," "It Don't Make Sense."

**CAMPUS CONFESSIONS.** (1938 Paramount) For the first time Betty is given top billing, but no awards are waiting. Director: George Archainbaud. Cast: Betty Grable, Eleanor Whitney, William Henry, Fritz Feld, John Arledge, Thurston Hall, Roy Gordon, Lane Chandler, Matty Kemp, Sumner Bitchell, Hank Luisette.

**MAN ABOUT TOWN.** (1939 Paramount) Betty does her comedic best with Dorothy Lamour in an all Jack Benny romp. Director: Mark Sandrich. Cast: Jack Benny, Dorothy Lamour, Edward Arnold, Binnie Barnes, Phil Harris, Eddie Anderson, Monty Woolley, Isabel Jeans, Betty Grable, E.E. Clive, Leonard Mudie, Pina Troupe, Peggy Steward, Patti Sacks, The Matty Malneck orchestra. Songs: "Strange Enchantment," "That Sentimental Sandwich," "Man About Town," "Fidgety Joe," "Bluebirds In the Moonlight."

**MILLION DOLLAR LEGS.** (1939 Paramount) Betty dons her cheerleader costume again and brings Coogan along once more. Director: Nick Grinde. Cast: Betty Grable, John Hartley, Donald O'Connor, Jackie Coogan, Buster Crabbe, Peter Hoyes, Dorothea Kent, Thurston

Hall, Roy Gordon, Matty Kemp, William Tracy, Joyce Matthews, Russ Clark, Wallace Rairden, John Hart, Billy Gilbert.

**THE DAY THE BOOKIES WEPT.** (1939 RKO) Betty gets female lead in a Penner comedy. Director: Leslie Goodwin. Cast: Joe Penner, Betty Grable, Richard Lane, Tom Kennedy, Thurston Hall, Bernadene Hayes, Carol Hughes.

**DOWN ARGENTINE WAY.** (1940 20th) Betty's career finally takes hold in this winning musical. Director: Irving Cummings. Cast: Don Ameche, Betty Grable, Carmen Miranda, Charlotte Greenwood, J. Carroll Naish, Henry Stephenson, Kay Aldridge, Leonid Kinskey, Chris-Pin Martin, Robert Conway, Bobby Stone, Charles Judels, Edward Fielding, Edward Conrad, Frank Puglia, Nicholas Brothers, Thomas and Catherine Dowling, Six Hits and A Miss, Flores Brothers, Bando De Luna. Songs: "Two Dreams Met," "Menita," "Sing To Your Senorita," "I Want My Mama," "Doin' the Conga," "South American Way."

**TIN PAN ALLEY.** (1940 20th) It's a sister act with Betty and Alice Faye, and the last time Betty will receive second billing for many years. Director: Walter Lang. Cast: Alice Faye, Betty Grable, Jack Oakie, John Payne, Allen Jenkins, Esther Ralston, Nicholas Brothers, Ben Carter, John Loder, Elisha Cook, Jr., Fred Keating, Billy Gilbert, Lillian Porter, Brian Sisters, Robert Brothers, Princess Vanessa Ammon, Tyler Brooke, Hal Dawson, William Davidson, Lionel Pape, Billy Bevan, Dewey Robinson, Robert E. Keane, John Sheehan, George Watts, Jack Roper, James Flavin, Franklin Farnum, Harry Strang. Songs: "You Say the Sweetest Things Baby" (only original song), "America I Love You," "Goodbye, Broadway, Hello, France," "Moonlight Bay," "The Sheik of Araby," "K-K-K-Katy."

**MOON OVER MIAMI.** (1941 20th) This time Betty plays sister to Carole Landis. Director: Walter Lang. Cast: Don Ameche, Betty Grable, Robert Cummings, Charlotte Greenwood, Jack Haley, Carole Landis, Cobina Wright, Jr., George Lessey, Robert Conway, Condos Brothers, Robert Greig, Minor Watson, Fortunio Bonanova, George Humbert, Spencer Charters, Lynn Roberts, Larry McGrath. Songs: "Solitary Seminole," "Loveliness and You," "You Started Something,"

"Hurray For Today," "Miami," "I've Got You All To Myself," "Is That Good?," "Kindergarten Conga." This is a remake of the 1938 film "Three Blind Mice."

**A YANK IN THE R.A.F.** (1941 20th) Betty does a straight role in a nonmusical without Technicolor. Director: Henry King. Cast: Tyrone Power, Betty Grable, John Sutton, Reginald Gardiner, Donald Stuart, Norton Lowry, Ralph Byrd, Richard Fraser, Bruce Lester, Denis Green, Lester Matthews, Frederic Worlock, Dennis Hoey, Stuart Robertson, Lynn Roberts, Fortunio Bonanova, James Craven, Guy Kingsford, Charles Irwin, John Meredith, Howard Davies.

**I WAKE UP SCREAMING.** (1941 20th) Once again it's black and white film, and a dramatic role for Betty in this mystery thriller. Director: H. Bruce Humberstone. Cast: Betty Grable, Victor Mature, Carole Landis, Laird Cregar, William Gargan, Alan Mowbray, Allyn Joslyn, Elisha Cook, Jr., Chick Chandler, Morris Ankrum, Wade Boteler, Ralph Dunn, Brooks Benedict, Forbes Murray.

**SONG OF THE ISLANDS.** (1942 20th) Betty is in Technicolor for her grass skirt cavorting with Victor Mature. Director: Walter Lang. Cast: Betty Grable, Victor Mature, Jack Oakie, Thomas Mitchell, George Barbier, Billy Gilbert, Hilo Hattie, Lillian Porter, Hal K. Dawson, Harry Owens and orchestra, Amy Cordone, Bruce Wong, Alex Pollard, Harold Lishman. Songs: "Blue Shadows and White Gardenias," "O'Brien Has Gone Hawaiian," "Malalo Mawaena," "What's Buzzin' Cousin?," "Down On Ami-oni-isle," "Sing Me a Song of the Islands."

**FOOTLIGHT SERENADE.** (1942 20th) It's black and white again for this backstage musical. This time choreographer Hermes Pan shows up in front of the camera in peppy dance routine. Director: Gregory Ratoff. Cast: John Payne, Betty Grable, Victor Mature, Jane Wyman, James Gleason, Phil Silvers, Cobina Wright, Jr., June Lang, Frank Orth, Mantan Moreland, Irving Bacon, Charles Tannen, George Dobbs, Sheila Ryan, Frank Coghlan, Jr., Harry Barris, Trudy Marshall, Don Wilson, John Dilson. Songs: "Living High (On a Western Hill)," "I'll Be Marching To a Love Song," "I'm Still Crazy For You," "I Heard the Birdies Sing," "Are You Kidding?," "Land On Your Feet."

**SPRINGTIME IN THE ROCKIES.** (1942 20th) Betty is lovely in Technicolor, but the Harry James band and Carmen Miranda are given the most attention. Director: Irving Cummings. Cast: Betty Grable, John Payne, Carmen Miranda, Cesar Romero, Harry James and his Music Makers, Bando De Luna, Charlotte Greenwood, Edward Everett Horton, Frank Orth, Harry Hayden, Jackie Gleason, Trudy Marshall, Chick Chandler, Iron Eyes Cody, Bess Flowers. Songs: "I Had the Craziest Dream," "A Poem Set To Music," "Pan American Jubilee," "Run Little Raindrop Run," "I Like To Be Loved By You."

**CONEY ISLAND.** (1943 20th) Betty plays a showgirl (Technicolor). Director: Walter Lang. Cast: Betty Grable, George Montgomery, Cesar Romero, Charles Winninger, Phil Silvers, Matt Briggs, Paul Hurst, Frank Orth, Phyllis Kennedy, Carmen D'Antonio, Andrew Tombes, Harry Seymour, Hal K. Dawson, Bud Williams, Alec Craig, Herbert Ashley, James Lucas, Francis Sales, Tom Dugan, Trudy Marshall, Claire James, Tene Ramey, Gus Reed, Delos Jewkos, George Grumlick. Songs: "Take It From There," "Beautiful Coney Island," "Miss Lulu From Louisville," "Get the Money," "There's Danger In a Dance," "Old Demon Rum," "Cuddle Up a Little Closer," "Everybody Loves a Baby."

**SWEET ROSIE O'GRADY.** (1943 20th) Betty plays a singer from Brooklyn who becomes the toast of London (Technicolor). Director: Irving Cummings. Cast: Betty Grable, Robert Young, Adolphe Menjou, Reginald Gardiner, Virginia Grey, Phil Regan, Sig Rumann, Alan Dinehart, Hobart Cavanaugh, Frank Orth, Jonathan Hale, Stanley Clements, Byron Foulger, Lilyan Irene, St. Brendan's Choir, Leo Diamond and his orchestra, Oliver Blake, Edward Earle, James Metcalfe, Bruce Warren, John Dilson, Paul Maxey, Sam Wren, Hooper Atchley, Joe King, Dorothy Granger. Songs: "My Heart Tells Me," "The Wishing Waltz," "Get Your Police Gazette," "My Sam," "Going To the Fair," "Where Oh Where Is the Groom?"

**FOUR JILLS IN A JEEP.** (1944 20th) Betty does a cameo spot in this black and white movie. Director: William A. Seiter. Cast: Kay Francis, Carole Landis, Martha Raye, Mitzi Mayfair, Jimmy Dorsey and Band, John Harvey, Phil Silvers, Dick Haymes. Guest Stars: Alice Faye, Betty Grable, Carmen Miranda, George Jessel. Songs: "Crazy Me," "You

Send Me," "How Blue the Night," "How Many Times Do I Have To Tell You," "Ohio," "It's the Old Army Game," "You Never Miss a Trick," "Heil, Heel Hitler."

**PIN-UP GIRL.** (1944 20th) Betty, a Washington, D.C. secretary sends pin up photos to military men. Again, she and Hermes Pan, the choreographer of the Technicolor film, do a dance number. Director: H. Bruce Humberstone. Cast: Betty Grable, John Harvey, Martha Raye, Joe E. Brown, Eugene Pallette, Dave Willock, Condos Brothers, Charley Spivak and orchestra, Dorothea Kent, Marcel Dalio, Roger Clark, Gloria Nord, Irving Bacon, Mantan Moreland, Hermes Pan and Angela Blue, J. Farrell MacDonald, Lillian Porter, Max Willenz. Songs: "Pin-Up Girl," "Once Too Often," "Yankee Doodle Hayride," "The Very Merry Widow," "Don't Carry Tales Out of School," "Red Robins," "Bob Whites and Bluebirds."

**BILLY ROSE'S DIAMOND HORSESHOE.** (1945 20th) Betty is once more a showgirl (Technicolor). Director: George Seaton. Cast: Betty Grable, Dick Haymes, Phil Silvers, William Gaxton, Beatrice Kay, Carmen Cavallaro, Willie Solar, Margaret Dumont, Roy Benson, George Melford, Hal K. Dawson, Kenny Williams, Reed Hadley, Eddie Acuff, Ed Gargan, Julie London, Cyril King, Milton Kibbee, Virginia Walker. Songs: "I Wish I Knew," "The More I See You," "In Acapulco," "Play Me An Old-fashioned Melody," "A Nickels Worth of Jive," "Moody," "Welcome To the Diamond Horseshoe," "Cooking Up a Stew."

**THE DOLLY SISTERS.** (1945 20th) Betty and June Haver play Jenny and Rosie Dolly in Technicolor. Director: Irving Cummings. Cast: Betty Grable, John Payne, June Haver, S.Z. Sakall, Reginald Gardiner, Frank Latimore, Gene Sheldon, Sig Rumann, Trudy Marshall, Collette Lyons, Evon Thomas, Donna Jo Gribble, Robert Middlemass, Paul Hurst, Lester Allen, Frank Orth, William Nye, Herbert Ashley, Mae Marsh, J. Farrell MacDonald. Songs: "I Can't Begin To Tell You," "Old-Fashioned Girl," "Give Me the Moonlight," "Give Me the Girl," "We Have Been Around," "Carolina In the Morning," "Powder Lipstick and Rouge," "Darktown Strutter's Ball," "Smíles."

**DO YOU LOVE ME.** (1946 20th) Betty does a bit part at movie's close as a gag with Harry James. Director: Gregory Ratoff. Cast: Maureen

O'Hara, Dick Haymes, Harry James, Reginald Gardiner, Richard Gaines, Stanley Prager, B.S. Pulley, Chick Chandler, Alma Kruger, Almira Sessions, Douglas Wood, Harlan Briggs, Julia Dean, Harry Hayes Morgan, Eugene Borden, Lex Barker, Harry Seymour, Sam McDaniel, William Frambes, Jesse Graves, Evelyn Mulhall, Betty Grable. Songs: "I Didn't Mean a Word I Said," "As If I Didn't Have Enough On My Mind," "Moonlight Propaganda," "Do You Love Me."

**THE SHOCKING MISS PILGRIM.** (1947 20th) Betty plays a suffragette (Technicolor). Director: George Seaton. Cast: Betty Grable, Dick Haymes, Anne Revere, Allyn Joslyn, Gene Lockhart, Elizabeth Patterson, Arthur Shields, Elisabeth Risdon, Charles Kamper, Roy Roberts, Stanley Prager, Edward Laughton, Hal K. Dawson, Lillian Bronson, Pierre Watkin. Songs: "Aren't You Kinda Glad We Did," "For You, For Me, Forevermore," "But Not In Boston," "Stand Up and Fight," "Changing My Tune," "One, Two, Three," "Sweet Packard," "Waltz Me No Waltzes," "Waltzing Is Better Than Sitting Down."

**MOTHER WORE TIGHTS.** (1947 20th) Betty forms a vaudeville team with Dan Dailey (Technicolor). Director: Walter Lang. Cast: Betty Grable, Dan Dailey, Mona Freeman, Connie Marshall, Vanessa Brown, Robert Arthur, Sara Allgood, William Frawley, Ruth Nelson, Anabel Shaw, Michael Dunne, George Cleveland, Veda Ann Borg, Sig Rumann, Lee Patrick, Senor Wences, Maude Eburne, William Forrest, Kathleen Lockhart, Chick Chandler, Will Wright, Frank Orth, Harry Chesire, Billy Green, David Thursby, Tom Stevenson, Ann Gowland, Karolyn Grimes, Joan Gerians, Anne Baxter (narrator). Songs: "You Do," "Kokomo, Indiana," "There's Nothing Like a Song," "On a Little Two-Seat Tandem," "This Is My Favorite City," "Rolling Down To Bowling Green," "Fare-Thee-Well Alma Mater," "Tra-La-La-La."

**THAT LADY IN ERMINE.** (1948 20th) Betty plays an Italian countess (Technicolor). Director: Ernst Lubitsch–Otto Preminger. Cast: Betty Grable, Douglas Fairbanks, Jr., Cesar Romero, Walter Abel, Reginald Gardiner, Harry Davenport, Virginia Campbell, Whit Bissell, Edmund MacDonald, David Bond, Harry Carter, Thayer Roberts, Don Haggerty, Duke York, Francis Pierlot, Joe Haworth, Harry Cording, Belle Mitchell, Mary Bear, Jack George, John Parrish, Mayo Newhall, Ray Hyke. Songs: "This Is the Moment," "The Melody Has to Be Right," "There's Something About Midnight," "The Jester's Song," "It's Always a Beautiful Day."

**WHEN MY BABY SMILES AT ME.** (1948 20th) It's backstage again with Betty and Dailey a husband and wife team (Technicolor). Director: Walter Lang. Cast: Betty Grable, Dan Dailey, Jack Oakie, June Havoc, Richard Arlen, James Gleason, Vanita Wade, Kenny Williams, Robert Emmett Keane, Jean Wallace, Pati Behrs, Lee MacGregor, Charles Tannen, Noel Neill, Lu Anne Jones, Joanne Dale, Dorothy Babb, Hank Mann, Edward Clark, Charles Latorre, Lela Bliss. Songs: "By the Way," "What Did I Do," "When My Baby Smiles At Me."

**THE BEAUTIFUL BLONDE FROM BASHFUL BEND.** (1949 20th) Betty, complete with six-guns, invades the old West (Technicolor). Director: Preston Sturges. Cast: Betty Grable, Cesar Romero, Rudy Vallee, Olga San Juan, Sterling Holloway, Hugh Herbert, El Brendel, Porter Hall, Margaret Hamilton, Emory Parnell, Chris-Pin Martin, J. Farrell MacDonald, Marie Windsor, Esther Howard, Chester Conklin, Mary MacDonald, Snub Pollard, Frank Moran. Songs: "Everytime I Meet You," "Beautiful Blonde From Bashful Bend," "In the Gloaming."

**WABASH AVENUE.** (1950 20th) A reworking of *Coney Island* with a different setting (Technicolor). Director: Henry Koster. Cast: Betty Grable, Victor Mature, Phil Harris, Reginald Gardiner, James Barton, Barry Kelley, Margaret Hamilton, Jacqueline Dalya, Robin Raymond, Hal K. Dawson, Colette Lyons, Charles Arnt, Walter Long, Billie Daniel, Marion Marshall, Percy Helton, Henry Kulky, Alexander Pope, Dick Wessel, Peggy Leon, Bill Phillips. Songs: "Wabash Avenue," "Clean Up Chicago," "Wilhelmina," "May I Tempt You With a Big Red Apple," "Baby, Say You Love Me."

**MY BLUE HEAVEN.** (1950 20th) Betty and Dan play radio personalities who want a family (Technicolor). Director: Henry Koster. Cast: Betty Grable, Dan Dailey, David Wayne, Jane Wyatt, Mitzie Gaynor, Una Merkel, Louise Beavers, Laura Pierpont, Don Hicks, Irving Fulton, Billy Daniels, Larry Keating, Minerva Urecal, Mae Marsh, Noel Rayburn, Phyllis Coates, Barbara Pepper, Myron Healy, Lois Hall, Frank Remley. Songs: "My Blue Heaven," "Live Hard, Work

Hard, Love Hard," "The Friendly Islands," "It's Deductible," "Halloween," "Don't Rock the Boat Dear," "What a Man," "I Love a New Yorker," "Cosmo Cosmetics."

**CALL ME MISTER.** (1951 20th) Betty is a USO girl entertaining troops in Japan (Technicolor). Director: Lloyd Bacon. Cast: Betty Grable, Dan Dailey, Danny Thomas, Dale Robertson, Benay Venuta, Richard Boone, Jeffrey Hunter, Frank Fontaine, Harry Von Zell, Dave Willock, Lou Spencer, Art Stanley, Bobby Short, Bob Roberts, Jerry Paris, Ken Christy, Dabbs Greer, John McGuire, Harry Lauter, Jack Kelly, Paul Burke, Geraldine Knapp. Songs: "Japanese Girl Like American Boy," "I Just Can't Do Enough For You, Baby," "Love Is Back In Business," "Whistle and Walk Away," "It's a Man's World," "Lament to Pots and Pans," "Call Me Mister," "The Going Home Train," "Military Life."

**MEET ME AFTER THE SHOW.** (1951 20th) Betty dances like never before with Gwenn Verdon (Technicolor). Director: Richard Sale. Cast: Betty Grable, MacDonald Carey, Rory Calhoun, Eddie Albert, Fred Clark, Lois Andrews, Irene Ryan, Steven Condos, Jerry Brandow, Arthur Walge, Edwin Max, Robert Nash, Gwen Verdon, Max Wagner, Al Murphy, Rodney Bell, Harry Antrim, Lick Cogan, Billy Newell. Songs: "Let Go Of My Heart," "Meet Me After the Show," "Bettin' On a Man," "It's a Hot Night In Alaska," "No Talent Joe," "I Feel Like Dancing."

**THE FARMER TAKES A WIFE.** (1953 20th) Betty is a cook on an Erie Canal barge, in black and white. Director: Henry Levin. Cast: Betty Grable, Dale Robertson, Thelma Ritter, John Carrol, Eddie Foy, Jr., Charlotte Austin, Kathleen Crowley, Merry Anders, May Wynn, Noreen Michaels, Ruth Hall, Mort Mills, Gwen Verdon, Gordon Nelson, Ed Hinton, Emile Meyer, Lee Phelps, Ted Jordan.

**HOW TO MARRY A MILLIONAIRE.** (1953 20th) Betty's first film in Cinemascope (Color by De Luxe). Director: Jean Negulesco. Cast: Marilyn Monroe, Betty Grable, Lauren Bacall, David Wayne, Rory Calhoun, Cameron Mitchell, Alex D'Arcy, Fred Clark, William Powell, Tudor Owen, Emmett Vogan, Charlotte Austin, Richard Shackleton, Eve Finnell, Benny Burt.

**THREE FOR THE SHOW.** (1955 Columbia) Again in Cinemascope, Betty moves to Columbia to play a girl with one too many husbands. Her first film away from Twentieth in fifteen years. Director: H.C. Potter. Cast: Betty Grable, Marge Champion, Gower Champion, Jack Lemmon, Myron McCormick, Paul Harvey, Robert Bice, Hal K. Dawson, Charlotte Lawrence, Willard Waterman, Gene Wesson, Aileen Carlyle, Rudy Lee, Eugene Borden. Songs: "Someone To Watch Over Me," "I've Got a Crush On You," "Friendship," "How Come You Do Me Like You Do," "Down Boy," "Which One," "I've Been Kissed Before."

**HOW TO BE VERY VERY POPULAR.** (1955 20th) Betty returns to free-lance in this Cinemascope musical remake of *She Loves Me Not.* Director: Nunnally Johnson. Cast: Betty Grable, Sheree North, Bob Cummings, Charles Coburn, Tommy Noonan, Orson Bean, Fred Clark, Charlotte Austin, Alice Pierce, Rhys Williams, Andrew Tombes, Noel Toy, Emory Parnell, Edmund Cobb, Hank Mann, Leslie Parrish. Songs: "Shake, Rattle and Roll," "Bristol Bell Song," "Bunny Hop."

## INDEX